2004 - 2014

OSPREYS IN WALES
THE FIRST TEN YEARS

Copyright © 2014 by Emyr Evans

Published by Emyr Evans

First Edition - November 2014

No part of this publication may be reproduced, stored in a retrieval system, or transmitted in any form or by any means, electronic, mechanical, photocopying, recording, or otherwise, without written permission from the author.

For information regarding permission, write to

ems11@btinternet.com

ISBN 978 0 9930990 0 7

All rights reserved.

Cover and book design by jenksdesign@yahoo.co.uk

Printed by Cambrian Printers, Aberystwyth

2004 - 2014

OSPREYS IN WALES

THE FIRST TEN YEARS

Emyr Evans

I Mam a Dad

Caru chi am byth

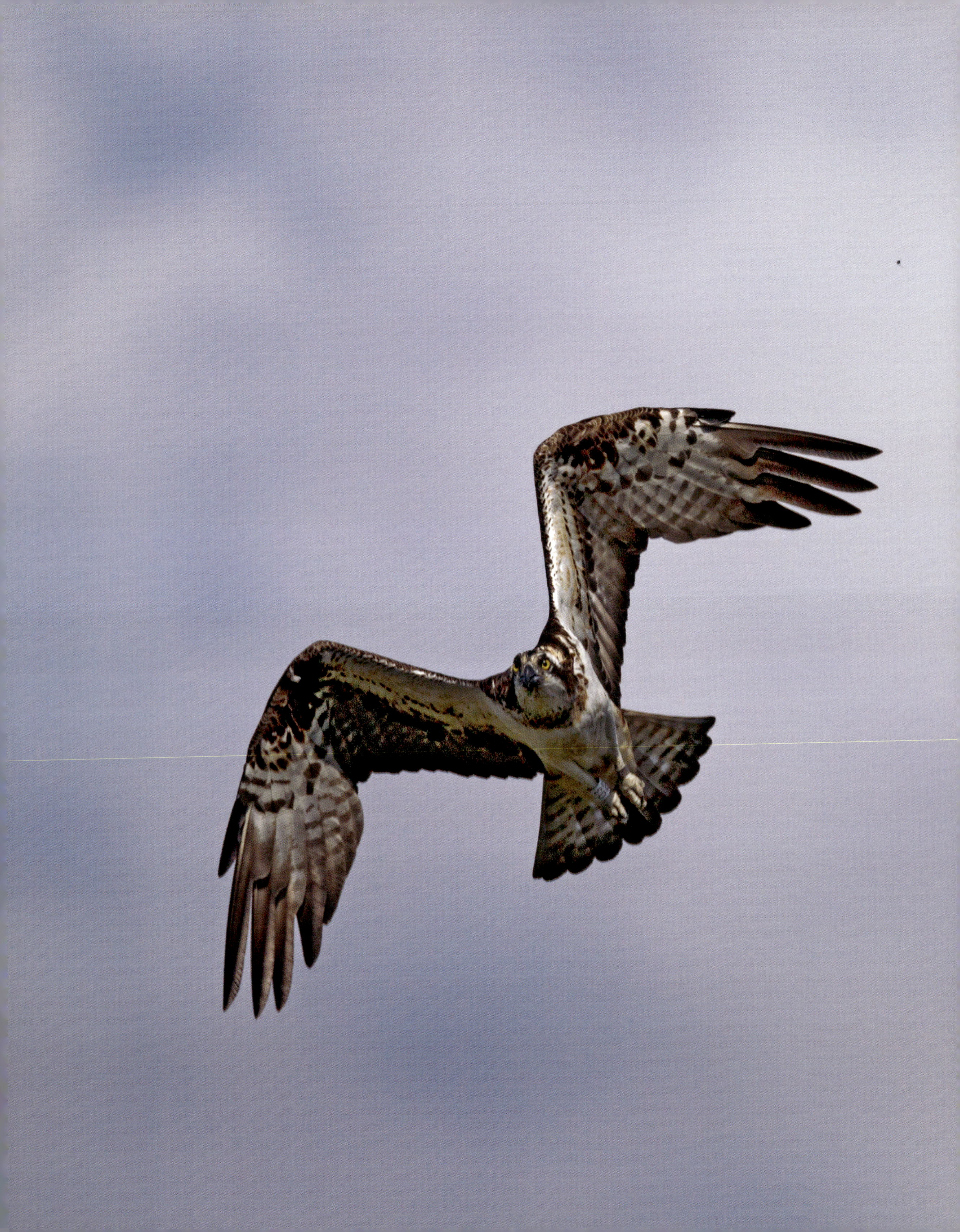

Contents

Foreword by *Iolo Williams*	i
Preface	ii

Introduction
The History of Ospreys in Wales	iii
Persecution in the UK	vii
Ospreys in the Modern World	ix
A Personal Relationship	xii
Photographing Ospreys	xv

2004
Buses	1
The Discovery	2
Who's Who?	3
The Rutland Translocation Project	4
What's Your Name?	5
Disaster	8
Working Together	9
Building for the Future	10
Welshpool	12

2005
In at the Deep End	15
The Ospreys Return	17
Operation Pandora	22
Pont Croesor	25
Ecstasy	28
From Strength to Strength	29

2006
Extended Honeymoon	33
The Only Pair of Ospreys in Wales	35
A Scottish Trip	36
Tri Chynnig i Gymro	38
Bittersweet	41
A Community Affair	46

2007
Lights, Camera, Action	49
Who Are You...?	52
Seeing is Believing	54
Protecting 24:7	57
Lightning Strikes Twice	59
Ringing Success	61

2008
Pioneering Ospreys	65
Protecting in the Dry	66
Ospreys Everywhere	67
The Holy Grail	69
The Dyfi Dynasty	73
A Welsh Osprey Returns	75

2009
A New Start	78
Confusing Ospreys	81
Monty	83
Scraggly	85
The Odd Couple	87
Glaslyn Grandchildren	90
Yellow Gold	92

2010
Mirror Image	94
A Hat-trick of Hat-tricks	96
Another Returnee	97

Ospreys Everywhere on the Dyfi	99
Scraggly Returns	102
Black 80	104

2011
So Many Questions	106
Monty Returns	107
Flaming Nora	108
Bonding Together	112
Ospreys of Higher Resolution	113
Glaslyn Record Breakers	114
Making History	118
Practicing New Behaviours	119
Einion, Dulas & Leri	120
On Track for Africa	124

2012
The Big Pull	128
And Then There Were Three	134
Another Glaslyn Osprey – White 91	135
The Perfect Storm	137
The Intervention	143
Ceulan	147
The Scottish Trip – Part II	150

2013
Where's Nora?	156
Females Everywhere	157
Another Glaslyn Osprey Returns	161
And Then There Were Five	164
Happy Tenth Anniversary	165
Glesni's Reign	167
Clarach and Cerist	170
The Search Party	173

2014
A Room with a View	179
Blue 24 and Dai Dot	180
The Big Fight	185
Under New Management	188
Come in White 91	191
High Fives – A Fifth Glaslyn Osprey Breeding	193
Glaslyn Empire Building	194
Dyfi Double	196
Gwynant and Deri	199
Dai Dot	204

Stats
Marmite	209
Glaslyn and Dyfi Key Dates	210
Glaslyn and Dyfi Egg Data	212
Glaslyn and Dyfi Chick Data	214
Dyfi Sightings and Glaslyn Offspring	216
Welsh Osprey Nests	218
Dyfi Fish Stats	220
Fish Pies	222

And Finally...
The Legacies	224
Superospreys	229
The Monty Mystery	232
The Next Ten Years	235

Glossary	242
More Osprey Books	244
Acknowledgements	245
Photo Credits	246

Foreword

Ospreys are different. Like most large birds of prey, they are beautiful, noble, magnificent and regal, but they also stand apart from their raptorial cousins. Ospreys are long-distance migrants, they are piscivorous and they plunge into water from a great height in pursuit of their prey. To watch a hunting osprey is to witness poetry in motion. The all-seeing orange eyes, the powerful wings and grasping talons are tools honed to perfection by millions of years of evolution.

You never forget that magical moment when you see your first osprey. Like watching man's first landing on the moon or Wales winning a rugby Grand Slam, you remember exactly where you were at that moment in time. For me, it was a visit to the RSPB's famous Loch Garten ospreys in the early 1970s at a time when only a handful of pairs nested by remote lochs in the Highlands of Scotland. I can also clearly recall my first Welsh osprey, seen on a sunny autumn day in the Elan Valley when my eyes were drawn skywards by a group of gulls noisily mobbing a long-winged bird of prey that was desperately trying to gain height to escape its pursuers. As I focused my binoculars on what I thought was a distant red kite, at first I couldn't believe my eyes. An osprey in mid-Wales? Surely not; but there it was, in all its majesty, slowly rising above the gulls and drifting away southwards on its long journey towards Africa.

Since that day, I have had dozens of further encounters but even at the turn of the Millennium, I would have laughed at anyone who would have claimed that fifteen years later, we would have several pairs of ospreys nesting in Wales. I remember my disbelief when I found out that we had not one but two pairs nesting in Wales in 2004, both of which may well have been present the previous year. The Glaslyn pair, although it failed in that first year, has gone from strength to strength and thanks to hundreds of volunteers, it has now become one of north-west Wales' principal tourist attractions. Although the pair that reared one young near Welshpool never returned to the site in following seasons, the nearby Dyfi Estuary birds have also become major attractions with successive appearances on the BBC's popular 'Springwatch' programme attracting fans from all over the globe.

Emyr Evans has been at the forefront of osprey conservation work in Wales, from the early years at the Glaslyn to the present day as head of the team safeguarding the pair nesting at Cors Ddyfi near Machynlleth. Emyr is ideally placed to write about the first 10 years and without his knowledge and enthusiasm, osprey conservation in Wales would certainly be a very different story. With four pairs now known to be nesting in the country, surely it can only be a matter of time before we see these wonderful birds nesting on every estuary and every large lake in the Principality. I, and thousands of other wildlife enthusiasts all over the country, certainly hope so.

Iolo Williams
September 2014

Preface

I grew up in North Wales, just a few hundred metres from the Menai Straits overlooking Foryd Bay. I loved living by the sea and only really appreciated how lucky I was when I moved away at the age of 18. The calls of distant curlews and the high-pitched piping of redshanks and oystercatchers were part of my everyday life – as well as the raucous squawking of herring and black-headed gulls of course, which I had a deep fascination for, and still do.

When I was 16, I bought my first 'proper' camera – an Olympus OM10. Wow, it was amazing. A lens soon followed, a Tamron 500mm catadioptric mirror contraption I bought second hand in Colwyn Bay; it was a kind of poor man's telephoto lens but I didn't care. Suddenly all the birds of my childhood were a heck of a lot closer. I loved nothing better than to spend an early morning or late afternoon creeping up to whimbrels or goldeneyes or what ever the tide or the wind had brought in that day, and get the best shot I could. After getting my Kodachrome slides developed and processed, I used to pick the most decent (and most in focus) slide and take it down to Gray-Thomas gallery in town and get it printed and framed. I remember vividly the anticipation and excitement of ripping off the brown paper wrapping and seeing my compositions for the first time in their frames. I still have most of them, in the attic probably.

If you had told me then I would write a book many years later about birds, I wouldn't have believed you. If you had told me then I would write a book about ospreys breeding in Wales, I would have laughed out loud!

I never intended to write a book about anything, least of all ospreys. I guess most people don't set out to write a book, not a non-fiction one anyway, but find themselves at some stage in their lives with a headful of stories, diaries full of notes and albums full of photos stashed away somewhere, just waiting to be arranged and catalogued in some kind of orderly fashion that may be of interest to someone. I suppose that is what has happened to me.

I've been incredibly lucky to have observed at close quarters the osprey's revival in Wales, right from the start almost. With a bit of photographic know-how and a slightly better lens than that monstrosity from the 1970's, I found myself in that very fortunate position with a story to tell. And what a story it is.

The recolonisation of the osprey in Wales has seen a decade's worth of tears and sweat, laughter and happiness, sometimes all rolled up into one. It has captured the hearts of thousands of people and with the help of social media recently and countless TV programmes, the osprey is now an icon amongst British birds. Back from the dead in the UK and back after several hundreds of years in Wales.

My sole objective in writing this book has been to get the story out there. So many people want to know what has happened, especially during those early years when Welsh ospreys were not on most people's radar screens. Some of the photographs in these early days were not brilliant, but I have included many of the important ones nevertheless. When ospreys first started breeding in Wales digital photography was in its infancy, still in the pram; but I decided that despite the quality, it was their content that mattered. It's the stories the photos tell that are of significance, not the precision and artistry of the photographer or the technology at hand.

It has been an enormous privilege to have been immersed in the story of the osprey's fight-back in Wales over the last decade. This is their story, not mine; I'm only the ghostwriter with a few pictures and a laptop handy. I hope you find the osprey's adventures fascinating and their tenacity to survive inspiring; you never know, I might be back in 10 years' time with another instalment.

Emyr Evans
November 2014

Introduction

The History of Ospreys in Wales

I almost called this book "The Return of the Osprey to Wales", but for anything to return, obviously it must have been present at some time in the past. Herein lies the confusion and the start of endless discussion and debate regarding the historical fate of the osprey in Wales during the last few hundred years.

A pair of breeding ospreys – they must have been widespread in Wales many centuries and millennia ago.

Surprisingly, no official written records exist of ospreys breeding in Wales until 2004, although there are numerous references to them over the centuries. The medieval Welsh stories, The Mabinogion, tell the tale of "The Eagle of Gwernabwy", described as being "the one who has wandered most", attempting to catch a salmon from Llyn (lake) Lliw, so large that it is almost drowned. This 'eagle' could have been a white-tailed eagle, but is more likely to be a reference to the osprey judging by its behaviour. The coat of arms of the city of Swansea, granted in 1316, features an osprey suggesting that they once bred in the area. It was and still is, perfect habitat for ospreys. The coat of arms of West Glamorgan also bears an osprey.

A Flemish engineer working on wetland drainage systems on the Dyfi estuary, Mid Wales, in 1604 mentioned several "fishey hawkes" breeding close together along the banks of the River Dyfi. This is almost certainly a reference to ospreys as, unlike any other bird of prey in the UK, they have a habit of nesting in loose colonies.

During the last two hundred years or so, we have more concrete, albeit ignominious records that prove beyond doubt that ospreys were around in Wales. A male osprey was shot in the Gloddaeth area of Llandudno in 1828 and another near Caernarfon in 1937. Many ospreys were caught in pole traps including a bird at Clyro in Radnorshire in 1867 and another on the Berwyn Mountains in 1880. The fact that ospreys were in Wales and fishing at different watercourses is not in doubt. Were they nesting and breeding here though?

Perhaps there is a clue in the Welsh name for osprey. Just as with most birds that breed in Wales, there are numerous names for osprey in the language. Writing on the subject a few years back, naturalist and wildlife historian Twm Elias recorded at least ten different names. Surely ospreys used to breed in Wales in ancient times – why else would there be so many names for one species?

Here are some of them with their recorded date of use in brackets:

Môr Eryr – Sea eagle (1604)

Eryr y Môr – Eagle of the sea (1795)

Gwalch y Weilgi – Strait/Sea hawk (1800)

Eryr y Dŵr – Water eagle (1805)

Pysgeryr – Fish eagle (1805)

Barcud y Môr – Sea kite (1834)

Pysgodwalch – Fish hawk (1835)

Gwalch y Môr – Sea hawk (20th century)

Gwalch y Pysgod – Fish hawk (20th century)

The agreed and accepted Welsh name for osprey nowadays is 'Gwalch y pysgod' (fish hawk). Things were not so simple a few hundred years back.

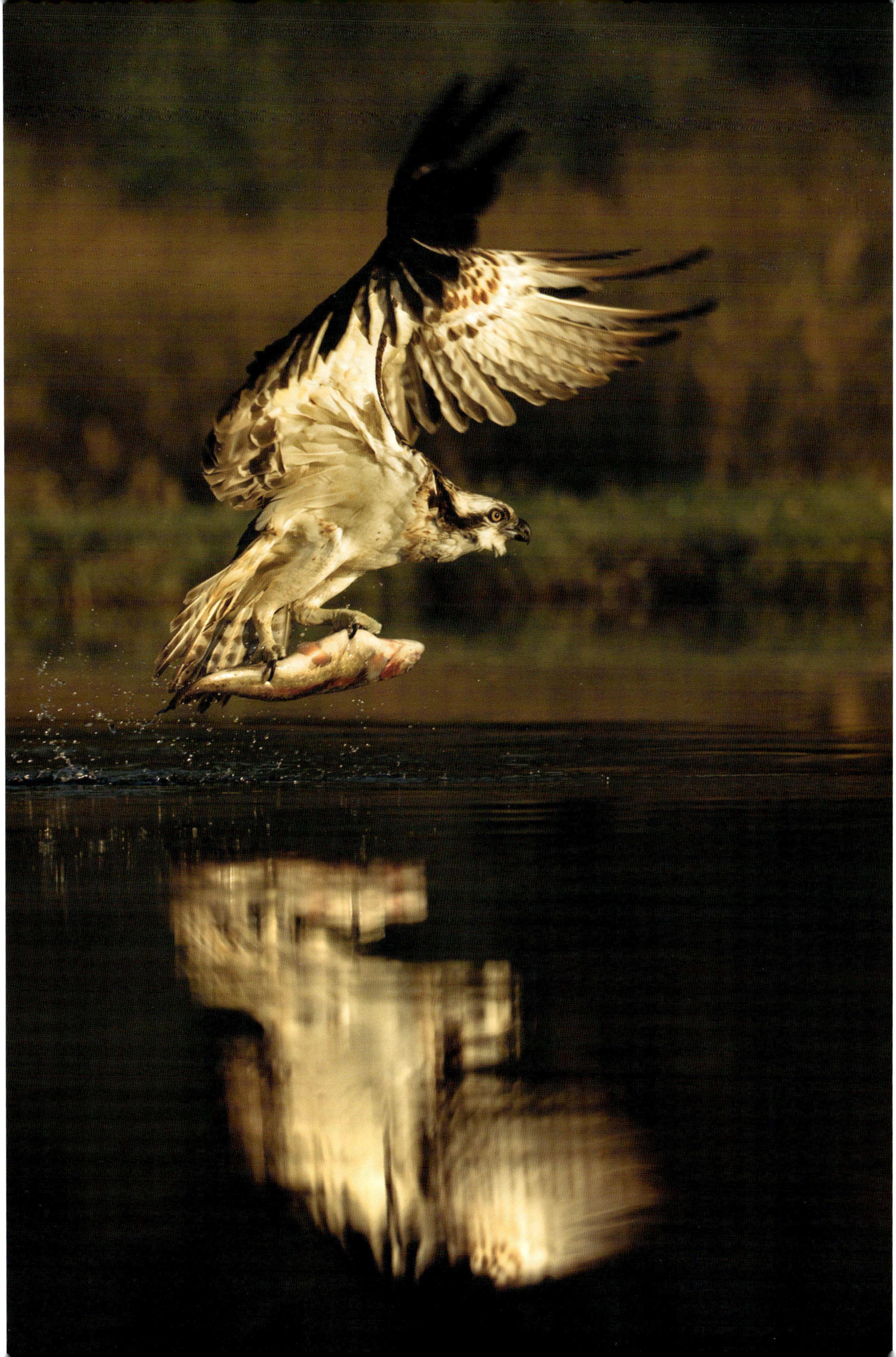

By the time Shakespeare wrote his Greek tragedy Coriolanus, the osprey was already on the decline.

The problem was that Wales was a rural, largely mountainous country with a low human population. A couple of hundred years ago there simply wasn't anywhere near the same interest and appetite for recording wildlife, bird sightings and breeding as there is today. People were far too busy trying to eke out a living and staying alive. True, some of these words may have been used for what we call the white-tailed sea eagle today, which is in itself interesting that they could have been breeding in Wales. But there seems little doubt really that ospreys used to breed in Wales, and not just a few pairs either; they most probably flourished here a millennium ago and had done so since the glaciers thawed out at the end of the last ice age, some 11,000 years back.

It's what I call the common sense rule. Ospreys had been recorded in practically every county in England and were even written about by Shakespeare 400 years ago – they must have been common then. And Stratford-upon-Avon isn't a million miles away from the Welsh border is it? Just because they were never officially recorded as breeding in Wales, doesn't mean that the osprey never had.

Just imagine Shakespeare sitting on the banks of the River Avon some four centuries ago, quill and parchment in hand as a large male osprey swoops imperiously in front of him and swipes a trout clean out of the river, water splashing everywhere. I bet he would have given his favourite swan quill for a pair of binoculars!

"I think he'll be to Rome
As is the osprey to the fish, who takes it
By sovereignty of nature."

William Shakespeare, Coriolanus 1607

Persecution in the UK

The historical decline of the osprey in Scotland and England is well documented; an apex predator at the top of the food chain stood little chance from the Middle Ages onwards in the British Isles. They were a nuisance, a pest and served no useful purpose in everyday life. Money had been invented and was in everyday use, people wanted prosperity and wealth – the only currency the top mammals and birds of the day could offer was once they were dead. Animals were persecuted to extinction in the UK, one after another whether it be for their pelts, their feathers, their eggs, for food, for safety, for ornaments, for clothing, or latterly, for 'sport'. Consigned to the history books and museum displays went the lynx, followed by the wolves, the beavers, the brown bears and the eagles. Thank goodness all of these animals managed to hold on in other European countries, otherwise the complete top of the biomass pyramid (remember them in school?) would have been sliced off for good.

Some species, however, didn't make it through this period of mass species extermination. The great auk survived into the mid 1840's and then, at exactly the same time as the osprey in England, disappeared; only in the auk's case, off the face of the earth. They would never come back; extinction is forever.

The osprey would suffer a capricious and torrid time during these dark persecution years. By the time people started making a 'hobby' out of taking their eggs for ever-growing collections in Victorian times, the osprey had already suffered greatly at the hands of a rather peculiar and extraneous cause, religion.

The tradition of Catholics fasting from meat on a Friday meant that fish was to be on the menu on this day, and every Friday of the year without fail. This caused obvious conflict with the osprey. Monasteries and large estates started to build large fish ponds (or stew ponds as they were called at the time) and as sure as your chaffinches and blue tits come to your garden attracted by the bird feeders, ospreys were similarly tempted to these stew ponds like magnets. They were unwelcome 'vermin' and had to be eradicated, so as to uphold the religious Friday fish-eating observance of the day.

The dark years – ospreys teetered on the edge of extinction in the British Isles for most of the 20th century.

By the early years of the last century, the beginning of the end was nigh for British ospreys. After centuries of suffering a host of draconian measures to wipe them clean off the avian map of the UK, the last recorded pair succumbed in Loch Loyne near Inverness in 1916. An egg collector of the day, William Dunbar, wrote in a letter to his friend (another prolific egg thief), John Wolley, *"I am afraid that Mr. St John, yourself and your humble servant, have finally done for the Ospreys".*

Ospreys in the Modern World

Of all the 320 or so bird of prey species that have been recorded, the osprey is the only one that forages exclusively on fish. It is found all over the world and on every continent apart from Antarctica and the osprey is generally split up into four sub-species: a North American population, a Caribbean population, a Palearctic population (Europe and all across the northern Hemisphere including Asia to eastern Russia) and an Australian and Tasmanian population, sometimes known as the Western osprey. This last race is arguably distinct enough from the other osprey populations of the world to warrant its own classification and full species status. It certainly looks quite a bit different from the other three; its morphology and genotype are also sufficiently distinct. There are also at least two species of ospreys that have become extinct; both lived around 13 million years ago, so nothing to do with us this time, thankfully.

Ospreys are large birds, with some of the bigger females (which are generally larger than males) having a wingspan of six feet (1.83m) and weighing up to five pounds (2.25Kg). Most osprey populations are migratory except those that already breed in hot climates such as the Caribbean, southern States of America, Mediterranean, Arabia and the Western osprey in Australia for example. They have a host of evolutionary adaptions conducive to their fish eating ecology, including valves in the nostrils that close to shut out water when the bird dives, strong enzymes and an elongated small intestine used to digest fish-bones, a toe that can be reversed to latch on to slippery fish and specialised spiny foot pads or 'spicules' to further grip its prey. Manufacturers of goalkeeper gloves could do a lot worse than take a closer look at what 15 million years of evolution has done to the osprey's foot.

The 20th century proved to be a pivotal time for ospreys. Persecution had reduced their numbers to shockingly low levels in Europe, including wiping them out completely in many countries. In North America the story was slightly different, it was bioaccumulation that was killing them there.

Dichlorodiphenyltrichloroethane (let's call that DDT!) is a chemical that had been used as an agricultural insecticide since the 1940's, protecting crops from insect damage. Some thought, however,

OSPREYS IN WALES *The First Ten Years*

Female osprey of the Palearctic subspecies – they are generally darker (head, chest belly, under-wing) than males and are typically 10% - 15% larger and heavier on average.

that DDT was also damaging the ecosystem and everything than existed within it. A particular heroine of mine, Rachel Carson, published a book in 1962 called 'Silent Spring', which documented the detrimental effects on the environment, and particularly on birds, of the indiscriminate use of pesticides, especially DDT. This chemical, once in the food chain, made it more difficult for birds to absorb calcium thereby resulting in the thinning of their eggshells. Osprey eggs, and those of many other raptors, were breaking open before the chicks inside were ready to hatch and osprey populations suddenly plummeted as a result. Because large birds like eagles and ospreys typically only lay one to three eggs at a time, losing one or two eggs due to shell thinning was having a dramatic impact on their populations.

Introduction

Rachel Carson blamed the chemical industry for spreading disinformation and accused public officials of accepting industry claims unquestioningly. The book was met with fierce denials and criticism from the chemical companies producing these pesticides, however it eventually led to the nationwide ban of various synthetic pesticides and laid the groundwork for the creation of the Environmental Protection Agency, which finally banned the use of DDT in 1972, eight years after Rachel Carson lost her fight to cancer. She was posthumously awarded the Presidential Medal of Freedom by President Jimmy Carter in 1980; not bad for a humble marine biologist. The osprey, and every other animal living at the top of the food chain, including us, has a lot to thank Miss Carson for.

By the end of the 20th century, things were looking better for the osprey. British law had made it a crime to kill or disturb them, or to steal their eggs. People's attitudes towards wildlife were also changing and deep inside the British psyche there was a cultural revolution going on. Men who once shot birds were putting their guns down and buying expensive binoculars and telescopes to watch them instead. Some exchanged bullets for paintbrushes and easels. Up and down the country bird feeders were going up in people's gardens and children were peering out of their bedroom windows and trying to work out which bird was which. I was one of them.

Wildlife tourism had also taken off big style; suddenly we wanted to know more about the natural world around us and how plants and animals coexisted. Words like 'ecosystems' and 'biodiversity' were creeping into everyday language and were no longer the geeky rhetoric of conservation officers in their corduroy trousers and knitted tank tops. Nature reserves were being created and people were actually invited along to them to explore and learn more about nature. Normal, everyday people were taking their families and travelling hundreds of miles to go and see red kites feeding, eagles soaring, ospreys fishing, pelicans and guillemots nesting on steep cliffs. Not too far from where I grew up around the slate quarries where my grandfather and his father slogged their guts out in atrocious conditions a century ago, thousands of people now visit. Not to split or extract slate from rock, but to watch a pair of crows nesting. What the chough is going on?

These things seem quite normal and commonplace to us today, but just a few decades ago, living memory for many people, they were as avant-garde as an iPad would have been to Darwin. I bet there isn't an app for that.

deep inside the British psyche there was a cultural revolution going on

A Personal Relationship

Spotting an osprey carrying a fish has an attraction and appeal that is hard to describe.

Finally, around 50 years ago, there had come a time when the poor osprey could metaphorically breathe a sigh of relief. Hundreds of years of relentless, divisive and calculated attempts at osprey annihilation were coming to an end. The population in Scotland was at last starting to increase again, visitor centres and hides were being constructed to see them and people were starting to build an emotional attachment with the osprey.

Unlike Iolo, I had to venture slightly further afield than the Cairngorms to see my first ever osprey. Some 20 years ago I was sitting at a beach bar in Mexico on holiday, camera in one hand and a plastic glass of cheap, all-inclusive cocktail in the other. Pelicans and laughing gulls mingled in-between sunbeds strewn with sweaty, sunburnt tourists as the beach sellers were doing their rounds, aloe vera (and other botanical specimens) in hand. From the corner of my eye I spotted a large bird of prey in flight, it was flying parallel to the shore going left to right of me around 50m away, fish in talons. Well it had to be didn't it? I jumped out of my seat and gave chase, running along the beach as quickly as I could screaming "OSPREY…OSPREY" at the top of my voice. I didn't get close enough to take a photograph, but there was no doubt as to what it was.

I walked back to my bar stool panting and managed to regain some composure. I'm not sure the human beach dwellers were especially impressed with me, nor the pelicans for that matter – and the gulls definitely weren't laughing. I remember asking the barman what 'osprey' was in Spanish. He never did work out what I was attempting to ask him, but that tequila sunrise, or whatever it was with the umbrella in it, didn't half taste better than it had 10 minutes previously. So did the next one…

The osprey has some sort of special powers, I'm sure of it. It has appeal and charm that people find alluring and seductive. You remember the first time you saw an osprey, but why is that? I don't remember the first time I saw a buzzard or a marsh harrier. Maybe it's the persecution story and the osprey's battles with man over the centuries – a real David and Goliath scenario. Maybe it's the fact they only eat fish, or the fact that they migrate to an exotic beach somewhere, thousands of miles away only to return to the exact same nest the following spring. Perhaps it's simply because they are beautiful birds. Maybe it's all, some or none of these things, but whatever it is, people in this country, and many others for that matter, have acquired an affinity with ospreys and are somehow drawn in and captivated by them.

The British Trust for Ornithology started placing leg rings on birds at around the time the last pair or two of ospreys were hanging on for dear life in Scotland a century ago. What a great idea – to somehow put a marker on a bird and then rely on 'recoveries' to be sent back to a central processing office and information about species' movements collated, researched and published. An elegant and effective scientific instrument that has helped us understand more about birds than any other tool over the last hundred years. Where they go to, how long they live, the rate of natal dispersion, survival rates, who's related to who, the amount of inbreeding, immigration, emigration, and much, much more. The more we know about birds, the more we can help them, especially those that desperately need help.

Over the last 10 years or so, osprey ringing has generated a surprising and unpredicted advantage that has benefitted their conservation and status in the UK. Identifying ospreys as individuals, by way of their leg rings, has enabled their stories to be told on a much more personal level and to a much wider audience. That endearing little robin that has come for bread to the bird table throughout the

camera in one hand and a plastic glass of cheap, all-inclusive cocktail in the other

Red 8T – a 'famous' Scottish osprey. We know what nest he comes from, how old he is (2001), what partners he's had, how many chicks he's fathered. We even know the route he takes to his wintering grounds in Senegal. Remarkably, we know the exact tree in the exact mangrove swamp on the Casamance River where he tends to roost each night!

winter – is it the same bird every day? Could he be the same robin that has been around for the last three years? If you knew the answers, would you not feel more attached to that bird, more connected?

As you will see throughout this book, distinguishing ospreys as individuals by their leg rings (and other features and behaviours sometimes) has endeared them to the general public. Watching an osprey fly past so close to you that you can hear its wings beat is one thing, but knowing who he or she is, who they are breeding with, their age, where they come from, who their chicks are, puts things on a completely different level. You feel you have a bond with that osprey, an emotional attachment. A visitor said to me a decade ago, "This is better than watching Eastenders", and how right they were. Ospreys make brilliant cast members for a soap opera, only there are no script writers here, the birds are the story makers and some of the things they get up to, you really couldn't write a script for.

Photographing Ospreys

Arguably the one defining factor responsible for connecting people with the osprey more than any other over the last 50 years has been photography, both still photography and video. As a child I used to collect the books of wildlife photographer Eric Hosking; he was a pioneer in many ways and some of his images have stood the test of time on many levels. Grainy, low-resolution black and white photographs have been replaced these days by clear, high-fidelity colour images. Today's digital cameras and lenses are incomparable to the equipment Eric Hosking had in his time: better glass, auto-focus, image stabilisation and telephoto lenses of insane lengths for those far away birds.

Nevertheless, taking record shots of ospreys with your latest mega-zoom, auto-everything camera is one thing; taking some of the best photographs in the world under strict UK licensing is another. I'm honoured and eternally grateful that my friend and award winning professional wildlife photographer Andy Rouse has helped me out with some of the photographs for this book.

Over a cod and chips dinner in the Riverside restaurant in Pennal overlooking the Dyfi River in September 2014, Andy graciously offered to donate some of his best images in order for me to tell the osprey's story. He didn't have to ask twice. All the photographs in this chapter are his, as are many more images scattered throughout the book.

A male osprey, laden with a large fish and soaked feathers, fights gravity to get himself and his dinner airborne.

2004

Buses

When I think back to 2004 I always think of buses. You know the old saying, you wait ages for a bus…

This was the case in the osprey world in Wales. No breeding for hundreds of years, and then as if by magic, two come along at the same time. Only it wasn't magic of course, there was a whole series of events leading up to 2004 that led directly to two pairs of ospreys breeding in Wales at the same time, after a void of several centuries. The osprey conservation work in Scotland for the past 50 years, and the translocation project of ospreys from Scotland to Rutland in the 1990s, had both played a huge part in this magic bus journey.

The Cob, Porthmadog, with Snowdon in the background, left.

It was only a matter of time really. A land of hills and mountains, a modest human population, a veritable wealth of rivers, lakes and man-made reservoirs and a border of mostly fish-rich coastal waters, Wales was a prime target for the eventual re-colonisation by the osprey. Reports of migrating birds started in the 1970s, leading to a frenzy of sightings by the late 1990s and early 2000s. Surely the inevitable would happen sooner rather than later, after all, some of the reported sightings were recorded in the high breeding season – May and June, a time when most ospreys are either nest-bound, or roaming around looking for suitable nest sites close to water.

A male osprey had been seen fishing along the 'Cob' in Porthmadog, North Wales, throughout the summer of 2003. The Cob is an estuarine habitat of shallow waters where two main rivers, the Glaslyn and Dwyryd, enter the sea. Perhaps of even greater interest was the fact that this male osprey had been seen displaying to a female.

No nest was found in the summer of 2003, but it was with high hopes and expectations that local people spent the winter and spring of 2004. Ospreys are highly site specific, when they settle in an area seldom do they move out of that locality once they return from their winter migration in West Africa or (rarely) southern Europe.

The Discovery

By May 2004, it was apparent that two ospreys were again gracing the skies over the Glaslyn Valley. The same birds, surely.

The pair was eventually spotted flying in the direction of Nantmor, a tiny hamlet a few miles north west of Porthmadog and just south of Beddgelert, but despite asking local farmers and landowners, a nest could not be located. On the evening of 18th May, a cyclist, Steve Watson, spotted an osprey flying upstream and carrying a fish. He contacted local community policeman and ornithologist Kelvin Jones, who stated he didn't know where the nest was, or if there was even a nest at all, but he believed the

Panoramic view – the Glaslyn River meets Cardigan Bay.

ospreys could be based near Nantmor. The following morning Steve was back on the phone to Kelvin, he had found the nest.

The initial excitement of finding the nest soon gave way to the realisation that any eggs present were at risk of theft by egg collectors, or predation resulting from general disturbance. This was the first ever pair of ospreys to be officially recorded breeding in Wales and their eggs would be highly prized and extremely vulnerable.

May 2004 – the female looks as if she is sitting on eggs in the nest.

Kelvin contacted the local RSPB office in Bangor and, facilitated by the Conservation Team, a monitoring scheme was quickly organised. Members of local organisations such as Cymdeithas Edward Llwyd, Wales Raptor Study Group, Cymdeithas Ted Breeze Jones, Glaslyn Birdwatchers, Cambrian Ornithological Society, Countryside Council for Wales, the Environment Agency, Snowdonia National Park and the RSPB volunteered to help, and soon a 24-hour watch was set up 300m from the nest site. It was a basic affair, just a camp chair and a borrowed telescope initially. Three weeks later, however, the loan of a touring caravan offered more luxurious species protection facilities!

Who's Who?

Around 40% of Scottish ospreys are ringed each year as chicks, usually with a small metal BTO (British Trust for Ornithology) ring on one leg and a larger plastic ring on the other leg. These larger rings are often called 'Darvics' after the type of pressed PVC plastic they are made from. So the big question, were either of these Glaslyn ospreys ringed?

Here's the problem... Darvic rings, despite being put there specifically to be read on a bird 'in the field', are incredibly difficult to read. Your typical UK osprey has a 'circle of confidence' from humans of at least 100m, but usually twice that and then some. Venture inside this circle of confidence and the bird flies off. Darvics are 20mm across and have two or three digits on them, repeated several times. The writing is 1mm thick. Some Darvics break, some fade and some simply fall off after a few years.

It was both a delicate and significant undertaking to get close enough to the new pair without disturbing them, but it soon became apparent that one of the birds, the male, was indeed wearing a Darvic. An ochre (orange) ring on the right leg. The fact that it was the right leg carried huge significance.

In Scotland, Darvic rings are placed on the left leg. Back in the late 1990's it was decided that all ospreys hatching south of the border would have the Darvic ring placed on the right leg when they were ringed as chicks, thereby making the distinction between Scottish and any other British born osprey easy, without having to get close enough to read the digits. At the time, ospreys had only bred successfully in Scotland, the last recorded breeding in England was back in 1847. It took until 2000 for a non-Scottish osprey to hatch in the UK at a nest in Bassenthwaite, Cumbria, where one chick fledged. Was the Glaslyn male this bird returning as a four-year-old? After all, Cumbria is not a million miles away from North Wales.

The first photograph – Glaslyn male osprey with an ochre-coloured Darvic ring eating a fish.

The Rutland Translocation Project

Ospreys are highly philopatric (see Glossary, page 242). When they are adults, ospreys (especially males) tend to come back to breed to the same nest areas where they themselves were born. This might be a successful reproductive strategy for ospreys as a species within a normalised ecosystem, but add in centuries of persecution, UK extinction and a recovering species scenario, and you have a big problem if you are in anyway inclined to try and help the osprey.

There are two things you can do really, for osprey conservation within this unnatural situation. Put up artificial nest platforms, then hope and wait (for centuries possibly). Or you can move young ospreys from an area where they are doing well, and where there is healthy competition within the adult population, to an area where ospreys have become extinct, but where the habitat is still good for them. In the mid 1990's, Leicestershire and Rutland Wildlife Trust did both.

From 1996 to 2001, and under the stewardship and guidance of world-renowned osprey expert Roy Dennis from the Highland Foundation for Wildlife, 64 six-week-old chicks were removed from nests (of two or more chicks) in Scotland and transported to specially built holding pens at Rutland Water in the heart of England.

The young birds would be fed two or three times a day and eventually released when they were old enough to fly, the birds returning to the pens to be fed as they would to a normal nest, until they would start their migrations south at the end of August and September. The young birds were also ringed, the Darvics this time going on the right leg from 1998 onwards, with each year having a specific coloured ring. The interesting question of course was, would returning birds in a few year's time be philopatric (return) to their original Scottish nest areas, or would they be sufficiently imprinted onto Rutland Water to return there as adults?

Almost two decades on from those early 'translocations' as they are called, the answer is most definitely the latter. Of the 13 translocated ospreys that have been recorded having come back to the UK as adults, 10 returned to Rutland and two to Wales. Only one bird, a female, returned to Scotland where she bred near Dundee, raising eight chicks in all.

So, to go back to our ochre ringed male eating his fish in the Glaslyn Valley in 2004, ochre was the colour used for the translocated ospreys in 1998. Surely this bird had to be one of the 1998 Rutland birds?

What's Your Name?

Digital cameras back in 2004 were never up to the job of rudimentary 'digi-scoping' – basically placing your camera to the eye-piece of a telescope, pressing the shutter button and hoping for the best. The sensors in those first generation cameras were crude and unrefined compared to today's modern high resolution, multi-million pixel devices. Much better in 2004 to use the old fashioned and tested approach; look through a telescope with your eye and jot down what you see. And that's exactly what Tim Mackrill and John Wright from the Rutland Osprey Translocation Project did when they visited the Glaslyn in early July 2004. Using a ditch as cover, John and Tim managed to get to within 250m of the ochre ringed bird and close enough to see the actual number inscribed on it, just. The number was 11. It was, indeed, one of theirs.

pressing the shutter button and hoping for the best

2004

Ringed ospreys in the UK are generally identified according to a specific naming system. Colour, then number, then the year hatched in brackets. So, the Glaslyn male would be Ochre 11(98). These days all Darvics used for British ospreys are blue with white writing, so the colour is often omitted from this naming protocol. Eventually of course, all British ospreys will be blue ringed as older birds die out. This country-specific colour system is also used in some other European counties; France uses orange rings, Germany black rings, Spain yellow rings, and so on.

From around 2010 onwards, British ospreys have been ringed with blue Darvic rings.

Tim recalls Ochre 11(98) as a chick in 1998... *"On 23rd July, before he could fly, 11(98) was brought to Rutland Water where he was held in a pen for two weeks. He appeared to be a very active and fairly dominant bird, frequently taking fish from the other birds in his pen.*

He was released on 7th August, took about an hour to leave the pen and then had a long maiden flight, lasting almost six minutes. Unlike the other birds of that year, and surprisingly considering his subsequent history, he stayed in the immediate locality of the reservoir for several weeks.

11(98) was last seen on 11th September 1998, when we presumed he began his migration to West Africa."

So by 2004, Ochre 11(98) (let's call him the 'Glaslyn male' from now on!) was six years old. Ospreys stay in Africa for their first summer and tend to return to the UK as adults at two years of age and older. So had this six-year-old male been back to Rutland from 2000 onwards before deciding to venture further afield to Wales? Quite possibly, but impossible to say for certain as he has never been positively identified anywhere other than the Glaslyn. What is more certain is the likelihood that he had been spending the summer around the Glaslyn valley in the years prior to 2004. Almost certainly in 2003 and most probably a year or two before this as well.

The female osprey of 2004 was un-ringed, so her origins could not be traced. There were two main realistic options: she was either hatched at a nearby nest that nobody knew anything about, or she was a Scandinavian, or more likely a Scottish female, that had returned to the UK and stumbled across the ochre ringed male displaying to her, a few hundred miles south of her intended destination. The latter seemed more realistic – there were around 160 breeding pairs of ospreys in Scotland in 2004. Either way, her ancestry could never be proven and neither could her age. The only safe bet was that she was at least three years old in 2004, the earliest age at which ospreys tend to breed, although there are, exceptionally, birds that breed at two years old.

So with no leg rings to help identification, was there anything else that could be used as a form of ID to help distinguish this female from other ospreys, especially if she returned in future years? Thankfully, there was.

All ospreys have distinctive head plumage markings as well as individual under-wing patterns. Their own bespoke fingerprint set in feathers. Photographing the head patterns, especially in 2004, was especially challenging, notwithstanding the fact that head markings can appear contradictory viewed from different angles. They can also look different when the osprey is wet, which happens quite often to a fish-eating raptor living in Wales!

A 2004 shot of the female with her 'bespoke' under-wing pattern.

Much better to get a decent shot of the under-wing 'cobbles', the individual spots of dark brown feathers that are unique to that bird.

Female ospreys are typically darker in overall appearance than males, especially around the head, chest and under-wing. This female however was especially dark. With the absence of leg rings, her markings were the next best thing we could have to identify her in the future.

Disaster

By June, the RSPB had taken the lead role in coordinating everything osprey related. On 28th June, Kelvin, accompanied by a wildlife cameraman, gathered on the side of nearby mountain, Moel Ddu, with a video camera and telephoto lens. The pair didn't have to wait long before the hairs on the back of their necks were standing on end.

Tragedy – both chicks died at around two weeks old after their nest collapsed.

Peering down the camera's viewfinder, the female osprey could clearly be seen leaning into the nest as if she was feeding a chick. The white shooting spray over the side of the nest a short time later, confirmed what everyone had been hoping for. The female osprey was indeed feeding a chick; at least one, maybe more.

A date for the official announcement was planned for Saturday, 3rd July on the BBC Radio Cymru programme, Galwad Cynnar. Tragically however, on the previous Wednesday, 30th June, a horrendous unseasonal storm hit the Glaslyn valley. The nest succumbed to the weather and most of it collapsed to the ground taking with it its precious live cargo – osprey chicks. There were two of them. The sense of euphoria and ecstasy had changed to dejection and helplessness quite literally, overnight. A subsequent post mortem revealed that the two chicks had died from injuries sustained in falling over 80 feet from the nest. They were 12 – 14 days old.

Working Together

A pair of ospreys recolonised Scotland in 1954 after possibly being extinct for several decades; 1916 was the last time ospreys had been recorded as breeding. Exactly fifty years on and ospreys were once again nesting in Wales – for the first time in hundreds of years. The great ornithologist George Waterston OBE had experienced successive attempts by egg collectors in the 1950's to steal osprey eggs at the Loch Garten nest in Speyside and in 1959, as RSPB's Scotland Director by then, he decided to change tack. Rather than keep everything osprey related quiet and hush-hush, which clearly hadn't worked, he went the opposite direction.

An observation post was set up and the general public was invited to come and see the rare and mysterious fish-eating bird of prey. Wardens and volunteers helped with protection shifts for the six weeks when there were eggs in the nest, and so started one of the greatest conservation stories of the 20th century. Three eggs were laid that year, all three hatched and all three chicks successfully fledged. It didn't stop egg collectors overnight, but it went a heck of a long way towards massively reducing their impact on the osprey's precarious fight back.

George Waterston's decision was courageous and visionary. Telling everybody, as opposed to nobody, was the medical equivalent of antibiotics – fighting fire with fire, and it worked. That template is still used today and it was used in the Glaslyn in 2004. Bringing several specialised organisations together and engaging the local communities of Porthmadog and the smaller villages of Prenteg, Llanfrothen and Croesor, was a direct replica of the model used in Scotland from 1959 onwards. And what better way of also connecting people and children with wildlife and environmental learning?

A makeshift viewing point was set up at Pont Croesor near the village of Prenteg and an incredible 9,500 people visited during the eight week period it was open. Just as in Scotland decades before, there was a huge appetite to see ospreys close up, and osprey viewing and learning in Wales was born.

the sense of euphoria and ecstasy had changed to dejection and helplessness quite literally, overnight

People gather to see ospreys in Wales for the first time in centuries.

Both adults sit out the remainder of the summer.

It was way too late for the ospreys to re-lay by July and they spent the remainder of the summer mating and rebuilding their nest. It was all part of the pair-bonding before leaving again in September and going their separate ways for the winter. The weather still wasn't on their side however, and much of their nest re-building work was frequently undone by strong winds.

Building for the Future

Over the winter it became pretty obvious that something needed to be done to help the ospreys the following year. The very top branches of the silver fir tree where the nest had originally been built were rotting away. Even if the ospreys would return the following year and the weather was calm, there was no guarantee that the tree could hold such a large and heavy structure.

OSPREYS IN WALES *The First Ten Years*

Up in Scotland, Roy Dennis had been erecting artificial osprey nest platforms and fixing broken ones for decades, it was a tried and tested formula and one that worked. Ospreys are very receptive to a bit of human DIY.

The rotting branches atop the silver fir were removed and a new nest built a few feet lower down. It was bolted and cable-tied together and securely fastened to a healthier part of the tree. If the ospreys were to return in 2005, they would have one less obstacle to successful breeding. Even the worst of Welsh weather wasn't going to budge this nest.

Local children from Ysgol y Garreg in nearby Llanfrothen helped with the nest building and a camera was placed at the highest point of the resculpted tree top, looking down into the nest. The significance of this £30 camera was lost at the time, but it would prove to be a shrewd investment in time to come.

A new home. If a man could stand in the nest comfortably, a couple of birds weighing less than 2Kg each should have no problems.

2004

OSPREYS IN WALES *The First Ten Years*

Welshpool

As the Glaslyn birds were taking all the limelight during the summer of 2004, something quite profound was also happening 45 miles away, just to the south of Welshpool in Mid Wales.

In 2003, Montgomeryshire Wildlife Trust had erected a nest platform on their Dolydd Hafren reserve, with the hope of attracting ospreys to breed there. Roy Dennis had tried to coordinate a Rutland style translocation to Wales in the late 1990's, but unfortunately could not obtain the necessary licenses, despite large swathes of Mid Wales being prime osprey habitat. Moreover, a German ringed (1996) female osprey had spent the summer in the area both in 1998 and 1999.

Ironically, a pair of ospreys did finally nest in 2004, but not on the Dolydd Hafren platform – they built their own nest. Fortunately this time, not only was one of the birds ringed, they both were.

The Welshpool osprey nest – 2004.

OSPREYS IN WALES *The First Ten Years*

The female had a red ring on her left leg with the inscription 6J. A quick phone call to Roy, who coordinates all osprey ringing in the UK, confirmed that this bird was ringed as a chick on the west end of Loch Tummel in Perthshire on 24th July 2001; so she was almost certainly a first time breeder at three years old.

Arguably of greater importance was the origin of the male. He had a white leg ring – 07. Unbelievably, he was another of the Rutland translocated ospreys, this time from the batch of eight birds moved down from Scotland in 1997, so he was seven years old. The efforts of Roy in Scotland and the Rutland team in England were starting to pay dividends – in Wales.

Enter Tim and John again. They visited the Welshpool nest on 13th July with Montgomeryshire Wildlife Trust's Conservation Officer, Clive Faulkner, and viewed the nest for several hours. What Tim and John said to each other after seeing a second Rutland osprey in Wales in as many weeks was never recorded. Even if it had been, no doubt it could not have been printed in any case!

The single osprey in the Welshpool nest at around six weeks old – the first osprey to fledge from a Welsh nest for centuries.

2004 13

Later that month on 26th July, Roy came down from Scotland to have a look for himself. On an adjacent tree Roy spotted another osprey nest which had been abandoned; probably the remains from a previous year's breeding attempt. Clive had asked Tony Cross of the Welsh Kite Trust and bird ringer extraordinaire, to also take a closer look, as it was thought that the new osprey pair could have young. Tony accepted the offer (he doesn't refuse many!) and duly arrived, cherry-picker in tow. Try as they might, they could not get the hoist bucket close enough and high enough to do any ringing. Tony did get close enough though to confirm one thing that he could see from his elevated vantage point... "ONE CHICK IN NEST" he shouted.

26th July, so near, yet so far. Tony Cross is unable to reach the Welshpool osprey chick in 2004.

That youngster, probably a male, went on to fledge the nest. After many hundreds of years, Wales finally had its first successful osprey nest.

2005

In at the Deep End

After initially volunteering at the Glaslyn, the RSPB offered me the post of Project Manager in the spring of 2005. I remember as if it were yesterday walking in to the protection caravan just before 6am and letting Elfyn, one of the Species Protection Officers, know the 'good news'. I think he was genuinely pleased, but not necessarily for me, more for the fact that the whole Glaslyn osprey initiative would now have a steer, a direction with somebody at the wheel. That was my sentiment too; all I remember feeling at the time was trepidation!

On one level my remit was simple enough. George Waterston had, after all, written the template up in Scotland almost half a century before. Embrace a pair of ospreys, run a public viewing site and a protection team, manage a few staff and volunteers, a bit of community liaison work, public relations, IT, licensing, photography, planning, media, and everything in two languages. What could be simpler? It was daunting to be honest, but something that I relished and wanted to grab with both hands. What a challenge. Not your run of the mill job, something without precedent in Wales up to then and something to emboss your own individual signature on.

Having been brought up just up the road in Caernarfon, I knew this community well and how it worked. Having bits of paper with qualifications on is one thing, but understanding the mechanics and nuances of a local community and how it operated was the best qualification I could ever have. I was on the right page, spoke the same language even.

At the time there was an undercurrent of mistrust within the local community. Nothing serious, just a kind of ambient, background rumbling that you couldn't quite put your finger on. If you asked, people would smile and brush it away with politeness, but it was there.

People on all levels can be unreceptive to change, but to be fair, the local Glaslyn community had suddenly been inundated with thousands of visitors into their rural, mainly agricultural community, some of them having travelled hundreds of miles to look at a couple of birds in a tree. On the face of it, what a strange thing to do? Yes, local people were used to tourism, we were in the middle of

understanding the mechanics and nuances of a local community and how it operated was the best qualification I could ever have

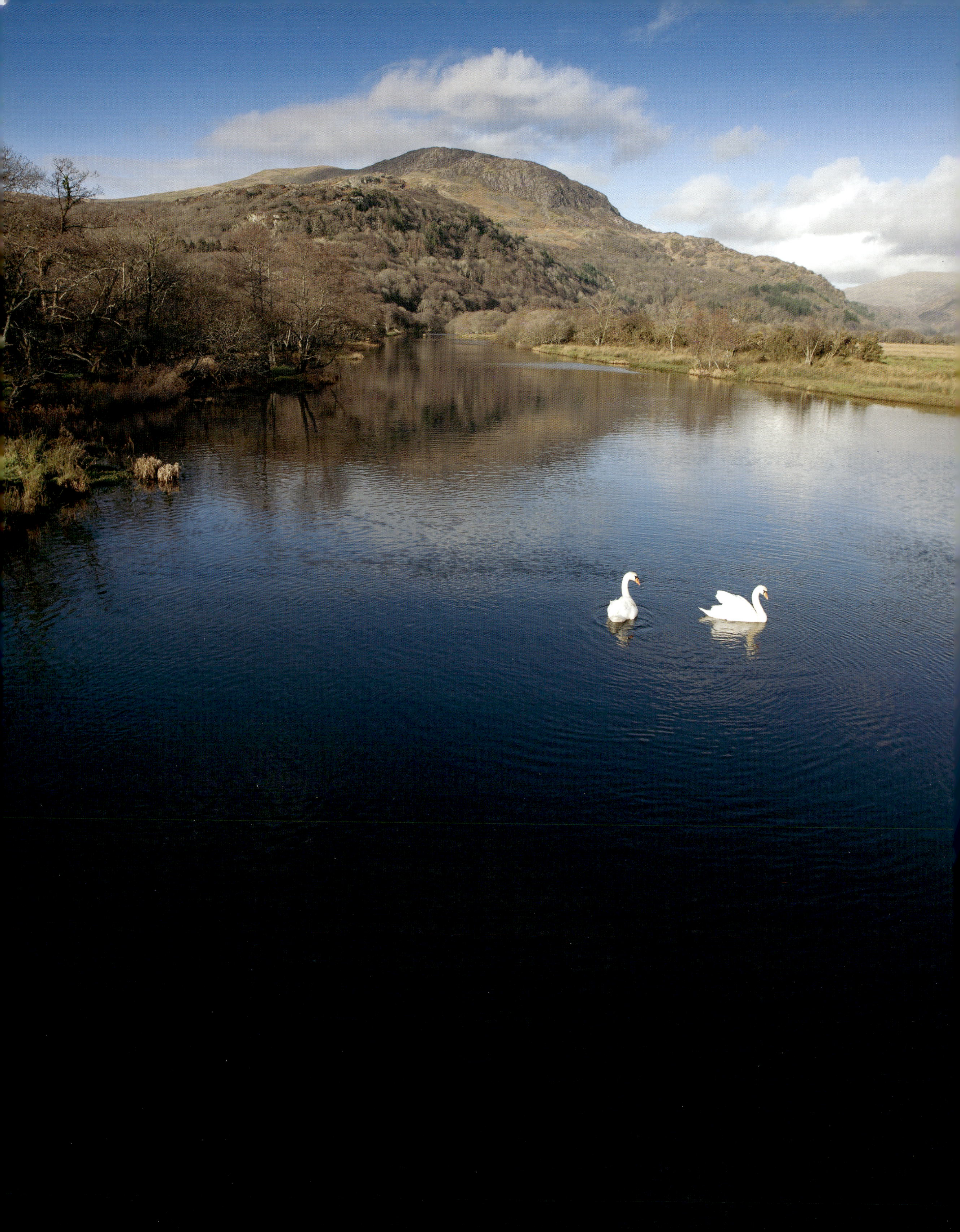

Snowdonia National Park of course, but several hundred people squished into a small field like sardines every day looking though tubes on tripods was a little bit different.

So started an initiative of community engagement. Talks, school visits, meetings, public consultations, newspaper articles, steering groups, radio and TV interviews. I would talk to everybody and anybody that would listen. The fact that the local community had someone speaking Welsh to them no doubt helped, but the clincher was someone explaining what all the fuss was about. Nothing beats cancelling out a fear of the unknown. A rare bird of prey that posed no threat to livestock, having never been properly recorded as having bred in Wales before, and a species that could potentially benefit the local community for years down the road. More visitors equals more money, equals more jobs, equals greater prosperity for all. Basic simple win-win economics, that everybody understands – and that's not to mention the conservational benefits to the ospreys themselves.

The formula was simple. Invite people to see the ospreys, make them feel part of the show, get them helping and volunteering, make them feel welcome. Soon the ospreys were 'theirs', people had a sense of ownership and belonging. Shoppers in the greengrocers in Porthmadog were saying, "we have ospreys"; bus drivers were telling people which stop to get off to see "our ospreys". Local people were now part of the osprey thing and not just bystanders looking at it through their windows behind net curtains. They were engaged and it felt good.

The RSPB wanted me to manage the Glaslyn ospreys, and everything to do with them, with the community at the heart of everything and I was only too happy to do exactly that. There was one thing missing though, and it was causing me some problems. What was this whole osprey 'thing' to be called? Glaslyn Ospreys was suggested, but what if another pair were to appear the following year and more in the future? Also, wouldn't people confuse "Glaslyn Ospreys" with some kind of North Walian rugby team?

I wanted to call it the "Glaslyn Osprey Project." The word 'project', to me anyway, sounded dynamic and progressive, something exciting to get involved with and get your teeth stuck into. Nobody had any serious opposition, so by May 2005 the Glaslyn Osprey Project was born.

bus drivers were telling people which stop to get off to see "our ospreys"

The Ospreys Return

With a new nest built over the winter, a little bullet camera installed, all that was left to do was wait. A new viewing hide had been erected in local farmer Dafydd Owen's field at Pont Croesor, just over a mile away from the nest, and by early spring it felt like the whole world was waiting to see if the two ospreys would once again return to the Glaslyn. Patience is a virtue, and there wasn't much of it around.

Winter 2004/2005, view of the Glaslyn River from Pont Croesor.

There were no high-tech recording and play-back systems back then, just the old fashioned pair of binoculars and a large amount of time and patience. Keen birdwatchers Heather and Janice Corfield had been following everything osprey related around Porthmadog right from those early sightings in 2003. They were as eager as anyone that the birds return. Taken from Heather's own diary…

probably a Scottish osprey on her final migratory leg home

Monday 28th March 2005 – The Male Returns.

Our first view of the newly re-built nest in March 2005 was from one of the few places the nest can be seen apart from Pont Croesor. Towards the end of March my mother and I, along with some local friends, were keeping a close look out for the returning pair.

During the Easter weekend we had made at least three trips a day to check things out and nothing. On Easter Monday after spending a couple of hours in Beddgelert, we decided to make one final check at 5pm. I was a little behind my mother, who was already stood with her binoculars pointed towards the nest. "He's There.." she shouted excitedly. I told her it was probably a branch she was looking at, as I raised my binoculars towards my eyes. "No, it is definitely him" she said. At precisely that moment I saw with my own eyes the stunning sight of the Glaslyn male sat atop the sawn off post above the nest. He was proudly surveying his nest as if he had built it himself. We rushed down to the stile at Pont Croesor to see whether any of our friends were there and met a gentleman from Corwen with a telescope, he had been there for most of the day and he had watched him fly in an hour before.

It was the same male osprey that had been around for the last two years; his ochre leg ring was plain to see. It was number 11 and he was back. As predicted, he took to the 'new' nest straight away and was quickly adding clumps of earth and sticks to it; he was alone and he seemed in a hurry.

The following Monday he was joined by a female, but this osprey looked different to the 2004 bird. She was un-ringed which is what we expected, but she seemed lighter in colour, the necklace not as pronounced. The new couple were not seen mating and exactly a week later the female was gone, it seemed that the male had refused to hand his dinner over once too often and that was enough for her. She wasn't the same bird.

Maybe the bond forged in 2004 (and possibly 2003) was strong enough for the male not to glibly start giving hand-outs to any old female that passed through his territory? Whatever the case, after spending exactly a week, 4th – 11th April in the Glaslyn, she had gone. Probably a Scottish osprey on her final migratory leg home.

*The same male osprey
returns 28th March, 2005.*

The female returns, but not until 22nd April. Is it too late to start breeding?

The male had been alone for 11 days and just as hope was fading that his partner from the previous year would return, on Friday, 22nd April, another osprey joined him on the nest. Was it the right one though? The two ospreys were quickly mating and by early evening the male had brought a fish back for his new mate. From the behaviours we observed, it looked a dead certainty that this was the same female – she was un-ringed and looked as if she had a very dark chest band, just what we expected. By the time I had managed to get a decent photograph of her a few days later, any doubts about her identity quickly vanished. She had the exact same chest, belly and face markings. The under-wing cobbles were identical to the female in 2004. It was her alright, no question, but was 22nd April too late to start breeding?

Almost every bird species on earth has an invisible ceiling, a cut off point where evolution has decided that there comes a point where producing eggs is just not worth it. No osprey wants to have eggs hatch on Christmas day in minus temperatures in Wales with just a few hours of daylight to catch several fish per day. This egg laying cut off point is somewhere in the month of May for British ospreys,

After waiting patiently at the protection caravan for most of the day, the female finally does a flypast close enough to photograph her. Three are out of focus, but the last picture comes out fine – it was the same female.

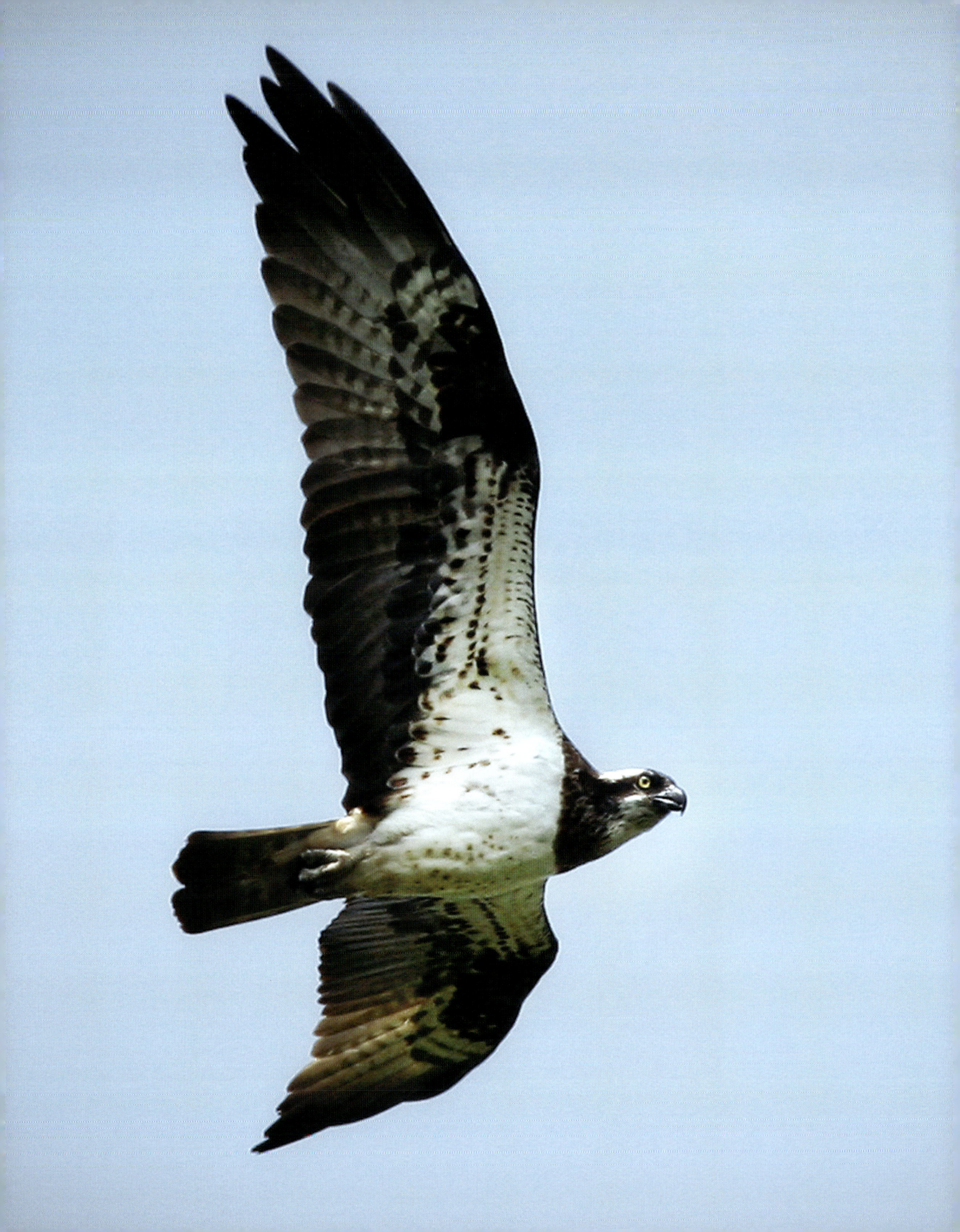

but when exactly? We had no reference to go by with this pair, nor any other pair for that matter in Wales. It was a case of wait and see. One thing was certain though, if the ospreys were not to lay any eggs in 2005, it would not have been for the lack of trying!

Operation Pandora

Over the winter local ornithologist and policeman, Kelvin Jones, with his Wildlife Crime Officer's hat on (or should that be helmet?), had done a great job in setting up a species protection protocol for the ospreys if they returned. The loan of surveillance equipment from North Wales Police, a communication procedure with 999 operators, ground nest sensors and anti-theft 'tar' for the nest tree, training for staff and volunteers, community liaison – and the whole thing was to be called Operation Pandora.

Local policeman Huw Jones with a receiver for the ground sensors, and biochemically distinct, anti-vandal tar behind him on the nest tree.

The osprey as a species is classified as a "Schedule 1" bird of prey. They are afforded the highest level of protection under UK law (Wildlife and Countryside Act 1981) and it is a criminal offence to intentionally or recklessly disturb ospreys near, or on an active nest. The maximum penalty for actually harming or stealing ospreys, including their eggs, is six months in prison. There existed however (and it still does), a dark underground of people that will do almost anything to steal rare birds' eggs in the UK; eggs that are practically worthless in monetary value. It's a relic still with us from Victorian times – offenders are always men, British, white, and take great enjoyment out of stealing eggs and causing havoc to species on the very edge of extinction in this country.

There is a paradox here – the rarer a bird is, the greater the attractiveness of its eggs to egg thieves, and by taking the eggs the bird becomes rarer still, increasing further their desirability to the egg criminals. An abhorrent and sickening 'hobby'.

Let's be clear here and not beat around the bush – the osprey became extinct in the UK a century ago not because of mass habitat loss or pollution or any kind of natural catastrophe. They were wiped out by man – stealing their eggs and shooting them dead. We had Operation Pandora and we all took it seriously. We had to.

A female osprey usually takes between 10 and 25 days to lay her first egg after mating commences. This period can be highly variable however, and can depend on a lot of factors. The strength of the bond between the two birds is important; the male's proficiency at catching fish, the amount of matings, the weather, time of year, disturbance and intrusions from other ospreys – all play a role.

For the first few days after being reunited, the male was seen bringing very small prey items back to the nest – not the size of fish you would expect at this time of year where a male should be showing off – display flights and the sky-dancing, that sort of thing. The fish were so small in fact that the female was seen catching her own fish on a couple of occasions and bringing them back to the nest. If we were to see any eggs in 2005, surely the male needed to up his game?

Here cometh the first lesson of working with ospreys. Get a load of people together, call them experts as they know what they're talking about, get a consensus and then let everybody know what will happen next in the osprey world. You can guarantee the birds will do something else. It's as if they have a sixth sense and can see what you're forecasting and will do absolutely anything to do the opposite and prove you wrong. Inexperienced birds where the male has been catching tiddlers, should take much longer to lay eggs than established pairs that have been breeding for years.

At 9:50am on 2nd May – a mere 10 days after first being reunited, the female laid an egg. Right at the extreme early part of the range. Here endeth the lesson. Ospreys know best so stop trying to second-guess what they're going to do next. They'll make you look stupid.

they were wiped out by man – stealing their eggs and shooting them dead

Operation Pandora had up until then been something academic, a concept. A PowerPoint presentation, something written down on paper or burnt onto a CD. Suddenly it was real and tangible and a call to action was required, quickly.

Rotas were drawn up for volunteers, the night vision glasses were dusted down and taken out of their box, signs for public footpaths had to be printed and put up. There was suddenly a whole species protection mini-project to manage and not one of us had done this before. Organisation and good communication were needed as well as an overall calmness – no panicking here Mr Mainwaring. Truth was, we were all so excited none of us were calm on the inside.

Luckily, I had a lot of experience of designing and managing 24 hour rotas, so I put that to good use. We had five Species Protection Officers that year and over 30 volunteers – between us we would guard that nest 24 hours a day with two people being on duty for most of the time. Early shifts, late shifts and night shifts – all had to be covered. Egg thieves don't come ambling along on a Saturday afternoon with ladders and empty egg boxes under their arms anymore. They are shrewd, conniving and savvy. We needed to be too.

Three days after she laid her first egg, the female laid another and following three more days, a third. You could sense the excitement on everybody's faces and in their voices. You could cut it with a knife. We had all read about this in books and magazines from decades past up in Scotland, now it was happening right here in Wales, and we were all part of it. It was an amazing feeling.

May 4th, 2005. Volunteer John Parry takes over from the night shift at 6am.

Pont Croesor

The excitement was just as palpable a mile away down at the public viewing site at Pont Croesor too. News about the three eggs had spread quickly and visitors were gathering in their thousands to see their first ever sighting of ospreys in Wales. True, being a mile away from the nest presented its own problems in terms of viewing the birds, but it was the only practicable location where thousands of visitors could easily and safely be gathered, and their cars of course, without disturbing the ospreys. High-powered telescopes lessened the distance somewhat and the glorious panoramic views across some of the highest mountains in Snowdonia also mitigated the distance.

The male with his leg ring, Ochre 11, hovers over the Glaslyn River in front of the new hide at Pont Croesor, in search of surface dwelling fish.

The hide was situated right on the edge of the Glaslyn River itself where we would often see the male osprey slowly soaring down river looking for his prey.

On Sunday afternoon, 22nd May, there was a torrential hail storm, the likes of which only come around once every few years – in late May at any rate. It had been unseasonably cold and rather worryingly, it was more than just a quick passing weather front. The incubating female was suddenly transformed into a white ghost-like figure and her nest and everything around her became covered with small white balls of ice.

The male was nowhere to be seen and as the weather deteriorated, it became increasingly difficult to view what was happening inside the nest. The female had snuggled right down and was doing everything in her power to keep her three eggs dry and at an optimal incubation temperature of 36°C. What followed that week was my first real experience of working with birds in the public domain.

Visitors watch as the male osprey makes his way down river towards the Cob at Porthmadog; luckily the hide is directly underneath his flight path. The mountain on the right is Cnicht.

By the middle of the following week, I had received a stack of emails, voice messages, phone calls, text messages and visits from concerned followers. Were the birds okay? Can the male still fish? Will the eggs be alright? We had seen how the power of marketing had resulted in thousands of visitors coming to Pont Croesor, but suddenly being bombarded by masses of people wishing to know more about the welfare of a single female osprey and her eggs was an eye opener. Most of these people had never seen the ospreys, not even a photograph – these were the days before social media and Live Streaming of course. One lady rang me from Canada, worried about the egg temperatures – how on earth did she know about a hail storm and a pair of birds in Wales, several thousands of miles away? It was deeply heart-warming that so many people cared enough to pick the phone up or to write in, it was also a profoundly effective lesson as to the power of marketing. I would remember this lesson and use it again in the future.

For the next two weeks we were working at full speed ahead, all guns blazing. The species protection guys doing their thing around the clock and the people engagement team talking and answering questions as fast as they were being thrown at them down the road at Pont Croesor. That £30 camera was paying off big time, for both sets of teams.

A live camera link at the small visitor centre at Pont Croesor, the female incubating while the male looks on.

As we entered June the mercury on the excitement barometer was rising. Osprey incubation is around 37 days; the eggs were due to hatch around a week into the month. Would all three hatch? Would any hatch? I had been regurgitating the story of the hail storm for over a fortnight – European ospreys were rugged, robust birds, breeding in countries inside the Arctic Circle where daytime temperatures can barely struggle beyond 0°C in May, all the way down to the sizzling conditions in southern Europe and Arabia. Surely a bit of hail and some single figure temperatures for a few days in temperate Wales wasn't going prove anything more disruptive to the ospreys than a tenuous annoyance. Was it?

Ecstasy

we started hugging and kissing and jumping up and down. I hardly knew some of them

By Thursday morning, 9th June, the female osprey had started to change her behaviour. Gone was eating dinner on a favourite nearby perch, she was now eating in the nest. She was fidgety and restless. The male seemed to be around more than usual too, loafing around on the nest with his partner all day. He didn't even seem interested in catching any fish that afternoon. By 6pm we had closed the visitor centre to the public and rather than going home, I grabbed a sandwich and headed straight for the protection site.

A few volunteers had already gathered there, they too knew something was afoot. The female continued with her fidgeting – up, off the eggs, then down, then straight back up again, all the while rotating slowly like a sundial with each clockwise movement. At 8:30pm she sat down to incubate her eggs again and stayed there. I remember us all looking at each other thinking, well, this is a bit of an anti-climax.

Shortly before 9pm the female once again stood up off her eggs and spun around for a few seconds. It was just enough time to allow the eight of us that had squashed into the tiny caravan to see what was beneath her. There were only two eggs in there, intact eggs that is, the third was split in two and a tiny, delicate little purple chick was wriggling around in-between the egg shells. What followed was mass hysteria.

We started hugging and kissing and jumping up and down. I hardly knew some of them. Cups of tea and pens and diaries were jumping off the desk – how that caravan stayed in one piece that tranquil June evening I'll never know. There must have been half a ton of weight bouncing up and down in a miniscule caravan the size of a family saloon, in the middle of nowhere. It was like the eight of us had just heard that we had won a syndicate lottery Euro Millions jackpot. Actually, it felt better than that, not that I will never know.

In all the commotion, we failed to spot the male disappearing up river. There was an hour or so of daylight left, but he didn't need more than 10 minutes of it. By 9:15pm he was back with a small trout and the female swiftly grabbed it off him and started to feed her new chick. She most probably had only ever been in this situation once before, in 2004, and then only for a few days. The chick suffered a thwack over the head from the trout, but by nightfall had thankfully eaten a few mouthfuls. Apart from the night shift, we all went home happy; no make that delirious. I had been studying and photographing birds for almost 25 years, how could peering at a 12-inch screen with seven others in a small caravan in North Wales for hours on end make you feel so happy? It was something I had never experienced before, the feeling of euphoria and exhilaration was indescribable. I never did eat that sandwich.

From Strength to Strength

By 12th June, three days later, the second chick had hatched, only this time it was at lunchtime on a sunny Sunday afternoon when the visitor centre was packed. There must have been 40, maybe 50 people crammed into the small portacabin looking at the live video being beamed back from the nest. I remember not feeling the same kind of euphoria as when the first chick hatched, but more an overwhelming happiness that so many visitors had seen what a select lucky few of us had witnessed three days prior. It was such a good news story; you just wanted to share it with as many other people as possible. I like to think that ten years on, there are still people out there that remember their experiences of seeing that second chick hatch in the Glaslyn in 2005. A great 'I was there' moment.

The third egg didn't hatch (most probably it was the second egg laid) and by the time we came to ring the two chicks at around five weeks old on 13th July, it was removed from the nest, still intact. It was probably an infertile egg, quite a common occurrence.

Both the Glaslyn chicks were allocated yellow rings in 2005. Yellow 37 was given to the whiter looking offspring which we had hypothesised was a male; his weight of 1,430g reinforced this view (females usually weigh in excess of 1,500g). The other, darker chick was over 100g heavier at 1,540g, most probably a female and she was given ring Yellow 38. As this ring was put on however, it started to crack! Luckily, Roy had sent us three Darvics down from Scotland and Yellow 39 came to the rescue. The rings were placed on the right leg and the correct way up – to be read from the foot up, so with the '3' nearest the talons. The odd ring has been put on upside-down in the past (and still are!), which makes identification years down the line extremely difficult, not to mention confusing.

The rest of that summer seemed to whisk along and by the time we closed the Glaslyn Osprey Project at the start of September, almost 75,000 people had visited – an insane amount of people just to view a pair of birds in the middle of a field in the rural countryside of Snowdonia. We had experienced a proper honeymoon period; more people visited the Glaslyn that year than in any single year since. I

by the time we closed the Glaslyn Osprey Project at the start of September, almost 75,000 people had visited

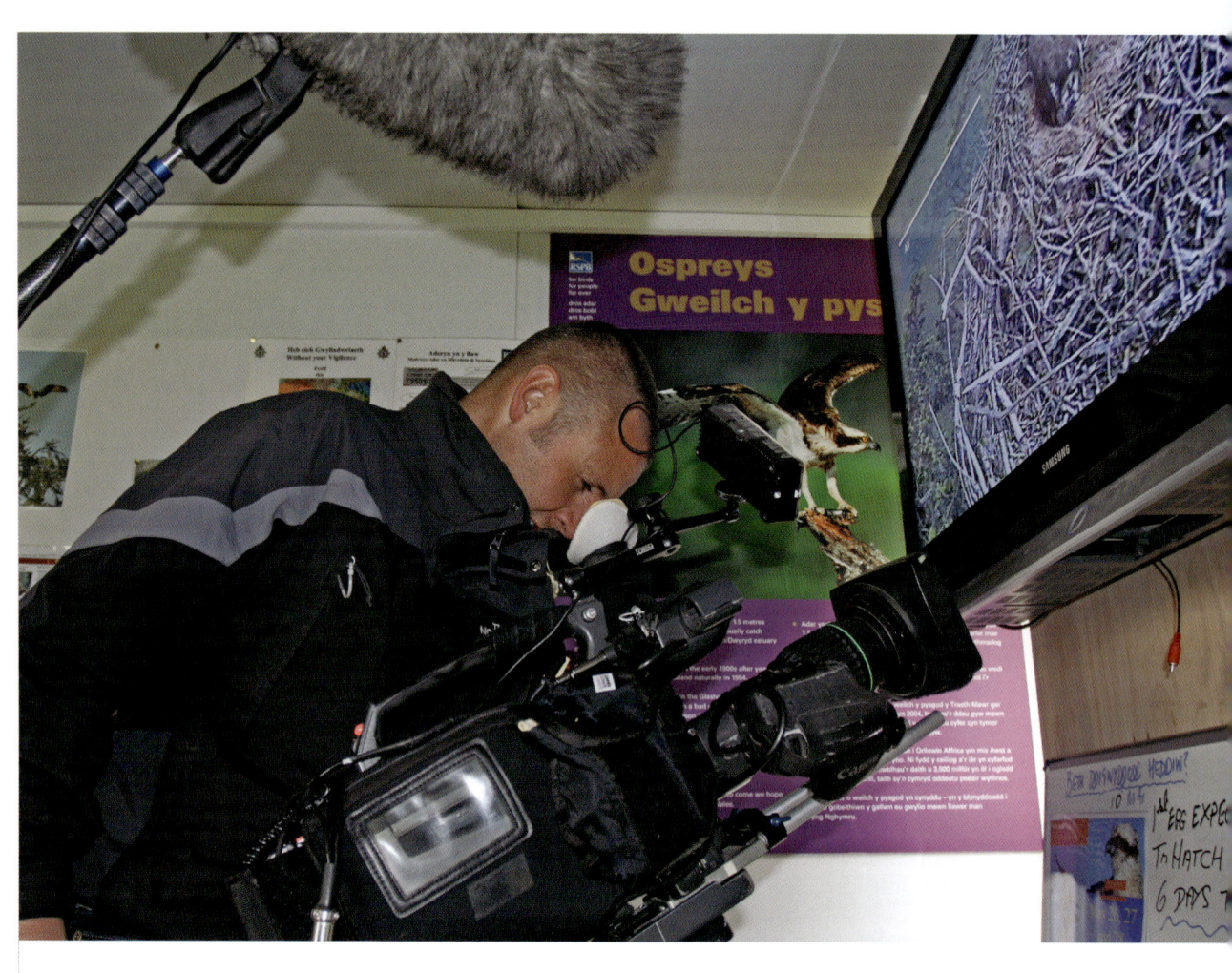

The Glaslyn ospreys become television stars in 2005.

remember thinking about the late George Waterston and how he must have felt after that brave decision he took in 1959 and witnessing, with several thousand others, the three Loch Garten chicks fledging in August of that year after several seasons battling, unsuccessfully, with egg thieves.

The Glaslyn male chick, Yellow 37, flew for the first time on 30th July at 51 days old. His sister, Yellow 39 fledged at 52 days old on 3rd August. We last saw the female on 1st September that year, but the male hung around until the middle of the month, he was the final osprey to leave.

In the autumn of 2005 I embarked on a rather hectic community talk programme, taking a slide show and a head full of osprey stories and memories to different venues around North Wales. For a couple of days in October it was refreshing to take a bit of a break and travel up to the Lake District for an osprey conference that the guys at Bassenthwaite had organised.

Clive from Montgomeryshire Wildlife Trust had also made the journey up the M6, but with some disappointing news. The Welshpool female, Red 6J, had not returned to her nest in 2005 and the male, having arrived back at the same nest once again, had not paired up with another female. No further breeding took take place at the Welshpool nest, although it seems that the male, White 07, did return

OSPREYS IN WALES *The First Ten Years*

for some years thereafter. This nest would go down in the history books as having been the first successful osprey nest in modern times in Wales, but rather sadly, just one single osprey would ever be raised in it.

I had dinner with Roy Dennis that evening. He had pork chops and a glass of red wine. I have no idea what I had. I must have barraged him incessantly with questions for a good couple of hours and he had the grace and charity to answer every one of them. I had a lot to learn. Roy had over 40 years of osprey experience under his wing by 2005, I had barely one season. I scribbled down everything I could remember from our conversation (or interrogation depending which side of the table you were on) and stayed up into the small hours writing away in my hotel room. What better way to learn than to talk to the master himself. The next osprey talk I gave was at Bangor University the following week – it felt especially humbling.

BTO ring and Yellow 38 Darvic, which subsequently broke.

The Glaslyn ospreys having fledged their first ever chicks in 2005, would not start their migrations until the last day of August (female) and mid September (male).

2005   31

29th March 2006 – the Glaslyn female is back before the male and starts nest repairs almost immediately, mobbed by crows and gulls.

2006

Extended Honeymoon

A benchmark had been set in 2005 and we all realised by 2006 that there was a massive appetite for everything osprey out there. We had to make sure we could meet the demand. Glyn Roberts, who had been with the RSPB since those early days of 2004 when the nest blew down, was joined by two other People Engagement Officers: Mick Alexander, who had started in 2005, and Alwyn Ifans.

The male had arrived back from migration at the end of March the previous year, so we were all eagerly waiting for him to return for his third year of breeding from around the 25th onwards. True to form, my mobile phone started buzzing with text messages early morning on the 29th. I raced down to the protection site having already scribbled down some notes for a press release… "King of the Glaslyn returns", or some nonsense to that effect. Sure enough, as I approached the caravan I could hear the early shift volunteers and that characteristic chatter and laughing that could mean just one thing. There was an osprey sitting on the nest, only it wasn't the king of the Glaslyn that had returned – it was the queen!

On average male ospreys return back to their nests a day or two before the females, but this is by no means a foregone conclusion. She hadn't arrived until 22nd April the previous year so it was good to know that the Glaslyn female could be an 'early' bird now she seemed to be a settled breeder. The main window for British breeding ospreys returning from migration is anywhere from mid-March to the end of April, so any bird arriving in the month of March is considered early, especially in Scotland where the arrival times are slightly later (the colder the climate, the later ospreys from those countries typically return; Finnish ospreys for example don't tend to return until well into April).

The king is back, but not before the missus.

We didn't have to wait long for the male to arrive. Just two days later Species Protection Officer, Angharad, was texting me again, only this time it really was the king. By the time I had finished a radio interview that morning and raced back to the protection site at 11:00, not only was the male back, he had caught a large trout and had handed it over to his mate. An hour later they were mating at the side of the nest and the show was on the road for another year. Start the car.

There is something very special about seeing the same osprey returning to the same nest each year, having being away for seven months or more. It's a sense of excitement mixed with bewilderment that they have travelled a round trip of seven thousand miles and returned to the very spot you last saw them the previous year. You find yourself asking all sorts of questions in your head… I wonder where you go? Which other ospreys have you seen? How do you know what time to set off? And many more.

The fact that our newly reunited ospreys were getting on like a house on fire was proof enough that both birds were exactly the same pair as previous years. The female looked the same, the male did too and he

Our boy is back – I could just make out the number 11 on his leg ring.

had leg rings of course. Remembering the 'ospreys will make you look stupid' rule however, I thought it best to check. Just in case.

Four days after he arrived, the male set off on a late afternoon fishing trip and, alerted by the guys at the protection site that he was heading for the visitor centre following the path of the Glaslyn River, I dashed out of the office with my camera, attached to the longest lens I had. Luckily enough, he flew close enough to the hide at Pont Croesor for me to snap a few shots. A quick look on the laptop a few minutes later confirmed what we all had assumed. It was indeed Ochre 11(98). Better to be safe than sorry.

The Only Pair of Ospreys in Wales

As sure as eggs is eggs, that's exactly what we got during the second week of April, only with an added bonus in 2006. The second egg was laid on Good Friday and the third on Easter Monday. What an absolute marketing godsend.

Easter eggs – three of them.

It was getting increasingly more difficult thinking of new ways to wrap up a perennial story. "Ospreys return for their third year to Wales" was fine, just, but if the birds were going to keep returning every year, some thought had to go into how we try and keep their profile going and the Glaslyn Osprey Project brand strong. The most obvious strapline I found myself repeating to visitors and the media was, "this is the only pair of ospreys in Wales" which was of course true. But what if the returning male at Welshpool were to find another mate, or the lone male at Malltraeth on Anglesey? This osprey had been around for some years by all accounts. There were reports of other ospreys possibly over-summering in Wales also.

It is not cheap delivering an osprey project. The RSPB were investing a lot of resources and cash into the Glaslyn Osprey Project, so we had to keep on our toes and think of ever newer ways of making people aware of the project and making it sustainable long term. My field of expertise was cameras – video and still photography, and by 2006, that £30 nest camera was looking a tad dated, a bit tired. It had served its purpose, but a better system was needed. That one mile distance between the nest and the hide wasn't getting any shorter, a new multi-camera set up would go some way in bringing visitors closer to the ospreys, if not in person, at least in the experience of viewing them.

2006

OSPREYS IN WALES *The First Ten Years*

A Scottish Trip

Reporter Roger Pinney from the BBC interviews the species protection team over the Easter weekend for a BBC evening news programme.

There were around 180 pairs of breeding ospreys in Scotland by 2006, not bad considering there were only three pairs 40 years before in 1966. Having spoken to Roy in the Lake District the previous autumn about Scottish ospreys and projects, I decided to make a whirlwind, one-week tour of various sites including the two largest osprey projects: the RSPB's Loch Garten and Scottish Wildlife Trust's Loch of the Lowes. The plan was pretty simple – to see how other projects, some decades old, were delivering on the same things as we were trying to do in Wales, and try to pick up tips and best practices from each and incorporate these into the Glaslyn Osprey Project.

50 years of ospreys breeding again in Scotland – at Tweed Valley.

I arrived to find most projects celebrating the 50th anniversary of ospreys breeding again in Scotland; the interpretation panels were still up from 2004, which was the actual anniversary date, 1954 – 2004. They looked awesome. I felt extremely humbled by all the people I met and how gracious they were with their time and advice. They couldn't have been more helpful in fact. What I found enlightening was the fact that no matter which project I visited, from the smallest to the largest, we all had one thing in common. The issues and difficulties that we were experiencing down in the Glaslyn were not specific or in any way unique to us – all osprey projects are continually battling the same problems, especially camera and IT difficulties. It really isn't easy getting quality pictures back from an osprey nest, usually located in the back of beyond, to a visitor centre (and let alone a website), without spending huge amounts of money. And that's exactly what wildlife charities don't have lots of, cash.

As I travelled from one osprey project to another, it became apparent that we all shared one common denominator, a love and passion for ospreys and their continued success and population expansion. We all had our slightly different ways of protecting the osprey eggs from those who want to steal them – all involved volunteers and they all worked. Kelvin had given us a great template of how to keep egg thieves at bay back in Wales.

The RSPB project officer at Loch Garten, Richard Thaxton, showed me their protection and surveillance set up. In their little hide where the residential volunteers would carry out their watch, they had a humongous set of binoculars. They looked like something out of a science fiction movie; they were in fact from a World War Two German U-boat. Now that got me thinking…

Osprey surveillance Scottish style – coffee, a log-book and a monstrous pair of binoculars off a German U-boat!

A male osprey intruding on the Glaslyn nest in May. He is carrying a stick – things are looking promising.

Tri Chynnig i Gymro

Back in Wales everybody was getting increasingly excited again about the three eggs – would we get all three chicks to hatch this year? That would be another first.

The first two weeks of May had been exceptionally wet, even for Wales. Both osprey parents had been doing a sterling job of keeping their eggs dry and shielded from the worst of the weather. The male had also been shielding another osprey away from his nest. On May 11th and 13th, a male osprey visited the Glaslyn and got quite close to the nest on several occasions. Not good news for the nesting pair perhaps, but certainly a positive

The Glaslyn male chases off an intruder osprey.

development in terms of osprey numbers and the possibility of another nest in Wales in the future. Maybe he was a two year old having just returned back from Africa for the first time (mid-May would be the right time for this), or possibly an adult bird looking for a suitable nesting place.

Unfazed by the weather or the visiting osprey, both parents continued incubating their clutch of three, the female spending the majority of the time on the eggs – around 80%. Their efforts were rewarded on Thursday, 18th May, when the first chick hatched. The weather had improved, the rain had gone and we were going to be inundated with visitors that weekend. The male was bringing copious amounts of fish to the nest and he needed to. On Saturday the second chick hatched and then shortly after 4pm on the Monday, with a visitor centre and hide stuffed to the rafters full of people, the female lifted off her two tiny chicks and assortment of egg shells to reveal a third tiny osprey. All three had hatched; it was the icing on the cake, the holy grail.

Iolo Williams takes a break from his filming schedule in May 2006 to see the ospreys for himself – through some new fancy binoculars.

People had inched their way closer and closer to the 42" plasma screen in the visitor centre that afternoon and by the time it became apparent that there were indeed three little heads bobbing around in the nest cup, they were almost in the nest with them. Gasps momentarily turned to silence, which quickly gave way to crying. Grown men crying. It was like 2005 all over again and the powerful emotions that Mother Nature can unleash on the unprepared were evident for all who were there to see. People were overcome by the emotion of the moment; it was proper heartstrings stuff.

Luckily the week before I had managed to track down a pair of Vixen astronomical binoculars on loan for the season. They didn't quite have the provenance (or weight) of the Loch Garten pair, but with 25 X 150mm optics, the ospreys had suddenly moved a heck of a lot closer!

We have a saying in Wales, "Tri Chynnig i Gymro", which loosely translates as three chances for a Welshman. The Glaslyn ospreys had returned for their third year and on their third breeding attempt had laid three eggs and all three chicks had hatched. Bendigedig.

Bittersweet

The weather was kind to the birds, and to us, for the rest of the 2006 summer. The differences in the relative size of the chicks, the eldest being four days older than the last to hatch, were quickly made up. Ospreys are strictly fish eaters – no siblicide (one chick killing another, usually for food or less competition) going on in an osprey nest thank you – we're British.

By the time all three chicks were between five and six weeks old, one of them had streaked ahead in terms of size making the other two look rather compact. It's at around 25 to 40 days old that a real growth spike occurs in osprey young, particularly the females as they weigh more generally. It looked like we had one female and

The three Darvic rings for the 2006 Glaslyn chicks.

OSPREYS IN WALES *The First Ten Years*

two smaller males and they would be ringed on 28th of June, when we could weigh and measure them, giving us a better idea.

Roy had sent black rings to us in 2006, Black 2J would be used for the larger chick and the two smaller offspring would get Black 5Y and Black 80.

As predicted, the larger bird was almost certainly a female weighing in at 1,640g; her two brothers being a more modest 1,460g (Black 80) and 1,350g (Black 5Y).

It is never an easy operation to ring osprey chicks due to the inaccessibility of some nests. We had no problems getting to the Glaslyn nest, but it did lie 25m up a silver fir with a myriad of branches and twigs restricting access for the tree climber. Thankfully, it only took the RSPB's Ynyshir warden and expert tree climber, Dick Squires, 10 minutes to ascend to the nest and before we knew it, all three chicks had been carefully lowered to the ground, each in its own bag.

Three osprey chicks in a nest in Wales – the first time this has happened for many centuries.

42 2006

Kelvin and I were waiting at the bottom of the tree along with licensed bird ringer Adrienne. Kelvin put the metal BTO rings on and Adrienne the Darvics. The whole operation took just over an hour with the least amount of fuss and disturbance to the ospreys.

Kelvin helps Adrienne with the ringing process.

The heaviest male chick is given his Darvic ring – Black 80, right leg reading from the foot up.

2006

The pitiful remains of Black 2J after the female has dumped her corpse over the side of the nest.

Sadly, it would be a bittersweet ending to the 2006 season. Despite our hopes that the ospreys might fledge three chicks for the first time, on a hot Friday afternoon, 30th June, the female chick died in the nest.

I was in the visitor centre with around 15 watchers and volunteers. We had been observing Black 2J furiously exercising her wings throughout the morning after a hearty trout breakfast. Shortly after 1pm, midway through a wing flapping session, she came to an abrupt halt and keeled over backwards. Her two brothers were moving around quite normally, but Black 2J was motionless, upside-down, one wing strewn open across the nest.

People were suddenly firing questions at me – is she ill? Is she tired? Is she alright? I immediately thought, like everyone else, that she had just burnt herself out after all the exercise and was taking a rest (albeit in a rather peculiar posture), but as the seconds became minutes, it started to dawn on all of us that this was no temporary respite. We couldn't see any movement, not even breathing. It was my first time seeing an osprey die in the nest; it's one thing an egg being infertile and not hatching, it's something else, however, watching a strong, seemingly healthy bird grow up only to suddenly keel over and die. You build a bond with a bird, an emotional attachment. It was a thoroughly sickening feeling, a helpless feeling too.

The parent ospreys carried on as normal and were seen trying to offer scraps of fish to the motionless chick. After three days the female, clearly realising by this time that her feeding attempts were futile, grabbed the remains of the chick and ditched 2J's corpse over the side of the nest, some 20m away.

The following day, Angharad and I quickly retrieved the body and took it away. Four days of hot temperatures and probably a fox overnight had left the corpse unrecognisable as an osprey. Feet were detached, as were some of the bones. Not nice.

Black 2J was 41 days old when she died in the nest without warning – an unusually mature age for a chick to suddenly perish without any obvious factors such as malnutrition or poor weather playing a role. I took 2J's body to a local vet and expert on bird physiology; he had a very plausible explanation as to what may have happened.

Birds of prey can suddenly become 'acutely hypoglycemic' he said. Low sugar levels in the blood can be brought on by exercise and hot temperatures (and it had been very hot) – a lethal combination to a six week old osprey that had suddenly entered that fast and furious wing flapping stage in her development. Seizures and death can occur if glucose levels fall below 80 mg/dl (milligrams per decilitre) – it looked as if this may well have happened to poor old Black 2J. Gutted.

Four days after suddenly dying in the nest, Black 2J's remains are almost unrecognisable as those of an osprey.

A Community Affair

It was nothing short of astonishing what happened after Black 2J died. People that had never been to the project before and knew very little about the ospreys were visiting and offering their 'condolences' and donating money. The whole community rallied together in an energised, cohesive and united way. They felt sorry for the ospreys and for the people who looked after them. It was a grieving process of sorts and the community was driven to stand up for the birds in a way I had never experienced before. Many of these people didn't know an osprey from an ostrich not too long back, but they did now and they cared.

I had organised another community weekend for the August Bank Holiday – an incredible 1,000 people visited each day. People came to sell stuff – artwork, home grown vegetables, books, jewellry; we had car-boot sales and it was all in aid of the ospreys. Anne-Marie from Staffordshire became our 50,000th visitor of the season, the media were there, the Brownies, various politicians popped in, Ffestiniog Highland Railway also had a stall. Glaslyn Osprey Project volunteer Tom Jones even won the Welsh Volunteer of the Year award for his 431 hours in 2005. There's unusual.

This was a million miles away from just two years back, with a desperate looking pair of ospreys moping around after their nest had blown down, with a handful of people looking at them from a makeshift hide. Ospreys and people had become bonded together; a connection had been built with wildlife that was the complete polar opposite of the last time ospreys were around in any great numbers. A hunger to persecute and destroy in the early 20th century had been transformed into a hunger for learning and conservation instead by the 21st century. How good was that?

To safeguard the prosperity of ospreys and the Glaslyn Osprey

Anne-Marie receives a celebratory book – she is the 50,000th visitor to the Glaslyn Project in 2006.

People from the nearby village of Prenteg with their stall at the community weekend.

Project in the future, we had to capitalise on this new-found coalition between people and wildlife. As devastating as it was to lose a healthy six week old osprey, Black 2J may have done her species an awful lot of good in the long run, certainly in Wales. I started a campaign of fund raising and bridge building in the autumn and winter of 2006. Forming new alliances with anybody with a stake in the project was essential. We had a shiny new pair of expensive binoculars, but we needed to change the camera if we were to reach new audiences and make the project better and financially secure long term. TV programme makers were screaming out for better video than we could give them, so were our visitors by the end of 2006. We had given people a taste of 'osprey world' and they wanted more. I even visited the Ospreys rugby team at the Liberty Stadium in Swansea – there was an obvious stakeholder connection there. For a North Walian 'Gog' like me, that *was* unusual!

Rachel (right) and Patience bring the local Porthmadog Brownies to the Glaslyn Osprey Project.

Spreading the osprey message at the Liberty Stadium, Swansea. Left to right. Sonny Parker, me, Ryan Jones, Stefan Terblanche and Brent Cockbain (and an osprey).

2006

Black 80 starts his journey south at 15 weeks old – would we see him again as an adult in years to come?

By the end of the first week of September, all four ospreys had departed, one less than we had hoped for, but a productivity of two (amount of chicks fledged) was still above the osprey UK average of around 1.5 per nest. The male was the last to go on 6th September; the king had left the building, well the Glaslyn at any rate, for another year.

2007

Lights, Camera, Action...

2007 would be a defining year and a game-changer for ospreys in Wales.

We had been lucky enough to secure funding, not only for a new three-camera system around the osprey nest from Environment Wales, but also a generous grant from Snowdonia National Park's CAE (Cronfa Arbrofol Eryri/Sustainable Development) Fund. This CAE money was used to buy a solar panel system at the protection site, so that we could run all the security devices, including the new cameras, without having to run a petrol-guzzling generator 24/7 as we had been doing.

With snow on the mountaintops, the electrical circuit boards are installed for the brand new osprey camera system.

RSPB Anglesey warden, Conrad Smith, places a high-resolution camera on a tree around 40m away from the osprey nest and at the same height.

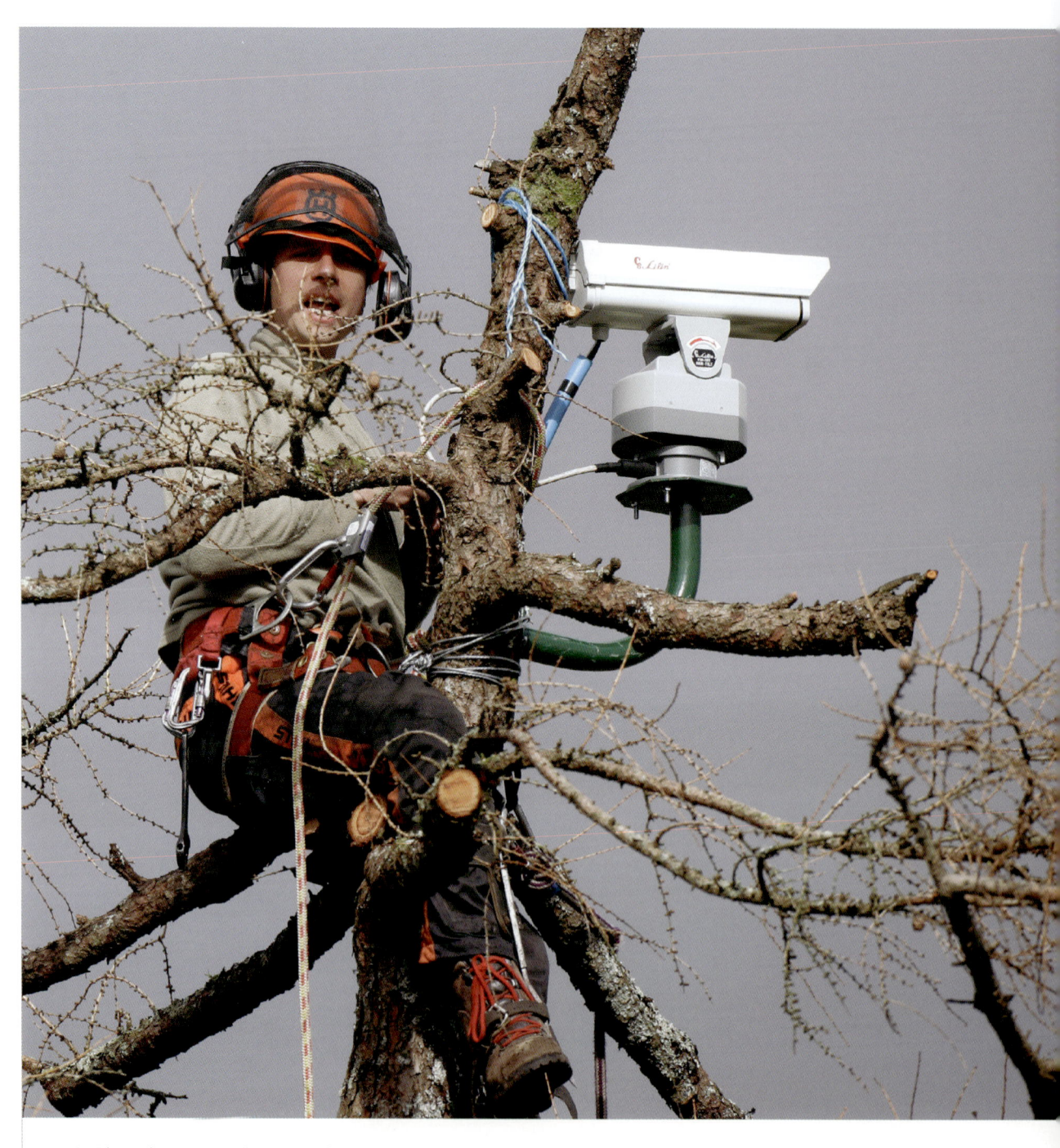

By Thursday, 1st March, St. David's Day, all the paperwork had been completed and we had the go-ahead to proceed. On a crisp, bitterly cold morning we started our installation work. Local company Criccieth TV were in charge of the electrical infrastructure, helped by several Glaslyn Osprey Project volunteers.

We had just about enough funding to buy three cameras. A high-resolution camera (it was in 2007!), a better bullet camera to replace the old one, and the *pièce de résistance* of the whole set up – a top of the range PTZ (pan/tilt/zoom) camera that we could operate from the protection caravan. State-of-the-art stuff in 2007.

Starting in March, we didn't have much time – the ospreys would hopefully be back by the end of the month. We had three weeks at most and we were praying for good weather. It's not the actual camera installation that takes time, it's all the infrastructure and testing that goes with it. There is one, hugely important, aspect to remember when you are installing cameras on an osprey nest – once the birds are back, that's it. If cameras break down or need tweaking in any way, tough. You have to wait until September and sort it out for the following season. That's a very long time to wait if your system has gone belly-up on 1st April with the ospreys having just returned. That would be an April fool's joke of the highest order.

Normally you would have enterprise-grade equipment and several back-up systems in this kind of situation, but these things cost money and lots of it. We had to get it right from the start and hope nothing would go wrong. The camera positions had to be dead level and precise so they're not pointing into the sun; the brackets had to be water-tight and secured well enough to withstand 100mph winds at the top of a swaying tree; the electric current had to be uninterrupted and, most importantly of all, the cameras needed to be far enough and high enough from the base of the nest so that you're not looking at PoopCam all summer long. Factor into the equation also that the ospreys will be using some parts of the nest more than others, choose lenses wide enough to include wing spans, takeoffs and landings, and most

Getting the angles right – Conrad gets the camera positions spot-on as I shout out measurements and angles from below!

Joy! After a four-hour battle with a 250m water pipe, volunteers Kelvin Jones and John Parry finally manage to push through the string and lead weight they had inserted at the nest-side end. The electrical and signal cables could now be pulled through the pipe and ultimately be attached to various bits of equipment in the protection caravan – and hopefully remain watertight!

critically, assume that the ospreys will add between a foot and two feet of nesting material; failure to do so will completely mess up your early March calculations by mid-July and you'll end up looking at a screen full of twigs. Remember – ospreys can, and will at every opportunity, make you look stupid.

Who Are You…?

Apart from being cold, the weather did stay kind to us and by 21st March we had everything up, tested and operational. All we needed now were two birds.

Five days later, just before dusk on 26th March, a male osprey showed up but he was un-ringed – probably an early Scottish bird passing through. The same osprey was around the following day too and I managed to get a distant shot of him from the protection site. He had a BTO (British Trust for Ornithology) ring on his left leg but no Darvic, how strange! The vast majority of ospreys in the UK are ringed both with a BTO ring and a Darvic ring.

Who was this mystery osprey with just one metal ring? What better test for the new camera system than to try to find out. Each BTO ring has a long number engraved into the metal, but this inscription is tiny. These rings are meant to be read on injured or dead birds in the hand, not from a few hundred metres away on birds that are very much alive. The first thing we needed to happen was for the osprey to land on the nest and stay still for a while. Well, that just didn't happen. Throughout that Tuesday, his first full day at the nest, he was frantically moving around, rearranging sticks and bringing more back. We could have a problem if the Glaslyn male returned to find this newcomer on his nest – would we see a battle for the nest?

This bird looks very similar to the Glaslyn male, but he doesn't have our male's distinctive ochre coloured Darvic ring on his right leg.

At 2:15pm the following day, 28th March, the Glaslyn female returned and by 3pm she was mating with our 'new' male. Ospreys don't tend to start the breeding process so quickly unless they were bonded birds from previous years; maybe there was a clue here as to the identity of the male? Just as the sun was setting and the last few rays of light illuminated the nest, we got him. Our new male osprey had disappeared shortly after 4pm, but at 5:15pm he was back – with a trout. Luckily, he decided to eat his dinner on the nest

Who are you? The new cameras were up and running, but this osprey wouldn't stay still for long enough to be able to zoom in on his small metal leg ring.

Gotcha – no Darvic ring, but the BTO ring was 1342758.

itself; this was our chance. Using the joystick I managed to zoom right in on the BTO ring and just before the light got too bad, the osprey had moved around enough so that the whole seven-digit number could be read. He had a leg ring number 1342758. Great, but what did that tell us?

It was still only early evening so I rang up Roy in Scotland; luckily he was in. I explained about our non-Darvic ringed osprey and read out the BTO number I had picked up with the help of the new PTZ camera. "Hang on a moment," he said, and the phone went silent for a couple of minutes. After checking his records he was back on the phone. "I've got an ID for you," he explained in that soft Hampshire accent of his… "1342758 was a translocated Rutland male in 1998 with ochre Darvic number 11". Well, well! It had been the Glaslyn male all along; he had obviously 'lost' it somewhere between leaving Wales the previous September and returning two days before. Cheers Roy.

Note – *occasionally Darvic rings do break and ospreys have been spotted without them. 'Henry' at Loch Garten lost his (also ochre coloured) Darvic ring in August 2003 when he (and the ring) was five years old. In 2008, 'Mr. Rutland' returned with his White 03 Darvic ring, but by mid-May he had lost it. He was just a few weeks short of his 11th birthday at the time, so the ring lasted that long. The Glaslyn male was almost nine years old when he returned in March 2007 without his ochre 11 ring. Another Rutland osprey, Maroon AA (2006), returned in 2008 as a two year old without his Darvic ring. He was later caught in 2011 and satellite tagged – he was also re-ringed, Blue AW. Maroon AA (or Blue AW – take your pick) is Blue 24's father – see chapters 2013 and 2014.*

Seeing is Believing

The female wasn't as interested as we had been in the fact that the male had lost some of his bling, she was more concerned with him catching a fish for her. After a bit of display flying he duly obliged and was back an hour later with a mullet. Our pair was back together again and on 31st March we opened the Glaslyn Osprey Project for the fourth consecutive year.

The new cameras had already helped us out with the mystery leg ring and they were to prove an absolute wonderment throughout 2007. The pictures coming back to the visitor centre at Pont Croesor were sensational. Gone was the old static camera looking down with its grainy, low resolution pictures; we were

The female returns 28th March and takes no notice of the new camera system, neither does her partner.

now practically in the nest with the ospreys and we could see an astonishing amount of detail. I had read a book about Howard Carter over the winter and his story of discovering Tutankhamun's tomb in Egypt. "Can you *see* anything?" asked financial backer Lord Carnarvon as he stood behind Carter peering into the tomb for the first time through a tiny hole he had drilled out; *"Yes, wonderful things"* came the reply. That's what it felt like – seeing things that you knew were there, but in all their microscopic glory for the first time. It was mesmerising – you could sit and watch the birds all day with this quality of imagery, and we very often did!

Unbelievable detail – osprey watching like never before. The female returns on 28th March.

Once we had got over the amount of detail we could now see, it quickly became apparent that we were witnessing new behaviours for the first time too. The male standing on one leg, the other neatly tucked away under his body; the female sleeping by closing one eye and then alternating with the other one; the discarded fish gill covers (opercula) in the nest – the only parts of the fish that ospreys don't eat.

Opercula – the hard bony flap coverings that protect the gills of fish. Ospreys tend not to eat these and many are discarded in the nest or on the ground next to feeding perches (singular – operculum).

The new cameras were a gateway into the very core of osprey lives. This was seeing 'osprey world' live and close-up for the first time. We would soon realise that many of the text books of the 20th century had got a lot of their osprey facts wrong; there is only so much you can extrapolate from watching a nest through a telescope on the ground and recording in a note pad, sometimes speculating, what was going on at the macro level deep inside the nest.

Protecting 24:7

Just 12 days after reuniting, the Glaslyn female laid her first egg of the season at 5:25pm on 9th April. Their increasing tendency of returning back from migration earlier each year was having a knock-on effect on the egg laying too. Two more eggs would be laid on 12th and 15th April, and everything was set again for another osprey season.

Protection volunteers Buckley and Dafydd see the funny side of the flash floods – thankfully the cameras and solar panels survived.

OSPREYS IN WALES *The First Ten Years*

No sooner had the 24-hour species protection and surveillance watch started for the year, than the heavens opened and we experienced an unseasonably wet period culminating in flash floods. The ospreys seemed to be coping fine, but the weather would prove a sterner test for our new fancy solar panel and camera systems.

Meantime, I had been sending some of the amazing sample videos from the new PTZ camera to different TV companies and programme makers. It wasn't long before the BBC got in touch – they wanted to record a feature on the methods we employed to protect the Glaslyn ospreys. The programme was called Animal 24:7 and by the time they had recorded some of the protection volunteers at work, they wanted to come back later in the summer and record the chicks being ringed – if we were to get any chicks that is.

BBC reporter, Tom Heap, recording a feature on the Glaslyn ospreys for wildlife programme Animal 24:7. It was too wet at the protection site so we had to do a lot of the filming at Pont Croesor instead.

2007

The Glaslyn article on Animal 24:7 developed and grew as the season progressed and ended up being a whopping 20 minute feature by the time the show was broadcast. Other than news items, it was the first national TV exposure for ospreys in Wales and it would put Welsh ospreys on the map, in more ways than one. It was a huge public relations scoop for us and we would reap the benefits for a long time to come. The programme is still repeated on satellite TV now and again, it's Series 3, Episode 10 of Animal 24:7.

Lightning Strikes Twice

All the species protection staff and volunteers had done a great job again in 2007 and kept a close vigil on the nest for the whole six-week incubation period. Their efforts were rewarded on 16th, 18th and 20th May when, for the second year running, all three chicks hatched.

Two out, one to go. Amazing close-up views of the first two Glaslyn osprey chicks to hatch in 2007.

For the remainder of May everything went swimmingly, even the weather improved. Two days into June however, I was sat in the visitor centre with volunteers Janice, Judith and Heather discussing the middle chick – it didn't seem to be feeding properly. The other two chicks were moving around quite normally and begging for food, but their sibling seemed out of sorts. He/she had taken a thwack in the head from a lively mullet the day before; maybe this had something to do with its seemingly lethargic behavior.

The following day the male brought in another mullet for breakfast, but again the middle chick didn't seem interested. By 11:45 it had stopped moving so we zoomed in the camera as much as it would go – it wasn't breathing. The female tried to nudge it a few times but to no avail. For the second year running a young osprey had died in the nest – this time at an earlier age, 16 days old. Lightning had struck twice in as many years and the feeling of euphoria had changed to gloom, again.

Later that Sunday afternoon the female returned to the nest with a fresh sycamore leaf. She carefully placed it over her dead chick's body and left it there for several hours. It was hauntingly sad to watch. We tried for days to come up with a scientific reason for the leaf placing – maybe she was attempting to sever her filial bond to the chick? We may never know. After two days the mother, as she had done the previous year, grasped her dead chick's body and disposed of it over the side of the nest. Maybe the encounter with the mullet had been more damaging to the chick than it looked, or maybe the youngster was diseased or had a congenital problem? The important thing now was for the remaining two offspring to get increasingly stronger and fledge the nest in a few weeks.

OSPREYS IN WALES *The First Ten Years*

The female osprey places a sycamore leaf over her dead chick's body.

Alwyn explains to visitors the sad news that one of the chicks has died in the nest.

60   2007

OSPREYS IN WALES *The First Ten Years*

Ringing Success

Both the remaining chicks flourished for the following few weeks and, accompanied again by the Animal 24:7 film crew, were ringed at between four and five weeks old on 19th June. Roy had sent us five Darvics through the post in 2007, they were all white and sequential, YA through to YE.

White Darvic rings, YA through to YE – surplus rings could be used the following year.

The day before the ringing, a mystery osprey had been seen around the Glaslyn valley. At around 9:30am it launched an attack on the nest, missing it only by inches. The Glaslyn adults were both on the nest at the time and protected the two chicks, shielding them from harm. The Glaslyn male then flew up and began chasing the attacker off, alarm calling all the while. Was this intruder osprey one of the two 2005 chicks returning to the UK as an adult for the first time? The timing would be spot on if it was. The mystery osprey didn't get close enough for us to see whether it had any Darvic rings; Yellow 37 or Yellow 39 may well have returned to their ancestral nest, but we would never know for sure.

We found the two chicks in the nest to be healthy and strong. The older chick weighed 1,600g and was probably a female; the youngest weighed much less – 1,320g and was almost certainly a male. The male was ringed with Darvic ring White YA, the female White YB.

Thankfully, the remainder of the 2007 season went without any snags. The youngsters fledged the nest on 8th July (White YB) and 10th July (White YA), and by the end of August all four of the Glaslyn ospreys had started their migrations south. For the third year in succession we had started the season with two ospreys and ended with four, a great result from

2007   61

The two Glaslyn chicks in the nest in 2007; white YA nearest to the camera. On the ringing day we saw the first ever coarse fish in the nest, the remains of the partially eaten rudd are on the right.

the only pair of ospreys in Wales. Things don't get much more precarious than one pair of any species, so to get another two young ospreys in the air was brilliant.

There was still no news from the Welshpool nest but there were some encouraging developments from the Dyfi estuary, another 30 miles down the Welsh coast. On 8th August I wrote these words on the RSPB Glaslyn Osprey Project diary page:

Glaslyn chick White YA.

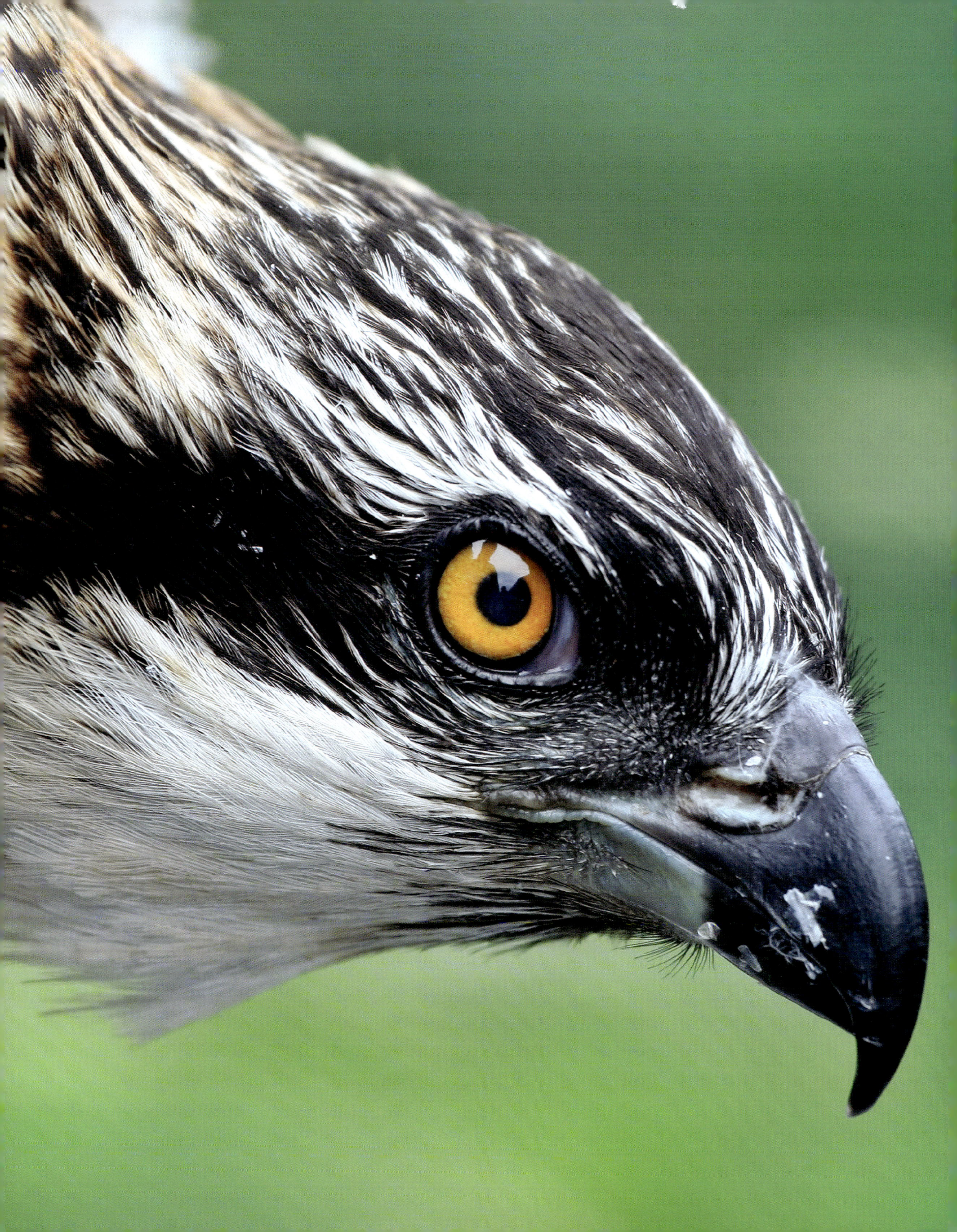

The Dyfi River winds its way to the sea – are there young ospreys around in 2007 looking for suitable nesting areas and mates?

Aug 8th *"Sightings of several different ospreys on the Dyfi estuary over the last week have prompted a flurry of excitement. Some have wondered whether these were the Glaslyn birds on migration already. They're not. The Glaslyn family are all present and correct, and though we are seeing less of them around the nest site now, all four of them are still being seen daily. The Dyfi sightings are more likely to be of other ospreys that didn't manage to pair up this season and are making an early start to Africa."*

On reflection, and knowing quite a bit more about osprey movements than we did back in 2007, it seems unlikely that these birds were in fact early migrators. The Dyfi sightings were of birds at the end of July and the first week in August – these must have been non-breeding adults, possibly young birds maybe two or three years old, prospecting for nest sites and mates. Interesting…

2008

Pioneering Ospreys

I remember thinking at the start of 2008 that the Glaslyn male would be a decade old that year. Not ancient by any means, in his prime most likely, but you still have to think about that awful time when a bird you've practically fallen in love with doesn't return. In terms of the bigger osprey picture, I felt more confident than ever that if one of the ospreys failed to return, we could have a situation whereby another osprey could take its place. The Glaslyn pair would still be the only pair of ospreys breeding in Wales in 2008, but we were seeing more birds with every passing year. 'Pioneering pairs' as they are called (one pair in isolation from a greater population elsewhere) do not have a good track record in terms of success; rarely does a viable population result from a pioneering pair. But with a growing osprey population in Scotland – over 200 pairs by 2008, it seemed reasonable to theorise two things. Firstly, one of the Glaslyn birds could be substituted by another osprey if one didn't return; secondly, there was an ever growing likelihood that other ospreys would not only be seen passing through, but actually start to settle, nest and breed in Wales.

Both ospreys return in 2008 at more or less the same time as they had the previous year – you could almost set your watch by them!

OSPREYS IN WALES *The First Ten Years*

The Glaslyn 'pioneering pair' returned as usual at the end of March. Here's an astonishing fact that ignites that sense of wonderment inside most of us... the male returned on the very same day as he had the previous year, 26th March, just two or three hours earlier in fact. The female returned at 7am on 27th March, less than 17 hours difference than in 2007 – unreal.

Protecting in the Dry

The flash floods of 2007 were a bit of a wake-up call for us. If the water level had risen a foot higher, the protection caravan could well have upped sticks and floated away. Coming soon to an estuary near you – the Glaslyn Osprey Project protection caravan…!

At the end of the 2007 season we towed it away to be scrapped – I had managed to acquire a 30-foot residential 'mobile home' as they are called, from Hafan y Môr Holiday Park, a few miles away from the Glaslyn. The new protection caravan was set up early for the 2008 season, which was just as well – the female had laid her first egg and true to form, she had broken her previous earliest egg record by one whole day. Three eggs were laid in all, on the 8th, 11th and 14th April, with the usual three-day gap between eggs.

Volunteer Janine Pannett working an early shift in the new, rather palatial protection caravan in 2008 – we didn't have to wait long for the first egg to be laid.

Just as the Glaslyn ospreys were becoming increasingly predictable with their arrival times, so was the Welsh weather. No sooner had we three eggs to worry about again than the heavens opened, only this time it was hail and snow. Thankfully, we had re-sited the caravan a few feet higher than in previous years so we were spared the worst of the floods in 2008. The ospreys had to brave it out however; just as well they have a highly developed uropygial gland that secrets oil from the base of the tail, which the osprey applies to its feathers through preening. The oil is used for waterproofing, which is not a bad thing to have in the heart of Snowdonia.

Ospreys Everywhere

I probably saw more ospreys in May 2008 than I had at any other time, in Wales at any rate. Following the usual 37-day incubation period, the chicks started to hatch and once again, all three made it out. Just as it had done the previous year, the new camera system was treating us to some amazing footage. The chicks hatched in the order their eggs were laid (which is usually the case, but not always) on 16th, 17th and 19th May. We could distinguish a particular egg from another by zooming in and studying the individual markings on them; they all had slight variations in the way the pigmentation process (maculation) distributed the reddish-brown pigments onto the shell just before laying.

The Glaslyn male sits out another snow shower on a dead branch just below the nest.

Amazing views of an osprey in the process of hatching.

It wasn't just the five Glaslyn ospreys at the nest we were seeing in the spring of 2008. From early April onwards we were recording more and more ospreys; some of them must have been migrating birds, but a few were hanging around. There was a female with a missing primary feather on her right wing seen several times during the third week in April; a male had been displaying to the Glaslyn female while she incubated her three eggs; there were also reports coming in of ospreys fishing in the nearby Dwyryd River as well as on the Glaslyn itself. They weren't our birds; most of these reports were during times when both of the Glaslyn adults were confirmed as either on, or very near their nest. How exciting! Could any of these birds be Glaslyn offspring from 2005 or 2006?

Saturday 29th March	Another osprey was seen flying over Llanfrothen.
Monday 7th April	A male osprey was spotted flying over the viewing site.
Friday 11th April	A female osprey was spotted flying over the viewing site.
Wednesday 16th April	An intruder osprey was spotted at the nest site.
20th and 23rd April	A female osprey around with missing primary feather on right wing.

Ospreys were being spotted further afield too, especially near lakes. The Malltraeth male was still around on Anglesey and there was a resident male now confirmed on Llyn Trawsfynydd, six miles to the south of the Glaslyn nest (I saw this bird many times myself). Another osprey was recorded regularly on Llyn Brenig, 24 miles to the east; a male osprey on Llyn Tegid in Bala, 19 miles south east and regular osprey reports were coming from the RSPB at their Llyn Efyrnwy (Vyrnwy) reserve, 26 miles south east.

These lakes seem quite fair distances away from each other to us, but only because the roads between them are so narrow and mountainous. Twenty-something miles to an osprey is an hour's flight and each bird would no doubt have a mental map of all these water bodies, having visited them in the past. Ospreys were also being reported further south in Wales. Clywedog Reservoir was a good spot for them, as were the many lakes and dams of the Elan Valley. There were regular reports of ospreys on the Cleddau River also, near Haverfordwest, Pembrokeshire. Things were looking up, and so were we.

Glyn on the lookout for intruding ospreys at Pont Croesor. Birds were now resident all summer and not just passing through on migration.

The Holy Grail

Four Glaslyn chicks had died during the previous four years since this pair had started breeding. Two perished in 2004 when the nest blew down and then one each in 2006 and 2007. Seeing these young birds die is heartbreaking enough, but when the success, or not, of a future Welsh osprey population could very well depend on just one or two of these chicks returning

in subsequent years, this made it doubly despairing. By the time we went to ring the class of 2008 on 20th June, we had high hopes that this year would be the one. The weather had been good, as had the fish deliveries to the nest, and the ospreys themselves were experienced parents by now. All we needed now was a little bit of luck for all three to survive and fledge.

An amazing view in Snowdonia – the only osprey nest in Wales in 2008 has three osprey chicks in it.

The three chicks were ringed with the white Darvics we had left from 2007. It was apparent from early on that we had two males and, despite being the youngest chick, a very heavy female by comparison.

In the order laid and hatched:

White YD - 1,390g - Male

White YC - 1,230g - Male

White YE - 1,540g - Female

That summer had already turned into a slightly humorous one; White YE was clearly a bit of a food monster. She would bully her two brothers into submission and dominate the nest, not only in terms of her presence but also loudness. That bird could scream! People would come in to the visitor centre and the first thing they would say was, "How's YE today?", "How many fish has she had?", "I can hear her from my house!"

On 4th July, White YD fledged – what a date to announce his independence! The following day his brother, White YC also took his inaugural flight. Interestingly, both the brothers fledged at 49 days – exactly seven weeks old. That is right on the extreme early end of the fledging age range, normally males are 51 to 52 days old with females taking a day or two longer on average. They were probably desperate to get away from YE and her torturous screaming!

White YE is the osprey equivalent of a food monster.

White YC – the younger of the two males in the 2008 clutch. He waits for a pause in the rain before taking his first ever flight at exactly seven weeks old.

Their sister did eventually fledge, but not until she was 53 days old, by which time she had put on so much body mass, we were starting to wonder whether she would be able to fly at all. Three ospreys had fledged a nest in Wales for probably the first time in many centuries. Jackpot – the Glaslyn pair had finally struck gold.

The Dyfi Dynasty

A couple of estuaries south of the Glaslyn on the Dyfi, there was some exciting news on the osprey front. In 2007, Clive from Montgomeryshire Wildlife Trust had, with the help of several volunteers and a 50 foot electricity pole donated by Scottish Power, erected an osprey nest platform on their Morfa Dyfi nature reserve in response to increased sightings of birds on the estuary in recent years. It didn't take long for the new nest to attract some interest.

On 22nd April, 2008, a male osprey was observed eating a mullet on the T perch next to the nest and a few days later he seemed to have taken ownership of it. On 24th June, he was joined by a female who had a moulting primary feather on her right wing. Was this female osprey the same bird as the one sighted at the Glaslyn a month earlier? The distance between the two nests is only 28 miles and both females had a missing primary feather on their right wing. Coincidence?

It was too late to breed by June, but both birds seemed to be pair bonding well, with the usual sky-dancing display flights being seen. If only these ospreys would return the following year, we would have two active nesting sites within one hour's flying time of each other – that would act as a huge magnet to other ospreys flying over. Ospreys are practically mesmerised by other nests, especially active ones with birds and chicks in them. It makes perfect sense; if an osprey nest is successful, it must be in a good place. The female was last seen in late August and the male set off at first light on 1st September. Time would tell if they were to return.

A nesting platform is erected on the banks of the Dyfi River in 2007 to try to attract passing ospreys.

Despite being the youngest, female YE (top) towers over her two brothers, YD (bottom) and the diminutive YC (left).

The Dyfi estuary has plenty of mullet and flounder in its shallow waters – perfect habitat for ospreys.

A Welsh Osprey Returns

Tuesday, 22nd of July, was like any other day at the office really. I was at Pont Croesor writing some emails when my mobile phone rang – it was a colleague of mine from Dumfries and Galloway, Scotland, Elizabeth Tindal. She was the council 'Ranger' up there and we would often talk about anything osprey related. She wanted to know my opinion about a Latvian ringed bird that had been photographed near Loch Ken, it definitely wasn't a Scottish bird she thought.

An hour or so later she sent me a picture taken by wildlife photographer, Keith Kirk. A couple of clicks of the magnify button in Photoshop revealed enough detail to be able to clearly make out the ring number. It was a Black Darvic with the number 80 – *but on the right leg*. I remember the next few moments as if they'd happened this morning. I just froze for around five seconds, I wanted to believe it was our 2006 bird, but was afraid to. Then all manner of things entered my head – Is it really him? He's only two years old, is this bird too young to be Black 80? Why is he in Scotland? Then I thought, well the ring doesn't lie; it just has to be him. The feeling must have been akin to realising your numbers have come up on the lottery, but you keep checking them, just in case.

I bolted out of the office and ran across the field to the viewing hide and then the visitor centre, screaming at the top of my voice… " BLACK 80, HE'S ALIVE; BLACK 80 HE'S BACK…"

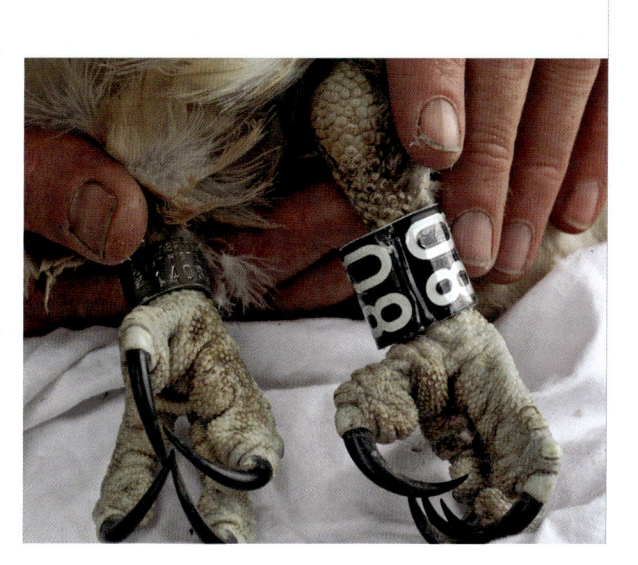

Our boy is back – a Welsh born osprey returns as an adult to the UK in 2008, the first ever recorded. Bottom photo – Black 80 being ringed as a chick in 2006.

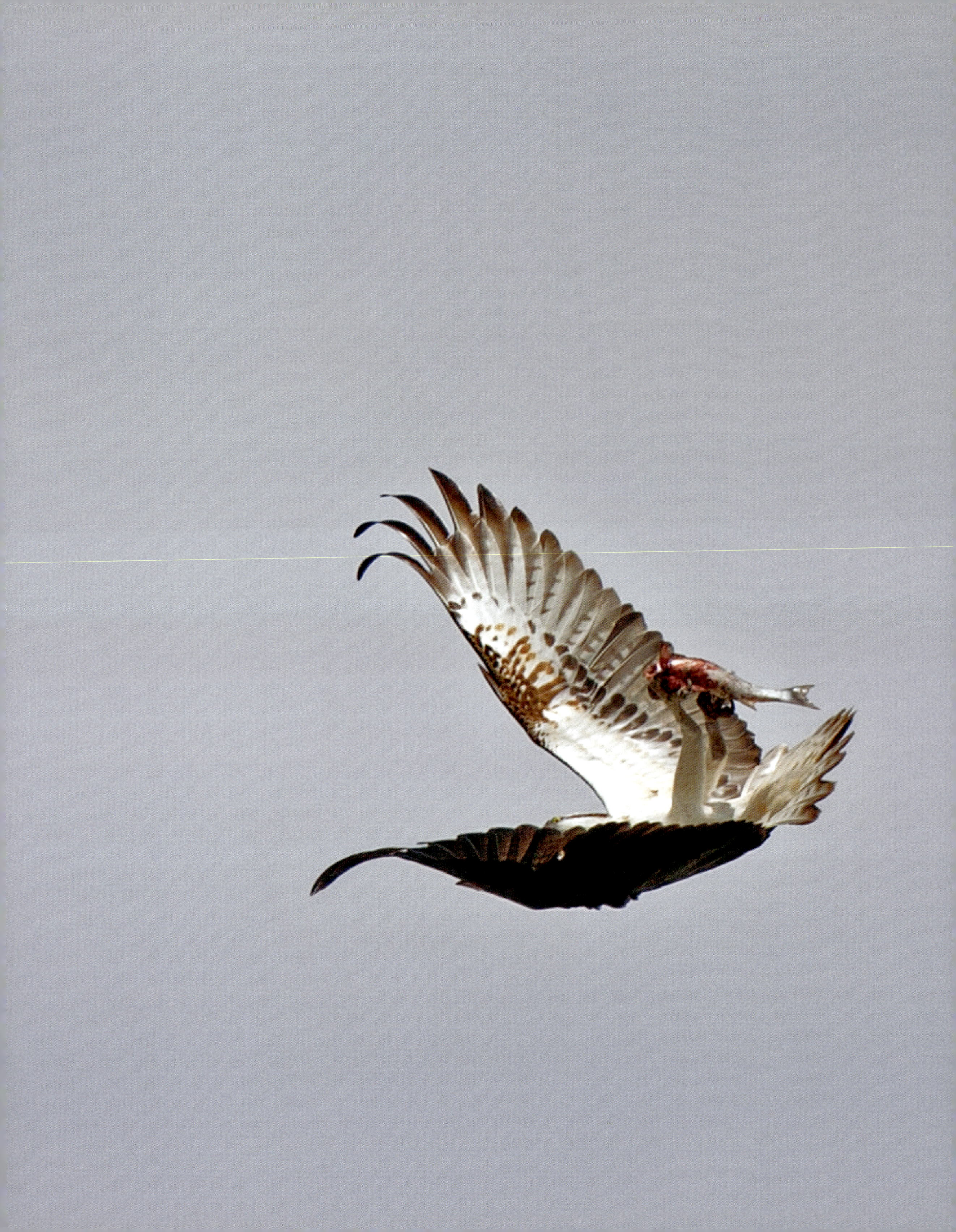

Normal visitors that day must have thought there was a mad-man on the loose, having just won some kind of bizarre Welsh bingo game. Well, in a way, I had; we all had – our numbers had come up and Black 80 was the jackpot ball. Glyn and Mick, who were working with me that day, knew exactly what had happened of course; one mad-man jumping and running around in a field in North Wales very quickly turned into three.

By the time we had all calmed down a bit and my voice had returned to normal pitch, I rang Elizabeth back in Scotland to tell her the news – she was made up for us. She explained that Black 80 had been around for a few weeks and was building a nest near Threave Castle. He was also catching fish – for two. He had a mate, an un-ringed female. It's normal for an osprey to return to the UK as a two year old, but to be nest building having seemingly attracted a mate is some going.

When I got home that evening and sat back to think about *that* phone call, it began to dawn on me the significance of it – it was huge. I must admit, I had a tear or two in my eyes. I thought about all the people that had made this event possible, from Roy and others in Scotland to the guys in Rutland and the RSPB and dozens of volunteers that had given their time so generously over the last four years at the Glaslyn to ensure Black 80's safety (and all his siblings). Long night shifts in the dark at minus temperatures, with only a torch, a flask and a fellow volunteer for company. This was their reward, their prize, this was their payback.

We ended 2008 on a real high. The male and female started their migrations on 5th and 4th September respectively, only this time, they had managed to fledge all three of their young for the first time. We were seeing more ospreys in the Glaslyn every day almost it seemed like, but by the end of the season, I found myself asking the same question over and over… that male that was around in June, was it Black 80 returning to his natal nest for the first time? It is very common for returnees to come back to the nest where they themselves hatched; could it really have been Black 80?

The Glaslyn male was seen doing some very acrobatic manoeuvres whenever the intruding male was around, a sort of sky-dance with a difference, very similar in fact to a courtship display. I managed to photograph him on one occasion when the male got too close; he was upside-down with a half eaten-fish in his talons, alarm calling at the other male. Was this other male his son? If it was, did he recognise him as his own offspring? We will never know the answer to that question; I guess some things are best left unanswered.

could it really have been Black 80?

The Glaslyn male ushers away another intruding osprey with some acrobatic displays – was this other osprey his son from two years back?

2009

A New Start

On a personal level, 2009 would herald a big change for me. In January, Montgomeryshire Wildlife Trust had asked me to meet them at their Cors Dyfi reserve to discuss the ospreys on the Dyfi. They were part-way through building a hide to allow people to watch the osprey nest, but they needed some help. We talked about cameras and electricity, visitor centres and osprey conservation. We also talked about setting up an osprey project and all the pros and cons of doing such a thing.

On the way home I remember thinking how much potential there was at the Dyfi for a project there, but also the difficulties Montgomeryshire Wildlife Trust would face in starting such an endeavor. Osprey projects are not easy things to set up, nor are they cheap.

By the time I arrived home I had received an email from the CEO of the Trust, asking me if I wanted a job! I slept on it over the weekend and emailed back on Monday morning. It was too good a challenge to let pass.

Cors Dyfi – January 2009.

The osprey nest was on a beautiful reserve teeming with wildlife, just like Loch Garten and Loch of the Lowes in Scotland. Cors Dyfi reserve was also just off the main coast road between Machynlleth and Aberystwyth (we call them 'main roads' in Wales, I believe they're called tracks in England); there was even a large caravan park next door with many owners who were keen birdwatchers. All the ingredients were there to build a really successful project, it had bags of potential.

First rule of project management – prioritise. The ospreys were due back in a couple of months and there was no time to waste; I needed to get electricity to the nest to run a camera and an infra-red lamp for protection work, and quickly. The nest was just 60m away from a train track, so I contacted Network Rail hoping they could do something for us. In a month they had given us our own six-amp electricity supply to be used solely for the nest – the best possible start. I also spoke with Scottish Power regarding getting power to the car park end; thankfully they were just as obliging. By the first week in April both Network Rail and Scottish Power had kindly sorted us out with electricity and they didn't charge us a penny.

A nest with a view – Pete Watkins saws off the root-ball of a washed-up ash tree before dragging it half a mile to the nest to use as a secondary osprey perch.

The nest that Clive had built two years previously was a free-standing structure on a telegraph pole – I needed to get something else near-by so that the ospreys could perch close to the nest. Natural nests are usually built near a dead tree or another high vantage point, so that the ospreys can monitor all around their nest and territory. Luckily, there was an uprooted ash tree that had washed up around half a mile away on a high tide – the race was on to drag this over to the nest site before another tide washed it away again.

We didn't have much to go on in terms of the Dyfi osprey's previous arrival times, but thankfully by 25th March we had managed to erect the ash tree 10m away from the main nest and put up two inexpensive cameras, one on the ash tree and one above the nest itself. No osprey had returned from migration so we managed to get things ready at the nest site just in time.

Back at the Cors Dyfi side I had managed to acquire a beaten-up portacabin for not much money and with a bit of cladding on the outside and some TLC on the inside, we turned it into a small visitor centre and office. By the second week in April we had two television screens up on one of the side walls

A shabby second-hand portacabin would soon be transformed into a 'brand new' visitor centre.

and we received live pictures back from the osprey nest for the first time. They weren't great, but they were the best we could afford – the signals were beamed back from the nest using a radio transmitter with a receiver at the visitor centre end. In just over two months we had the beginnings of an osprey project and by the last week in April we opened the doors of the Dyfi Osprey Project to visitors. We now had two osprey projects in Wales for the first time.

Confusing Ospreys

At 10:36 on Good Friday, 2009, an osprey lands on the Dyfi nest – but who is it?

All we needed now, after working non-stop for 10 weeks to get the show on the road, was a pair of ospreys. By the second week in April we had our first bird back from migration.

On Good Friday, 10th April, an un-ringed osprey landed on the nest to scenes of mass hysteria back at the visitor centre, which was still work-in-progress at the time. Alwyn had also come down to the Dyfi from the Glaslyn as a People Engagement Officer, as had Janine who had volunteered at the Glaslyn previously. We had been testing the new walkie-talkies earlier that morning, but suddenly now the airwaves were full of that familiar osprey chatter; it was exhilarating.

We had one main disadvantage in 2009, we didn't have a clue what the birds of previous years looked like and there were no photographs, nor records of any leg rings. The un-ringed osprey that landed on that Good Friday morning looked like a male, but he was especially dark for a male, particularly on the chest and under-wing. He had very dark orange-coloured eyes too, very unusual; adult ospreys usually have bright yellow eyes. Not a problem, once his partner returns we'll soon know whether he is a male!

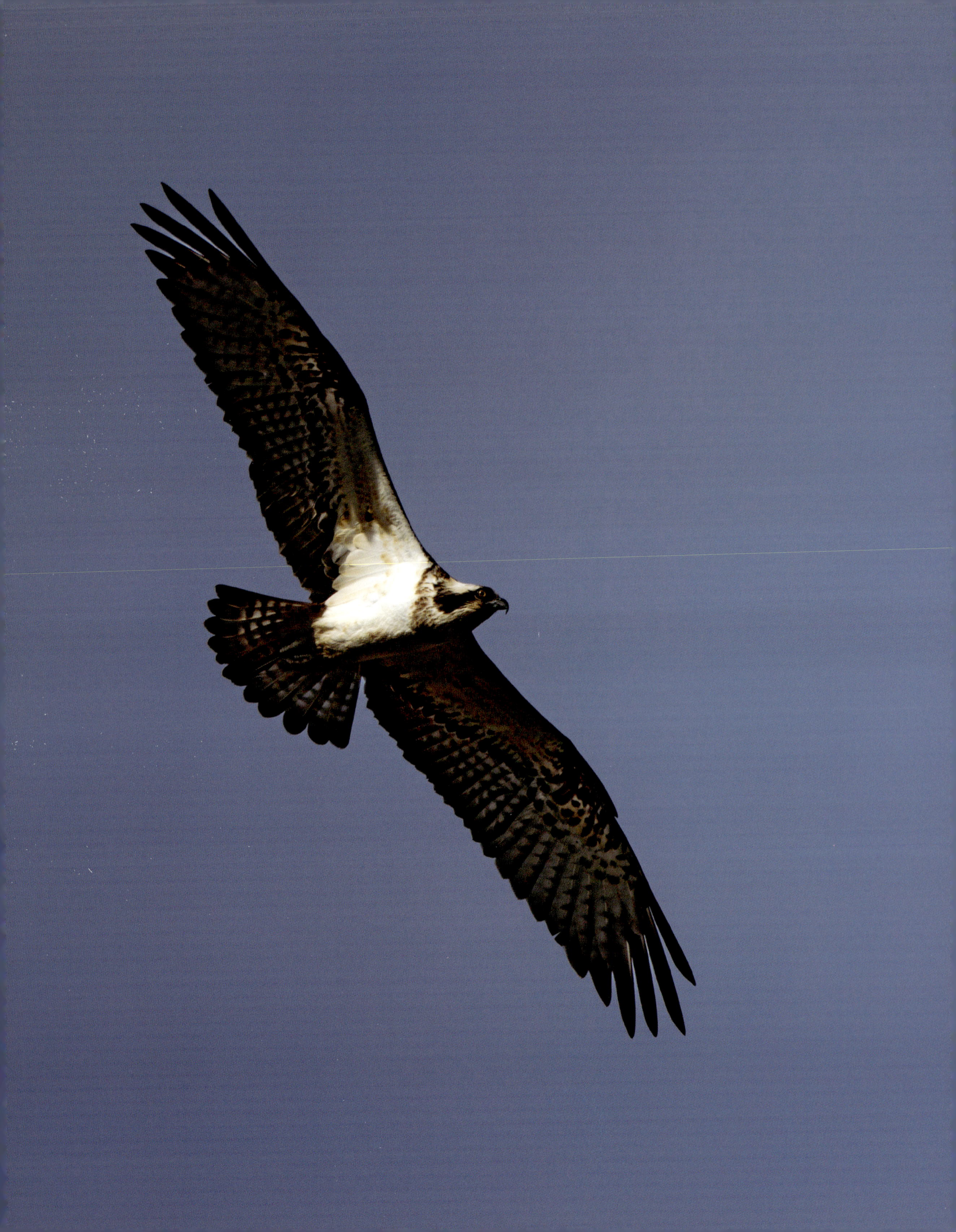

The male was still with us on 18th April when another osprey, a female, did indeed join him. Both birds were observed together on the nest, but they spent a lot of time away – we sometimes saw them displaying in the distance, but on 24th April the female disappeared. Unfortunately, we were having teething problems with the live pictures during that week, so we had no photographic record of this bird; she was probably just stopping off for a 'pit-stop' on her way to Scotland. Later that week the dark-eyed male flew directly over Cors Dyfi reserve and I managed to get a half-decent shot of him; it confirmed what we had thought – he was indeed a male, a very dark one, but all this was to change a few weeks later. Well, sort of.

Monty

On 25th April we officially opened the Dyfi Osprey Project to the public with the camera problems behind us. Everything was working beautifully.

Iolo Williams opens the Dyfi Osprey Project on Saturday, 25th April 2009. Wales has two osprey projects for the first time.

The first proper photograph of the orange-eyed osprey – male or female?

2009

Iolo was free of filming commitments that weekend and kindly agreed to officially open the project for us. Sadly, we only had one osprey to show him and the 500 or so people that turned up on the opening day; time was running out for any breeding on the Dyfi in 2009.

At least the cameras were working again and despite the commotion of all the new visitors milling around, Janine managed to get a really good close-up portrait of the male osprey as he preened himself on the ash tree perch; his eyes were even darker than we had previously thought. I knew of only one other adult osprey with the same colour eyes – a male bird named Henry that had bred on the Loch Garten nest from 2003 to 2007. I actually photographed Henry during my Scotland visit in 2006, but the resolution of the images was not good enough to meaningfully compare both birds. I was thinking, of course, whether they might be related.

"Lets call him Monty," Janine said; that way, if he did turn out to be a 'she', the name could still be used. "And Maldwyn in Welsh," proclaimed Alwyn. We had a name for our Dyfi osprey, named after Montgomeryshire, in both languages. Whether Monty was indeed a male osprey, however, was still in question!

"Monty" and his dark orange eyes – a view from the ash tree perch with Dyfi Junction train station in the background.

Naming birds is not to everyone's taste. Objectors usually decree two main grumbles: they are wild birds and shouldn't have a name, and anthropomorphism. What rubbish. Naming a bird doesn't make it any less wild and anthropomorphism is ascribing human behaviours to animals (a lizard looking pensive or a dormouse feeling jealous), nothing to do with naming anything. After all, isn't calling a bird 'osprey' naming it? How about '*Pandion haliaetus*', the osprey's Latin name? Naming birds is a great way of connecting them with people, especially children – heaven knows they need some positive limelight after what some of our ancestors did to them in the past. I've yet to hear of an osprey that had any objections to his or her name.

Scraggly

We saw Monty on a daily basis in April and May of 2009 and he was certainly treating the nest as his own, but following the female's departure on 23rd April, he had been alone. If Monty was the male osprey of the 2008 pair, and in all probability he was, his female mate had failed to return. What a shame.

At just before noon on 28th May, Monty was joined by another osprey and after a couple of hours eyeing each other up on the nest, they disappeared down the estuary together. Later that afternoon they both returned to the nest site at the same time, both with a fish. Monty landed on the ash tree perch with a huge mullet, but the newcomer landed on the nest itself, so we zoomed in and had a good look at him. It was a male!

There was no question about the gender of this new osprey – he was completely white-chested with only a sprinkle of under-wing spots. He was also tiny compared to Monty and looked quite disheveled. We were 100% sure this bird was a male, so what did that make Monty? Both birds were very tolerant

View at the visitor centre – 'Scraggly' on the nest (left) and Monty on the ash tree perch 10m away. Great to have a pair again, but what kind of pair were they!

of each other, even frequenting the nest for several hours, standing just inches apart, peering over the side like a pair of guards at the Tower of London.

We decided to call this male 'Scraggly' due to his tatty and rather unkempt appearance. He didn't half open a big can of worms though. Both ospreys didn't actually mate with each other, but they had a few attempts at, shall we say, landing on each other's backs. It was as if they knew each other or were young birds indulging in play behavior. We just didn't know and it didn't help either that a few hundred people were asking us every day in the visitor centre what the situation was – we were supposed to be osprey experts!

'Scraggly' appears in late May and quickly opens up a large can of worms.

It was the old adage again; ospreys will make you look stupid at every opportunity and they certainly had this time – with consummate ease.

I was really interested to know what the guys at Rutland thought of all this and whether they had encountered a similar situation there. In August, both Tim and John came over to the Dyfi, but they were as bemused as we were with the whole situation. I felt better in a way that neither Tim nor John had a full explanation, but on the other hand it didn't answer any questions either. Tim thought that Scraggly could even be a first-year bird, as he looked so emaciated and feather-bleached on his wings. Both Tim and John had experience of observing one-year-old ospreys in Italy and Africa, so they certainly knew what to look out for in terms of morphology. It is extremely rare, however, for ospreys to return to the UK as one-year-olds, but it would certainly explain a few things.

Irrespective of what gender Monty was, both ospreys were most probably young birds. The fact that Scraggly didn't show up until late May points to him being a two-year-old, or possibly even a one-year-old as Tim had suggested.

Ospreys are quite different to other birds of prey in terms of their reproductive ecology. Birds of the same gender tolerate each other's company very readily if the other bird doesn't pose a threat. There are many examples of all sorts of reproductive strategies from osprey populations around the world, which are far from monogamous, which an older textbook may allude to.

Ospreys can exhibit polygyny where a male has a second nest and female, usually near-by to his main nest. The polygynous male will feed both females if food is readily available and will sometimes successfully father chicks from both nests. Two females have even been recorded laying their eggs in the same nest in Scotland – how bizarre! Neither clutch succeeded.

Then we have a polyandrous set-up where a female on one nest has two males, both sharing incubation and fishing duties. Things are not as simple as they may at first appear in the osprey world.

Monty – most probably a young osprey.

Looking back at the events of 2009 now, a few years later, what seemed 'odd' to us at the time probably wasn't that uncommon at all. We know a lot more about the ecology of older, breeding ospreys than we do about youngsters; after all, who would be so dumb as to invest money in nest cameras and start an osprey project based on a few osprey sightings around a man-made nest that had never been used for breeding? Montgomeryshire Wildlife Trust had taken a brave decision in 2009 and it was certainly paying dividends in terms of increasing our understanding of the behaviours of (presumably) young, inexperienced ospreys that had not bred yet.

The Odd Couple

Whatever the actual dynamics between Monty and Scraggly, it was great to have them. Over 30,000 people visited the new hide at the Dyfi Osprey Project in 2009 and it was obvious that there was a huge appetite in Mid Wales too for everything ospreys, just as there had been when the Glaslyn started in 2004 - 2005.

Monty and Scraggly remained together for the rest of the 2009 season, very tolerant and at ease with each other, cohabiting the same nest. They took it in turns to bring nesting material back, they went

Volunteer Heather points out Monty and Scraggly to a young Machynlleth schoolgirl, Ffion, from the new osprey hide.

on fishing trips together, they even shared their food on a few occasions; they were the Jack Lemmon and Walter Matthau of the osprey world.

Assuming that Scraggly was either one or two years old, could we work anything out about Monty regarding his age? There's no question he was inexperienced and highly unlikely to have bred before, so he could be a three or maybe a four-year-old bird. However, if he was around on the Dyfi in 2008, and was most probably the osprey recorded in 2007 as well, that would push his date of birth back to around 2004, making him a five-year-old in 2009. Now that would make things interesting – that was the year the first osprey of modern times fledged in Wales at the Welshpool nest. That bird wasn't ringed either, as Tony Cross couldn't reach the nest with his cherry-picker. The Welshpool nest is less than 30 miles away from the Dyfi, so it would make perfect sense for a young adult osprey (especially a male), to come back to the area where he was raised. Maybe Monty was that young chick in the Welshpool nest in 2004 that Roy and Tony got so near to? Intriguing…

The odd couple: Monty and Scraggly take it in turns to bring nesting material back to the nest.

Glaslyn Grandchildren

Both the Glaslyn birds returned like clockwork again in 2009 and at their earliest arrival times yet. The male made it back on 21st March with his partner arriving just a day later. It is extremely early to have both birds of a pair back by 22nd March. Consequently, their customary three eggs were laid in record time too – 6th, 9th and 12th April.

The Glaslyn female – she arrives back on 22nd March in 2009, her earliest return date yet.

As the Glaslyn birds were getting on with their sixth year of breeding together, Karl Munday, Head Ranger at the Threave Estate, National Trust for Scotland, rang me with some wonderful news. The Glaslyn 2006 male offspring, Black 80, had returned to Threave and had again paired up with the same un-ringed bird he had been observed pair-bonding with the previous year. They had produced young also for the first time – two of them. A Welsh born osprey had been positively recorded as breeding for the first time ever, and what was more remarkable was that fact that Black 80 was only three years old, very young for a male osprey to breed successfully.

The Glaslyn dynasty was expanding in Wales as well as Scotland. Three chicks hatched from those three early eggs in mid-May and on 6th, 8th and 11th July the trio fledged in age order. The Glaslyn pair had successfully produced their successive hat-trick of youngsters. They were ringed with white Darvics again in 2009: White 90 and White 91 for the two females of the clutch and White YF for the male.

By 2nd September all three of the youngsters had left on their migration and the following day both their parents departed within hours of each other. Job done for another year.

The first grandchildren – two chicks in Black 80's nest on the River Dee in Dumfries and Galloway with Threave Castle in the background, top right.

Yellow Gold

With increasing regularity, we were hearing of more osprey sightings in mid-summer, especially at the Glaslyn but also on the Dyfi and elsewhere in Mid Wales.

In June and July there was a flurry of sightings of an osprey on the River Severn, very near to where the original Welshpool nest was sited in 2004. It was a male osprey and he was observed catching fish, bathing in the river and perching in nearby trees for a prolonged period in 2009 – several weeks. The big story regarding this osprey, however, was the fact that he was ringed – he had a yellow Darvic on the right leg. Had we struck gold again – was this bird the male chick from the Glaslyn nest in 2005, Yellow 37?

A yellow-ringed osprey sighted in Mid Wales in June and July 2009. Is he Glaslyn's Yellow 37 from 2005?

Unfortunately, nobody could get a close enough photograph to decipher the number, just the fact that it was a yellow ring and on the right leg. Then on 8th September, John Davies, a local bird tour guide in Mid Wales, reported a yellow-ringed osprey on the Dyfi – on the right leg again. Surely, this was the same bird that had been frequenting the River Severn just a few miles east for the previous two months?

By the end of 2009 things were looking much better for the osprey in Wales. Yes, we still only had the one breeding pair, but with more sightings of birds over-summering each year, hopefully it would only be a matter of time before a second pair got established. That was the dream, anyway.

Monty leaves the Dyfi in 2009 a year older and a year wiser, hopefully!

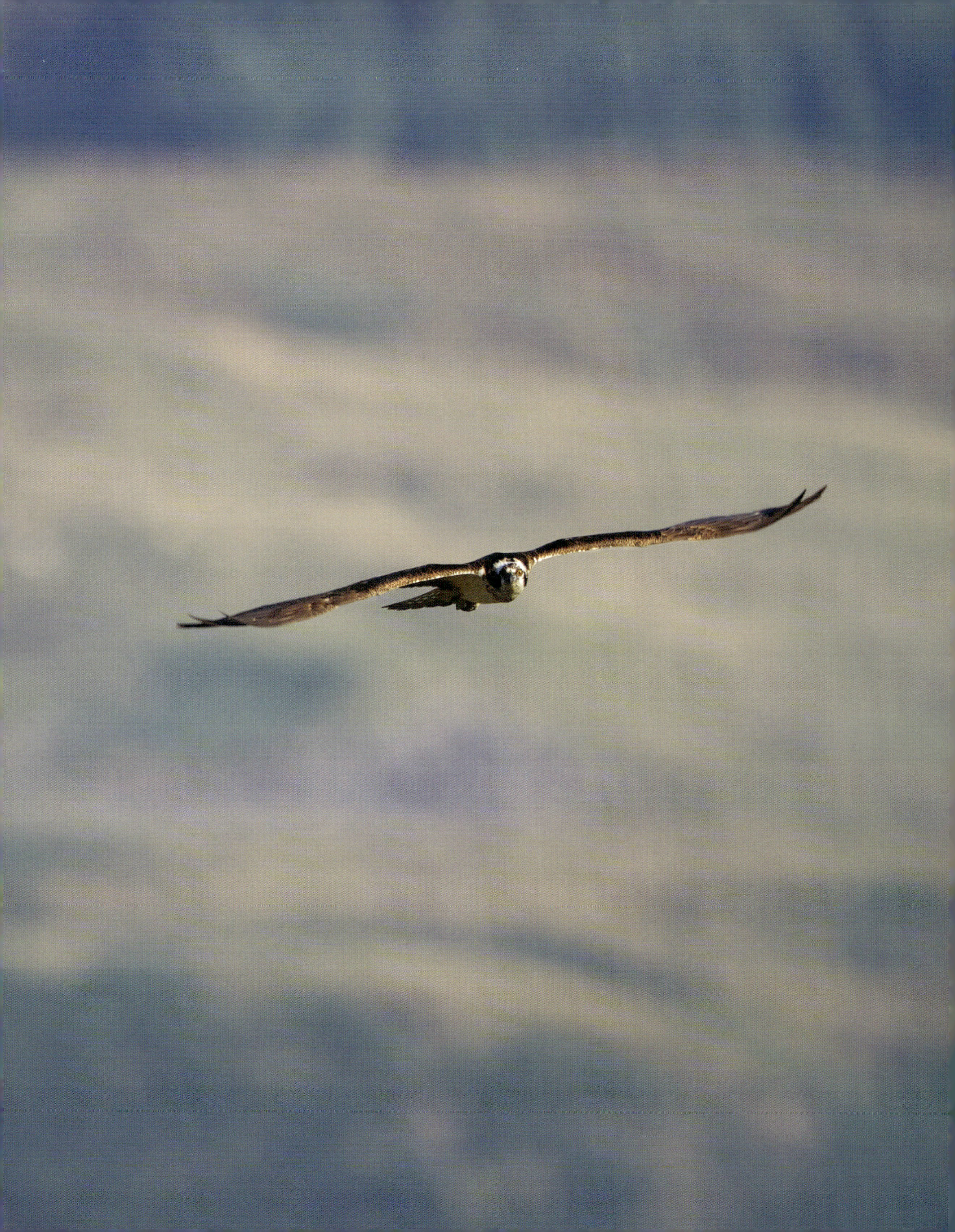

2010

Mirror Image

By the beginning of the second decade of this century we still only had one pair of ospreys breeding in Wales, however we were getting closer to a second pair establishing than at any time since 2004.

For the Glaslyn pair, 2010 would turn out to be a mirror image almost of the previous year. The male returned just a day later than in 2009 on 22nd March, and his partner was only a day behind, just as she had been the year before. The obligatory three eggs were laid 8th, 11th and 14th April, with the usual three-day gap in-between eggs.

The Glaslyn male arrives 22nd March, just a day later than in 2009.

The Glaslyn female – back for her seventh year of breeding in 2009.

I often compare measuring success (or otherwise) in wildlife conservation to turning the world's largest cruise ship around mid-ocean, while she's at full speed. It takes time.

It was promising that Black 80 had not only survived his first couple of years in Africa, but had bred for the first time at just three years old in 2009; especially as this is far from the norm. Ospreys sometimes don't breed for a decade or more and we can only establish that if we can spot them and identify them by their Darvic rings – which will have hopefully stayed intact during that time. It will take many years to fully gauge the success and significance of the Glaslyn pair's contribution to osprey population growth generally. For now, we just had to hope that they would keep fledging three young ospreys every year, conveyor-belt style. The more tickets you have, the greater chance of winning further down the road.

A Hat-trick of Hat-tricks

Sure enough, the Glaslyn pair did indeed manage to fledge three more young in 2010, their third successive year in doing so. Just as in the previous two years, all three chicks were ringed with white Darvic rings, and as in 2009 there were two females (White 92 and White 93) and one male (White 94).

So let's take stock here a moment. Including 2010, that's nine ospreys fledged during the last three years (3 x 3), and six from the previous three years (3 x 2). Nothing for the first year (2004), so 15 in all. That is a productivity of just over two birds per nest (2.14), each year for seven years (15 ÷ 7) – much higher than the UK average; the Glaslyn birds were doing fantastically well. There is one big spanner in this well-oiled engine however…

The return rate of young ospreys is low. Just one in three makes it back to the UK as an adult, and fewer still make it to full breeding age and produce young themselves. So the mathematics are pitifully simple. Out of every clutch of three, only one will ever make it back to the UK; out of the 15 offspring so far, around five should make it back. These are averages of course.

Young ospreys face a plethora of new dangers as soon as they become independent from their parents at around three months old. They have to start catching fish for themselves, and quickly; there's the weather and strong winds to contend with, in addition to a 3,000 mile journey – a third of it across the largest desert in the world. Assuming they make it to Africa in one piece, then starts a whole new ball-game of pitfalls and dangers – from scorching 40°C temperatures, to increased predation pressures, to competition for food and perching areas from other more mature ospreys that have done it and seen it all before. Survive all that and by November, an osprey will probably have seen the last of any rainfall

turning the world's largest cruise ship around mid-ocean, while she's at full speed

until the following May, by which time many of the fish-rich tributaries to the larger rivers will have evaporated to scorched earth; they don't call it the dry season for nothing. It's not easy being a young osprey – two-thirds never make it home again.

Another Returnee

Before we get too bogged down with the doom and gloom of the osprey return rate statistics, we received some positive news in 2010.

A white-ringed male osprey had been seen several times on the Dyfi. The ring was on the right leg, so it had to be a Welsh or English bird. On 8th July this bird actually landed on the Dyfi nest and caused a riot; both the resident male birds, Monty and Scraggly, were happy with their own company, but three males were definitely a crowd.

Scraggly (left) and Monty (right) are not overly impressed that another male has joined them on their nest on 8th July.

What a bizarre looking scene, three male ospreys on the same nest and not a female in sight! We had our suspicions that this intruding white-ringed bird was a Glaslyn offspring (White YA, YC or YD) from previous years, but we just couldn't get a clear enough shot of the leg ring to be absolutely sure. Hopefully, he would be back in 2011 and we'd be ready for him.

We also received another sighting in 2010, but not of a returning Welsh osprey as an adult this time; one of the 2010 Glaslyn youngsters was spotted in Europe on his migration south. He was not in a

Is this white-ringed male osprey one of the Glaslyn offspring visiting the Dyfi nest in 2010?

country you would expect to see a Welsh osprey migrate through, however, like France or Spain or Portugal – he was in Switzerland!

Swiss photographer, Martin Trachsel, was out photographing birds at Lake Klingnau, around 20 miles north of Zurich, when he photographed White 94 flying over. Why was White 94 in Switzerland? He should have been 500 miles further west. Western Europe had witnessed strong northwesterly winds that week and four days after he'd left the Glaslyn on 22nd August, White 94 had been blown off course in an easterly direction and had reached northern Switzerland by the time Martin photographed him at just before midday on 26th August.

One of the 2010 youngsters, White 94, is spotted on migration – in Switzerland! He was 500 miles too far east.

Whether White 94 later continued his migration south through Italy, or corrected his course and flew back west towards France and Spain to cross over to Africa via the Straits of Gibraltar (which is a more usual route for British ospreys), we will never know. White 94, the youngest of the three 2010 chicks, has never been spotted again, not that we know of anyway.

Ospreys Everywhere on the Dyfi

We opened the Dyfi Osprey Project on 27th March in 2010 with great optimism and hope that Monty or Scraggly would return and breed. We saw absolutely nothing for over a week, not even a passing osprey on migration, but on Easter Sunday, 4th April, we did. Four ospreys turned up!

A flounder-laden female at the Dyfi on 4th April 2010 – she stayed around for several hours, ignoring another male osprey just 10m away from her.

First to show at just before 10am was a beautiful looking female with a half-eaten flounder. An hour later a male joined her, but it wasn't Monty or Scraggly; he was un-ringed and stayed on the ash tree perch for a couple of hours whilst the female ate her flounder on the nest. Neither osprey interacted; they both seemed to be on a mission, probably their migration to Scotland – there was no real reason to socialise.

Next up was a distant osprey circling high over the river. We were hoping it might be Monty returning home, but we couldn't tell whether this bird was male or female. In the end it didn't matter, no sooner had it come into view than it disappeared north over the hills of Snowdonia.

By late afternoon both the other two ospreys had made their way north too, leaving us with an empty nest again. Just before sunset Alwyn rang me at home on his mobile phone; he had stayed on in the hide hoping that one of the three ospreys that day would return. They didn't, but another osprey had just landed on the ash tree perch: a dark male with deep orange eyes. It was the fourth osprey that we saw on that Easter Sunday and *the* one we had been hoping for. Monty was home.

Monty – back on his ash tree perch late evening on 4th April.

Other than Monty, we didn't see another osprey until 18th April when he suddenly sprang into life and got very animated – there was a female around and Monty was quickly up in the air displaying to her, sky dancing and performing any other trick he could pick out of his 'how to impress a lady' osprey-manoeuvres repertoire.

The female actually landed on the nest briefly with her half eaten mullet and spent most of the day around the Dyfi. Despite Monty's best efforts to persuade her to stay however, by the next day she was gone. Yet another Scottish female on her way north no doubt.

At least this osprey had spurred Monty to do something about his lack of success on the female front. We had hardly seen him on the nest, but following this ephemeral liaison with the mullet-female, he started taking a bit more interest in nest building – maybe the nest itself wasn't up to scratch? It makes sense that a female wouldn't want to invest her reproductive energies to it, and Monty, if it wasn't.

Monty adds a good six inches of nesting material (the browner, uppermost twigs) in a little over a week.

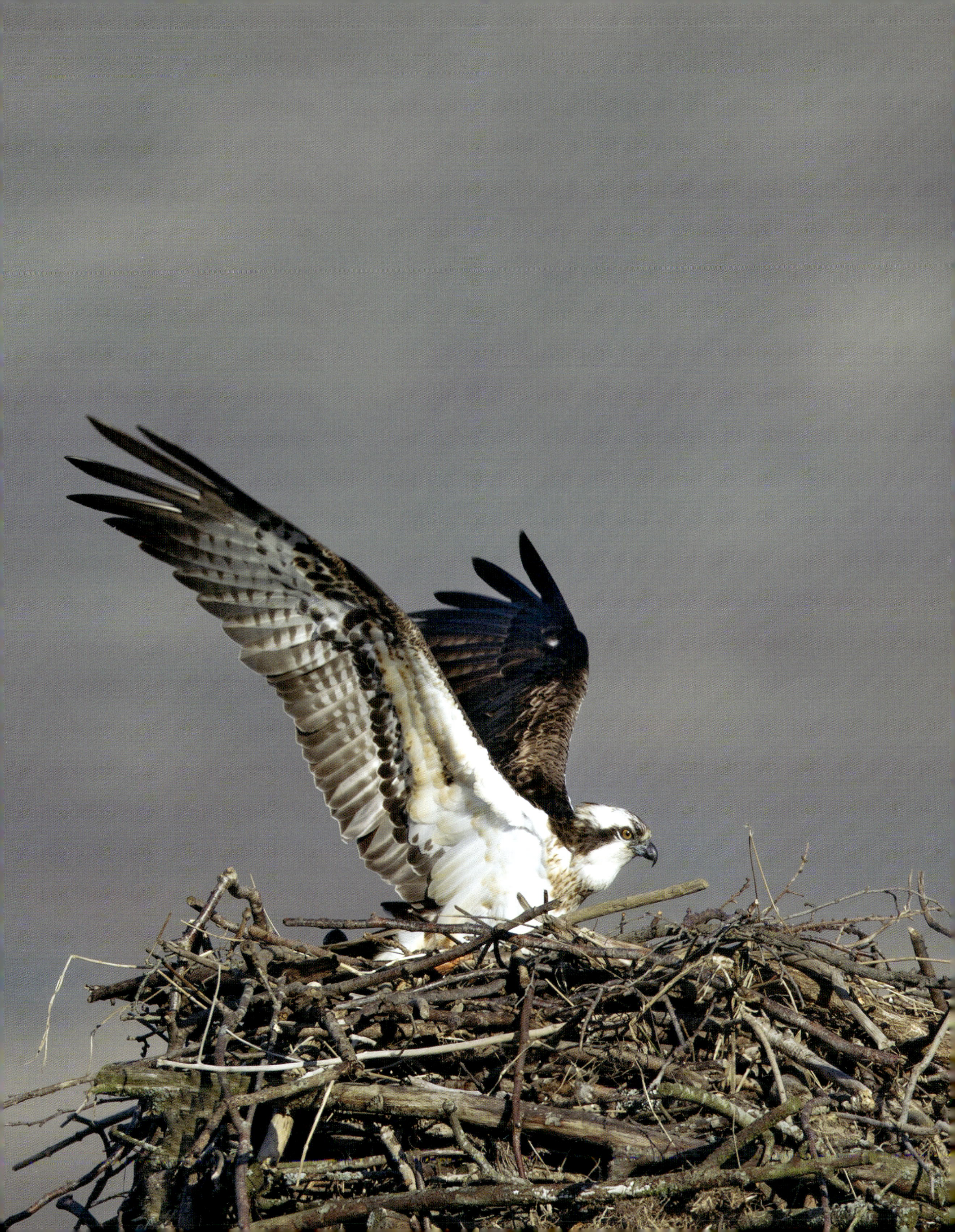

Thereafter started a spurt of intense nest building, if it was an inadequate nest that was the weak link here, at least he could do something about it.

Scraggly Returns

By mid-summer a few ospreys had passed through, but not one of them looked like staying despite Monty's attempts at commandeering them. Then on 29th June, another osprey thumped down onto the nest – a small, tatty-looking male; it was Scraggly. We'd assumed that he had either not made it back, or had decided to spend the summer in another area, but here he was.

For the next two months both Monty and Scraggly returned to the nest, regularly bringing with them nesting material, but at different times of the day. There were a few occasions where the two appeared at the nest together, but Monty often chased off the young male. Behaviourally, Monty seemed to have changed his approach to Scraggly. No longer did he tolerate him as readily as he had done in 2009; Scraggly was suddenly an adversary and a competitor. The Matthau and Lemmon arrangement was off.

Scraggly arrives back at the Dyfi nest in late June – where has he been?

In late July, another osprey landed on the nest, this one again had a white Darvic ring on the right leg. He was definitely a male osprey, so was it the same bird that visited at the beginning of the month – and possibly a Glaslyn youngster? It was so infuriating to be able to see the rings but not have enough definition to make out the characters inscribed on them. If only we had better cameras, high-definition ones, we would learn so much more about what was happening on the nest and who was visiting.

Despite my earlier forecast that there were enough ospreys around in Wales by now to replace another breeding bird if he or she failed to return one year, it was getting increasingly bothersome as to why the Dyfi nest with two (and sometimes three!) males could not attract a female. Maybe that was the problem – too many males. Females would surely be put off breeding with a male that couldn't even fend off another challenger?

We last saw Monty on 30th August in 2010 and Scraggly a few days before that. It had been a barren year once again with respect to breeding, but the fact that Monty was now defending his nest in a more determined and purposeful manner was promising. Maybe now he was old enough and mature enough to lay claim to the fact that his adolescent years were behind him? Not all male ospreys breed at three years old like Black 80, the average is more like five years old in Scotland. If the 'Monty-Welshpool 2004' theory was correct, Monty was only six in 2010 and considering we didn't have over 200 pairs of breeding ospreys like they had in Scotland, maybe we were too optimistic with our expectations of poor Monty? How was he supposed to attract a female if they all kept flying straight past him to Scotland!

Perhaps we needed to set up an osprey translocation project in Wales, but on a smaller scale than Rutland had done over a decade before. An injection of a few youngsters for a year or two with the hope that those birds, or at least a third of them, would come back to Wales to breed in future years. Dr. Chris Townsend, the Chairman of Montgomeryshire Wildlife Trust, and myself facilitated a few meetings with potential stakeholders in the summer of 2010, but for one reason or another, a mini-Welsh osprey translocation project proved logistically impractical to do.

At around the same time I visited a new viewing hide that the Countryside Council for Wales had built on their Cors Caron reserve, around 20 miles south of Cors Dyfi. Both reserves are similar with much the same habitat – wet, boggy, peaty reedbed (Cors means exactly that). It wasn't your everyday hide however, this was a swanky affair made of oak beams and a profusion of glass panels overlooking the reserve; it reminded me of an Air Traffic Control Tower.

Monty (left) looks on as Scraggly takes his flounder off him. The 'odd-couple's' relationship is wearing thin.

The osprey hide at Cors Dyfi with the nest-cam video receiver on the side – over 60,000 people came to watch Monty and Scraggly in 2009 and 2010.

If the Dyfi was so attractive to ospreys (well, males at any rate), maybe Montgomeryshire Wildlife Trust could build something similar on Cors Dyfi, but not on the ground – high up so that we would be on the same level as the osprey nest, and nearer to it? Over 60,000 people had watched the Monty & Scraggly show from the osprey hide at Cors Dyfi in 2009 and 2010, despite being 660m away from the nest. Soon work would start on making osprey watching and learning a much more personal and intimate experience on the Dyfi…

Black 80

Karl Munday (Threave Castle ospreys – Dumfries and Galloway) and I had kept in regular contact throughout the summer of 2010; we were all keen to know how Black 80 was doing. Sure enough, he had returned again to the same nest and had gone one better this time around; he and his un-ringed partner had produced three eggs and all three chicks had successfully hatched and fledged. Black 80 had only just turned four years of age in May 2010, and he had already sired five osprey youngsters in that time – that is some going!

Black 80 bringing in a flounder to his three offspring at his nest by Threave Castle, Dumfries and Galloway.

The Glaslyn pair had become grandparents (not that they knew it) for the fifth time and their dynasty was expanding, but not in Wales. Despite the fact that Black 80 had most certainly returned to Wales as a two-year-old in 2008, he had continued on to Scotland, just north of the border in fact, until he found a nest site he was happy with. We couldn't grumble really; his father was, after all, Scottish by birth – we had 'pinched' him via Rutland's translocation project in 1998, so it was only fair we gave Scotland one back.

If only we could do the same with a few rugby or football players. How about we translocate Lionel Messi or Christiano Ronaldo from Spain to Aberystwyth Town FC? Maybe not.

The Glaslyn male starts his southerly migration on 29th August in 2010, having now sired 15 young ospreys to fledging age. How many of these would come back to breed in future years?

2011

So Many Questions

This is where the osprey story really starts to warm up in Wales. We had a pioneering pair in the Glaslyn that was producing three young ospreys each year, 15 to date; there was the making of a pair on the Dyfi and there existed an ever increasing possibility of some of the Glaslyn youngsters returning as adults to breed. It was an interesting time to be involved with osprey conservation, you never knew what was around the corner and there were so many questions that could potentially be answered by just a quick click of a camera shutter or the focus ring of a telescope.

Monty returns on 6th April in 2011, but not to the nest initially.

Glaslyn's White YC would be three years old now, would he return? How about some of the other Glaslyn offspring, would we see them again? Would Monty finally find a female and start to breed? So many questions, would we find any answers in 2011? Put your seat belts on…

Monty Returns

The first week of April was a shocker in terms of the weather in Mid Wales. On 5th April a visitor to the Dyfi Osprey Project reported seeing an osprey fishing at the mouth of the estuary, but we had seen nothing through the rain and gloom; the nest was empty as it had been for the previous seven months. The following morning, Alwyn and I decided to go on a bit of an osprey search to see if the reported bird was still around. After looking for a few hours we found nothing over the estuary or the Llyfnant Valley close-by; as we drove back to the project, thoroughly drenched and dejected, we stopped off at one of Monty's preferred eating perches of the previous year, just to the south of Cors Dyfi reserve.

Monty – back on the ash tree perch wondering what all the fuss is about.

Monty was back. He had obviously heard that Alwyn and I had been looking for him all day, so decided to eat his mullet dinner out of sight on his favourite electricity pole and not return to the nest. Cue two grown men bouncing up and down excitedly in a steamed-up car, windows closed, in the middle of a field, howling hysterically. It can't have looked good to anyone passing by.

We radioed through to Janine at the project who was equally as excited at hearing the good news; by early evening that day the sun had finally come out and Monty was back on his ash tree perch next to the nest. It felt wonderful to see him again.

Flaming Nora

Three days later during the morning of 9th April, Monty was joined by another osprey – a female. This bird appeared a little different to the other females that had passed through Monty's patch in previous years; she didn't seem to have an agenda somehow. She lacked the purposefulness of the other females, probably because they were on their way to a final destination elsewhere.

I grabbed a video camera, set it on full zoom and started recording from the osprey hide at Cors Dyfi. Monty had been displaying to the new female, performing his tried and tested sky dancing routine, but as soon as she landed on the ash tree perch he joined her. Five minutes later the pair were mating, and proper mating too, *not the messing around stuff we had seen Monty and Scraggly get up to.*

This new female had a ring on her right leg. My first thought was that she must be one of the Glaslyn offspring – they had all been given white rings from 2007 onwards, but agonisingly I couldn't see the characters on the ring to identify her, she was too far away. As luck would have it, we had just lost the electrical supply to the nest due to scheduled maintenance on the rail track for a few days, so we couldn't check with the cameras either. How utterly torturous!

Try as we might we just couldn't read the ring number. The female was still with Monty three days later on 12th April when luckily, professional wildlife photographer Garry Ridsdale came to the rescue. He set up his camera equipment just before sunset to reduce any heat-haze, stacked several tele-converters onto his 800mm telephoto lens and focused, carefully. Garry was over 300m away, but he finally managed to get a clear enough shot of the female to be able to read the ring number. It was White 03.

This was a ring number I was unfamiliar with so I rang Tim at Rutland to see if he had any ideas. He almost fell off his seat – White 03 was one of theirs, a Rutland bird. She was a 2008 osprey whose

After three days of trying, we finally manage to get a decent photo. The female's leg ring is White 03.

parents were both first-generation translocated birds from Scotland to Rutland – her mother was Green 05(2000) and the rather famous 03(1997) was her father; more on him at the end of the book.

By now, we had started calling White 03, 'Nora'. When I took that video footage from the hide on 9th April, I had rushed home to upload a few seconds of highlights of Monty and White 03 mating onto the Dyfi Osprey Project's Facebook page – we had a massive 300 people following us then. In my haste I had quickly made my way back to the project to see what other developments were unraveling. Later that afternoon a visitor came up to me asking whether I was aware of the audio track that had also uploaded with the video. I turned white as a sheet – I never replayed the video back in full, such was my hurry to get back to the project. Just as Monty was mating with White 03 for the first time, I had shouted, "FLAMING NORA" (or similar…) and that was now in the public domain for all to see – and hear. I rushed home again to dub out the offending words, but by that time it was too late. Visitor after visitor were coming in asking how (ahem) Nora was, with a wry smile on their faces. Quite inadvertently, White 03 had acquired a name.

Even though she was allowing Monty to mate with her, in return for food of course, Nora kept disappearing for hours on end leaving Monty alone with all of us watching, biting our fingernails and wondering whether she would return. Early morning on her fifth day at the Dyfi, 14th April, she took off again and by 5pm she still hadn't returned – here we go again I thought, there goes another female Monty hasn't managed to hang on to. We did have another female osprey land on the nest that day though – a Scottish bird with a white Darvic on her left leg, White DA. She was from a clutch of two at a nest near Loch Ard in the Trossachs National Park, Scotland, and like Nora, she was also a 2008 bird so they were both three-year-olds. This was great news as the chances of either female having already paired up with another male were low.

From having too many males in 2010, we now have an abundance of females! White DA – a Scottish 2008 female osprey eyeing up Monty's nest and calling for food on 14th April.

Rutland's White 03(08), or 'Nora' as she quickly became known.

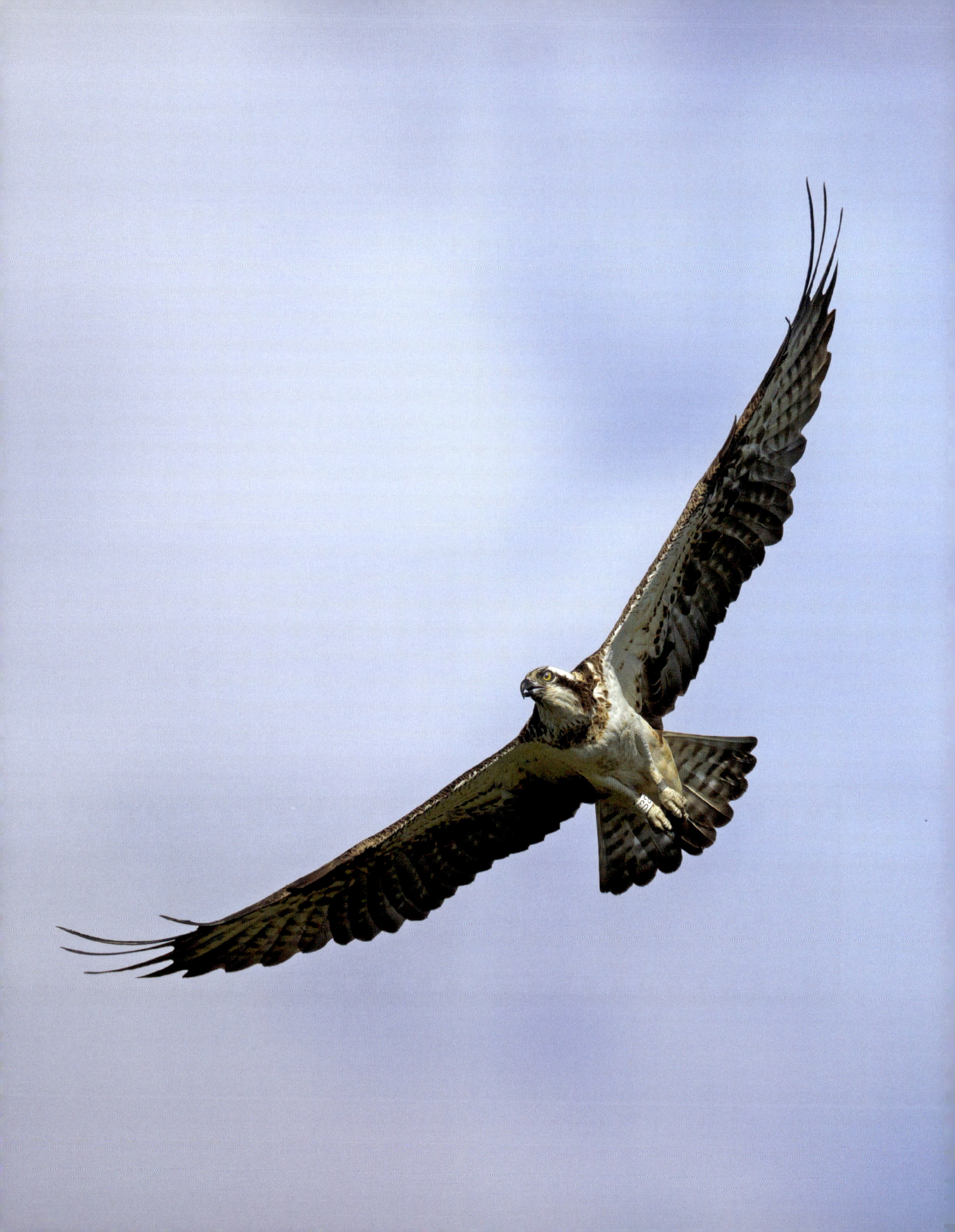

Bonding Together

Shortly before 6pm, Nora returned having been away all day only to find Monty gallivanting with another female. The appearance of White DA was possibly the best thing that could ever have happened. Nora saw White DA as a threat and a contender for Monty and his nest; she was having none of it. So ensued a girl-fight for the nest.

There is a kind of unwritten rule in the osprey world. Typically, males fight males and females fight females. Not always, but this is generally the case. It took Nora around half an hour of moderate airborne sparring to dispatch White DA, whose bond to Monty and his nest was a lot weaker than Nora's. The newcomer reluctantly gave up and she was on her way. Nora had demonstrated that she had grown an affiliation to Monty and the Dyfi nest during the previous five days, a bond that she was prepared to defend. Things were looking promising.

Once Nora returned that evening after being away for 10 hours and sending White DA on her way, she hardly left Monty's side. Suddenly, we had an osprey couple doing things straight from the textbook: Monty catching the fish and lots of bonding, nest building and mating. After a week, both birds were seen scraping out a nest cup and a week later Nora appeared so nest-bound, it was as if she was tethered to it. She was fidgety and seemed on edge – she had good reason to be.

On 25th April, 16 days after their first encounter, Nora laid an egg at 2:03pm with the visitor centre and hide full of people screaming and shouting. I'm amazed that the birds didn't hear us. Wales had its third nest of breeding ospreys after Welshpool in 2004 and Glaslyn; it was absolutely brilliant!

Three days later Nora laid a second egg and a third after another three days on 1st May. We had six eggs in two nests less than 30 miles apart – sensational.

Monty and Nora produce their first ever eggs; Nora is just three years old breeding for the first time and Monty probably around seven years old.

Ospreys of Higher Resolution

High-Definition cameras had been around for a few years by 2011, but not in the CCTV surveillance world, which was the technology we used to film osprey nests. These cameras are ideal for wildlife watching – they're rugged and weather proof and can be operated with a minimum of fuss and camera movement, just what we wanted. CCTV cameras had never been very high resolution though.

With the advent of IP (Internet-protocol) cameras, however, that was changing. I had been going to the largest CCTV exhibition in the world at the NEC, Birmingham, for the previous three years (yes, with my anorak) scouring around for the latest and greatest, hoping every year that this would be the year Full HD makes it to the market. Well thankfully by 2011, there were a couple of manufacturers that were bringing High-Definition cameras out to the consumer marketplace for the very first time.

I returned on the train from Birmingham International in May 2011 with a bag full of brochures and a head full of ideas… it was going to be great. Monty and Nora were breeding for the first time and we still had the inexpensive cameras that we put up in 2009 – they deserved better! Just like the Glaslyn in 2007, we needed a refresh.

After studying the camera brochures religiously to the point of being able to recite whole chunks off by heart, I came to the conclusion that the best cameras for our osprey application were made by a company called Axis, and by the end of August we had one of their reps visit the Dyfi Osprey Project with a sample camera I had read so much about. It was so new, it wasn't on the market yet; there were only two demonstration units in the country – and we had one of them to test for a whole day.

Two replica osprey eggs and a new HD camera demonstration – the images coming back to the visitor centre are astounding.

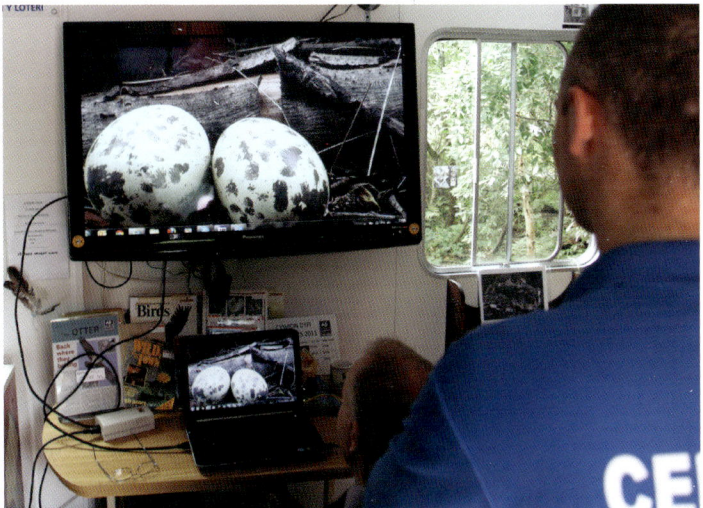

2011 113

I had placed two plastic replica osprey eggs in a nest that local schoolchildren had built just outside the visitor centre and then bolted the HD camera onto a nearby willow tree. Oh, my word – it was Howard Carter all over again and that 'I see wonderful things' analogy. The nest looked amazing and as we zoomed in, the eggs got larger and larger until they filled the Panasonic 55-inch screen we were ogling them on. It was insane – the clarity and definition of those plastic eggs was breathtaking. I even got Alwyn to poke one of the eggs from underneath the nest to simulate a chick inside chipping away at the shell – it was so good all I could do was laugh. The Axis camera rep, who was used to visiting shopping malls, airports and football stadia in the main, must have thought we were all bonkers.

The next day I started work on trying to secure funding to buy four Axis nest cameras for the following season. It seemed the right thing to do on so many levels. The BBC Springwatch programmes were being broadcast live from the RSPB's Ynys-hir Reserve right next door to Cors Dyfi at the time, and despite giving them some of our best footage, what they really wanted were HD pictures. Social media sites were becoming increasingly popular, and photographs and videos of HD quality would suit these new engagement platforms right down to the ground. Better cameras would open up a whole new world for the Dyfi Osprey Project, including possibly having a HD Live Streaming function directly from the nest to anyone, anywhere on the planet who wanted to see Monty and Nora. It was a brave new world, but for the time being we had breeding ospreys, and that was all we could ever have dreamt for in 2011.

Glaslyn Record Breakers

it was so good all I could do was laugh

While we were getting excited about Monty breeding for the first time on the Dyfi, the Glaslyn osprey production factory was in full swing again a few miles north.

Both adults arrived extremely early again and by 2nd April had laid their first egg, beating their own record by four whole days. By 8th April a clutch of three eggs had been laid – a phenomenally early start to a breeding season. I asked Roy later that summer about this first egg being laid on just the second day of April and he confirmed that was the earliest ever osprey egg recorded in the UK. Just to put that into some context – by the time the Glaslyn male was back at his nest on 16th March, probably half of all British ospreys would have been 3,500 miles away in Africa, not having set off yet.

Studies of various bird species over many decades have shown that pairs who breed earlier in the season tend to have a higher productivity than those who breed later. It is also true that ospreys that nest further south start breeding earlier than those in more northerly latitudes – it makes sense of course as the further south you are the warmer it is.

The Glaslyn male arrives back on 16th March in 2011 – a time when many British ospreys are still in Africa.

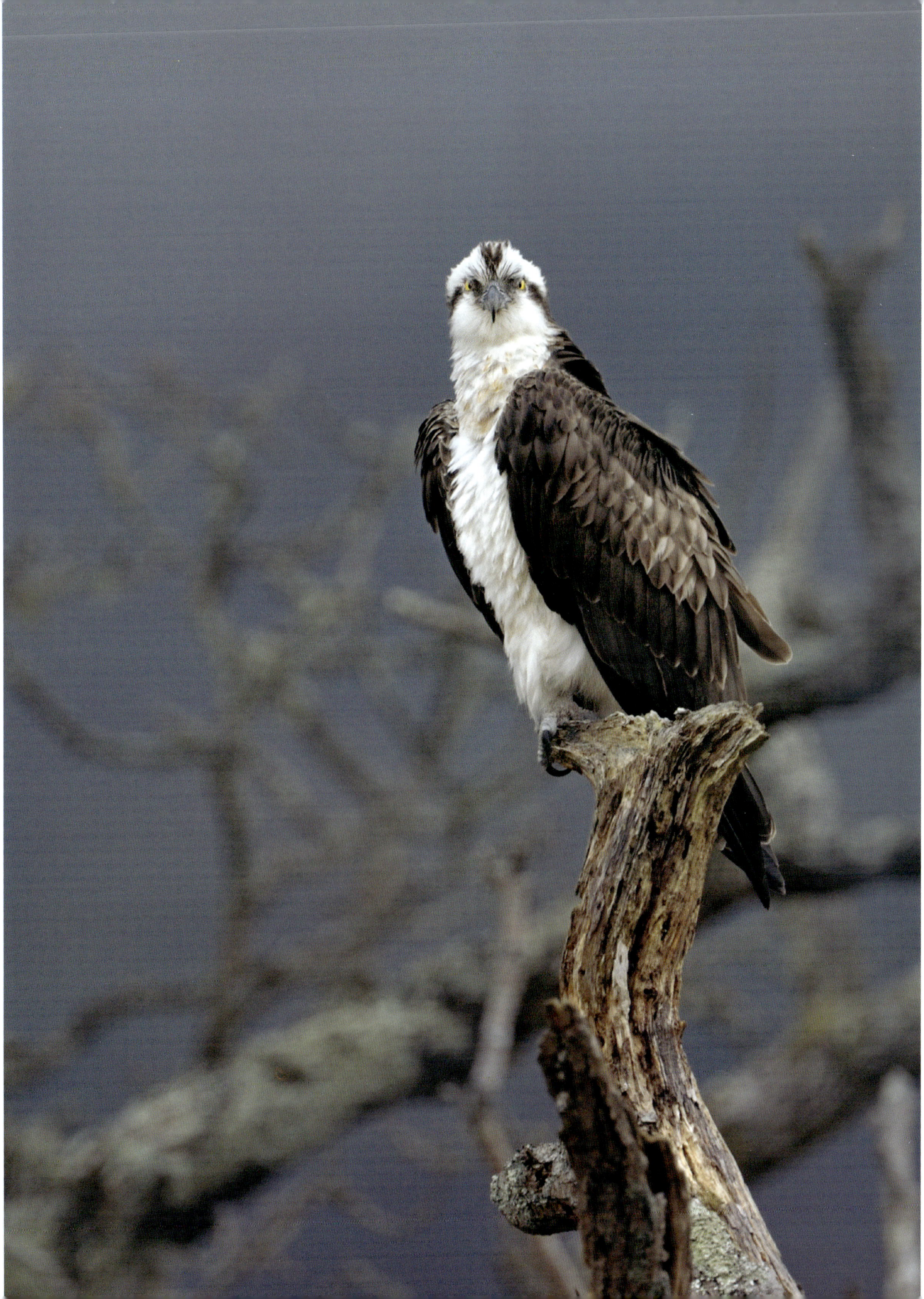

Glaslyn's White YC – being ringed as a chick in 2008 (left) and photographed on the Dyfi nest as a three-year-old on 18th May 2011. He was also spotted on his ancestral Glaslyn nest on 21st April and again on the Dyfi nest on 29th May.

So here is a great example of two birds adapting and changing their reproductive ecology over time to suit their environment. Being a Scottish bird by birth (and possibly Scandinavian by ancestry – remember Scottish ospreys were practically wiped out by the beginning of the 20th century), the male would presumably return later if he were still in Scotland, but because he was now several hundreds of miles further south, he (and the female for that matter) had progressively returned incrementally earlier each year. In 2005 and 2006 he returned on 28th and 31st March; by 2011 he had shaved two full weeks off these return dates. The female had also followed a similar pattern of returning earlier; she was a whole month earlier in 2011 than she had been in 2005.

Unsurprisingly, the Glaslyn pair went on to hatch and fledge three chicks once again: their 16th, 17th and 18th offspring to fledge the nest since 2004. By 2011 Roy had started using blue Darvic rings for ospreys in the UK, but the tradition of ringing on the right leg in England and Wales, and left leg in Scotland would continue. Accordingly, the Glaslyn chicks were ringed Blue 77 (female), Blue 78 (male) and Blue 79 (male).

Up in Scotland, the Glaslyn 2006 offspring was also doing well. Black 80 sired two more chicks to fledging age in 2011 with the same un-ringed female that he had been breeding with since 2009. That was seven offspring for the pair in just three years.

Arguably the best news of all concerning the ever-expanding Glaslyn osprey dynasty in 2011 was the return of another offspring. Those grainy pictures of a white-ringed osprey we took on the Dyfi the previous year were probably the Glaslyn male chick of 2008, White YC. Why him? He was back again in 2011.

2011

OSPREYS IN WALES The First Ten Years

I remember feeling a great sense of euphoria upon seeing White YC again; the last time I had seen him was on the Glaslyn nest as a youngster in 2008. We photographed him three separate times on the Dyfi during the 2011 season, and on several other occasions too I'm sure, when we couldn't quite get the cameras positioned and focused quickly enough. No doubt White YC was prospecting for suitable nesting sites and a female during the summer of 2011; the big question was, would we see him again in future years breeding?

White YC as a five-week-old chick in 2008. He is back in Wales as an adult in 2011 – would he come back to Wales to breed in the future?

OSPREYS IN WALES *The First Ten Years*

Making History

Back on the Dyfi the mercury in the excitement meter was rising. I had set up a 24-hour egg-watch protection based on the Glaslyn's Operation Pandora model and it had worked a treat; people appeared out of nowhere to volunteer – they were keen to be part of the surveillance team for the historic event unfolding on the Dyfi.

The excitement had turned to unease and concern however by 4th June – 40 days had passed since the first egg was laid and there was no sign of anything happening on the hatching front, despite being three days past the average incubation period. Nora hadn't incubated the first egg 'properly' for the first three days or so back in late April, and not at all during those three nights. I knew this was sometimes typical in a few bird of prey species, but it was something I had not witnessed at the Glaslyn; the female there started incubating the moment the first egg was laid.

The second egg laid is the first to hatch – we thought at 41 days the first egg was a gonner.

The following morning, Sunday 5th June, would go down in osprey history, if there is such a thing, as one of those special days that stays with you forever. By lunchtime, the second egg had developed a small crack in it – we thought. It was very difficult to see with the cameras we had in 2011. By 3pm the egg was almost split in half and we could see a tiny little chick inside fighting to get out. By the time Nora stood up again at 3:35pm the chick had hatched, it was completely free of its eggshell. The place went nuts. People were cheering and shouting, phoning and texting friends and relatives, it was pandemonium – it was wonderful to experience and very emotional. The first osprey chick had hatched on the Dyfi for hundreds of years and we had all been there to see it unfolding live.

The chick in the second egg had hatched at 38 days, about right, and we resigned ourselves to the fact that the first egg laid was never going to hatch, probably due to insufficient incubation at the very start.

As the delirium was finally starting to die down just a little bit, a very well known osprey watcher who had been with us in the visitor centre, glued to his seat watching the events unfold on the two TV screens, suddenly became very animated. "HANG ON," he shouted in his Northern Irish accent, "THERE'S A CRACK IN EGG NUMBER 1". Everybody scrambled to the front of the visitor centre again, trying to catch a glimpse of the first egg. The wily old cat was right – after a mammoth 41 days, the chick inside that first egg was hatching. Hallelujah.

The young bird didn't fully make it out of its egg until 6:40am the following day, so at 42 days that little chick holds the record for one of the longest osprey incubation periods observed in the UK. On Tuesday, 7th June, the third chick hatched; the whole lot of them had made it out and by that time we were all running on adrenaline. What an amazing feat – two ospreys, both first-time breeders, had not only laid three eggs, but all three had hatched. Someone had brought us a bottle of Champagne back in 2009 and it had stayed in the little fridge we had for the next two years. It was finally time to bring it out, and the cake, and the crisps.

Nora's first attempt at feeding her new chick was a disaster

Practicing New Behaviours

The next few weeks turned out to be a revelation in osprey watching and something I'm quite sure I will never witness again. Nest cameras are invariably put into nests where ospreys have already bred, but on the Dyfi nest, the cameras were filming a pair of birds trying to breed for the first time.

Experienced birds, on the whole, are more successful than first-timers, especially when both birds of the new pair are breeding for the very first time. They have no experience to fall back on and often take wrong decisions. We were seeing new behaviours in 2011 that had possibly never been recorded before – two ospreys trying to raise three chicks against the odds.

Nora's first attempt at feeding her new chick was a disaster. The youngster had survived those fraught head-bobbling first few hours to a point where he could sit upright. However, Nora wasn't getting anywhere near close enough to him to pass over any food. And even if she had, the pieces of fish she had prepared in her beak were either far too large or impossibly small. The learning curve was huge. She seemed scared to get too near her young offspring despite having curled up her massive talons into a ball to lessen the risk of accidental injury. She tried desperately for over two hours, but in vain.

Mullet in talons, Nora dragged the fish to the side of the nest, tore off tiny pieces and started to feed imaginary chicks at the nest's edge. Stretching her neck and lowering her head repeatedly as if feeding young chicks, she continued for around 30 seconds. It looked exactly as if she was practicing how to feed, having got it all wrong during the preceding hours. Was this really practice behaviour?

Purists would call this 're-directed behaviour'; a behaviour generated as a result of an animal's instinct or drive to do something specific becoming immobilised, the animal being unable to reach the intended target – in this case feeding chicks. Whatever name we put on it, the next time Nora tried to feed her chicks the following morning, she was successful; it had worked. Ospreys can live to be 20 or 30 years old and this type of behaviour may happen only once in their life times and last a mere few seconds. What a privilege to have witnessed this live as it happened. I had never heard, seen or read of this type of behaviour before – fascinating stuff. The decision to put up the cameras in 2009 was proving to be an inspired one.

Nora trying in vain to feed her first ever chick – she is standing too far back.

The weather was kind to the new couple in 2011 and as each day passed, you could almost sense Nora and Monty making fewer mistakes and becoming better parents. Monty caught lots of fish to feed his young family – they were flourishing and it was awe-inspiring to come to work every day to see them.

Einion, Dulas & Leri

Rather than the three chicks acquiring names by some unfortunate event as had happened with their mother, I had thought long and hard about what to call them. My only two criteria were they had to be Welsh names (and relatively pronounceable for non-Welsh folk!), and they weren't to be named after people – far too problematic and political.

Ospreys eat fish and fish live in rivers – perfect; why not call the three chicks after local rivers? I grabbed a map of Mid Wales and summoned volunteer Posh Pete to the office. Pete speaks the Queen's English (despite coming from Wolverhampton!) and has the worst Welsh pronunciation skills I have ever heard, even though he's lived in Aberdyfi for the past 20 years (he can say 'bore da' on a good day, but that really is pushing it).

Einion, Dulas and Leri at around six weeks old – the first osprey chicks to hatch on the Dyfi in centuries.

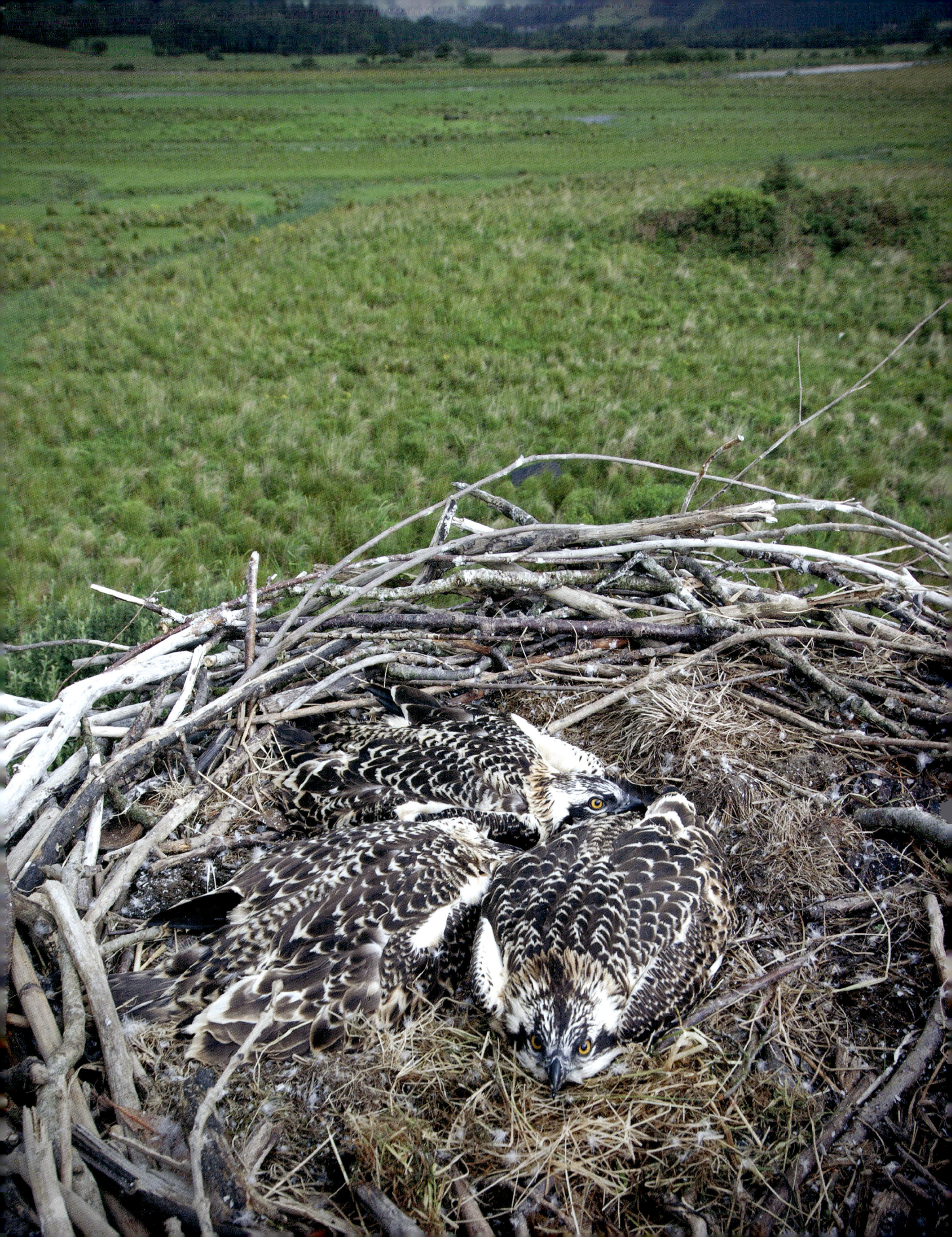

OSPREYS IN WALES *The First Ten Years*

Roy Dennis (left) and Tony Cross talk to Janine back at the project – they need to know which side of the nest the chicks are in before raising the ladder.

After a painful and utterly hysterical couple of hours, by process of elimination we had finally settled on three names, those that received the fewest laughs.

At six weeks old all three chicks were weighed and ringed. Roy Dennis came down from Scotland especially to satellite tag them; we had two males – the oldest two chicks, and a female. We decided to call the first chick Einion and his record-breaking (42-day incubation) brother, Dulas. Their sister was Leri. These are all tributaries of the Dyfi River.

Einion and Dulas shared almost identical weights, 1,470g for Einion and 10g less for Dulas. Their sister, despite being the youngest, was around 10% heavier at 1,610g.

All three chicks fledged successfully. Einion was the first to go at 52 days old and his brother Dulas took advantage of another day's worth of 'helicoptering' practice before he took his maiden flight. Leri was the last to fledge on 3rd August at 57 days old.

Einion just before he launches himself into the sky for the first time at 52 days old, his brother and sister are lying flat in the nest behind him.

	Name	Darvic ring	Weight (grams)
	Einion	DH	1,470
2011	Dulas	99	1,460
	Leri	DJ	1,610

2011

Once young ospreys fledge their nest, that's when you really get a feel for their true character. They have their own personalities and their own little ways of doing things. Einion was a free spirit and extremely independent. Rarely did he interact with Dulas or Leri, who were much more on the same wavelength and bickered with each other constantly. Einion seemed to be an intelligent bird, as though he always thought things through; he never got himself into difficulties and was always one step ahead of his brother and little sister in the maturity department.

It was no surprise really that he started his migration first. At 9:04am on 31st August, he took off from the nest and shot straight up, turning in clockwise circles as he gained altitude and then he was gone. No fuss, no big song and dance, he seemed as determined as he had been for most of his short life up to then. He started his migration at just 87 days old.

Dulas and Leri stayed on for another two weeks, constantly vying for attention and food from their remaining parent, Monty. Nora had started her migration on 14th August, leaving her partner to catch the last few fish of the season for their three youngsters. It is quite normal for females to leave first – Nora would have lost weight and condition bringing up three chicks whilst hardly getting airborne in that time; her job on the Dyfi was done, she needed to get herself fit again for her long journey south.

Next to go was Monty himself on 11th September. He'd obviously decided that Dulas and Leri were not in need of any further paternal investment from him and at 4:05pm he was gone. Dulas followed the next morning, but Leri hung around for another full day screaming and shouting for food before finally realising that her orange-eyed father had delivered the last fish to her two days previously. At 8am on 13th September, Leri finally departed south, the last of the five ospreys to go.

Dulas calling for food on the ash tree perch a few hours after his father had departed. The following morning he too would start his migration south.

2011

OSPREYS IN WALES *The First Ten Years*

Leri is the last of the ospreys to migrate on 13th September 2011. She left at 98 days, the exact same age as her brother Dulas, 14 weeks old.

On Track for Africa

At around the time Einion, Dulas and Leri were a fortnight old, Martin Hughes-Games, one of the BBC Springwatch presenters and producers rang me with a request. The BBC had featured the Dyfi ospreys on their 2011 Springwatch series in June, which had just come to an end; "We've fallen in love with Monty and the Dyfi ospreys," said Martin… "Would there be any chance of satellite tracking the chicks to Africa?" Martin had previously made a programme with Steve Leonard called "Incredible Animal Journeys" in 2005 about ospreys breeding in Martha's Vineyard, Massachusetts, and their migrations to South America.

With the help of Roy Dennis, the BBC and several hundred people that donated via a very quickly arranged appeal on the Dyfi Osprey Project's Facebook page, we raised enough money to buy three trackers, just in time.

When they were ringed, Roy tagged all three chicks with a 30g satellite tracker. These are unobtrusive devices that weigh the same as a small packet of crisps – just 1½ to 2% of the bird's body weight. They have a small solar panel which powers the tiny device, sending back data every hour about position, altitude, temperature, speed etc, at a predetermined interval – every two to five days typically. This was the first time that any Welsh osprey had been satellite tracked and I was hoping that by following them on migration, it would allay a big fear that Roy and I had about young Welsh ospreys heading out to sea on their first migration.

Young Scottish ospreys tend to start their migrations in a slightly southwesterly direction, taking them towards the northern coast of France. The fear was that if Welsh ospreys, which were already located quite a way west, took a similar initial southwesterly turn, it would take them straight out into the Atlantic Ocean and if the winds were not favourable, they would be lost at sea. Roy and I had spoken at length about this, but we needn't have worried.

Einion (31st August) – left the Dyfi at 9:04am and was directly over Llanelli by 12:40 doing 22mph (quicker than driving there!). By 6pm he had reached Looe, just west of Plymouth where he roosted for the night. He continued at first light the following day, roosting in Brittany before crossing the Bay of Biscay on Day 3. A week after leaving Wales he was crossing continents from Gibraltar in southern Spain to Morocco, where he stayed for the next three weeks, just to the south of Casablanca.

By 28th September, Einion had made it to Senegal where he stayed for the remainder of 2011 at Somone Lagoon Reserve, a perfect spot for ospreys jam-packed with flamingos, darters, frigate birds and great white pelicans, and fish of course.

Dulas (12th September) – there was a horrific storm passing through the UK during the second week of September; we were all hoping Dulas and Leri would hang around on the Dyfi for a few days until things calmed down. They didn't.

Dulas started his migration during the worst day of the storms and no sooner had he set off than the strong southwesterly winds started blowing him off course. He started his migration at 6:40am and by noon was flying east at an altitude of 310m – over Milton Keynes! We thought he had died that evening as his tracker was sending coordinates from the same location in the sea, 10 miles off the coast of Clacton-on-Sea, Essex. We were hoping against hope that he had found some sort of vessel to shelter on during the night from the worst of the 80mph winds. Thankfully, he had done better than that; Dulas had spent his first night alone 10m up on a gantry platform of a wind turbine (Gunfleet Sands) in the North Sea!

The following morning Dulas had made it to Belgium and, continuing directly over Paris, he had reached the Pyrenees just three days after setting off from the Dyfi. He crossed into Africa four days later heading over Gibraltar, just as his brother had done a fortnight before him. By the end of September, Dulas had made it to the Gambia where he stayed for the remainder of 2011, mostly frequenting one of the tributaries of the Gambia River itself.

Rather than heading south, Dulas is blown off course and spends his first night 10m high on a wind turbine gantry in the North Sea.

Leri (13th September) – leaving a day later than her brother, Leri was also blown easterly, but nowhere near as much as Dulas. She flew directly over Swindon at 3:10pm and roosted for the night in a farmer's field on the outskirts of Basingstoke. Leri had reached Bognor Regis by mid-morning the following day, before making the channel crossing over to Normandy at noon.

Leri followed a slightly different route down Europe than her brothers had, favouring instead to fly over the Mediterranean Sea; exactly a week after leaving Wales she flew directly over Ibiza at an altitude of 1,230m. She took the most easterly route over the Sahara Desert, but also the most gruelling and time consuming – she would have gone without food for at least a week, maybe more.

OSPREYS IN WALES *The First Ten Years*

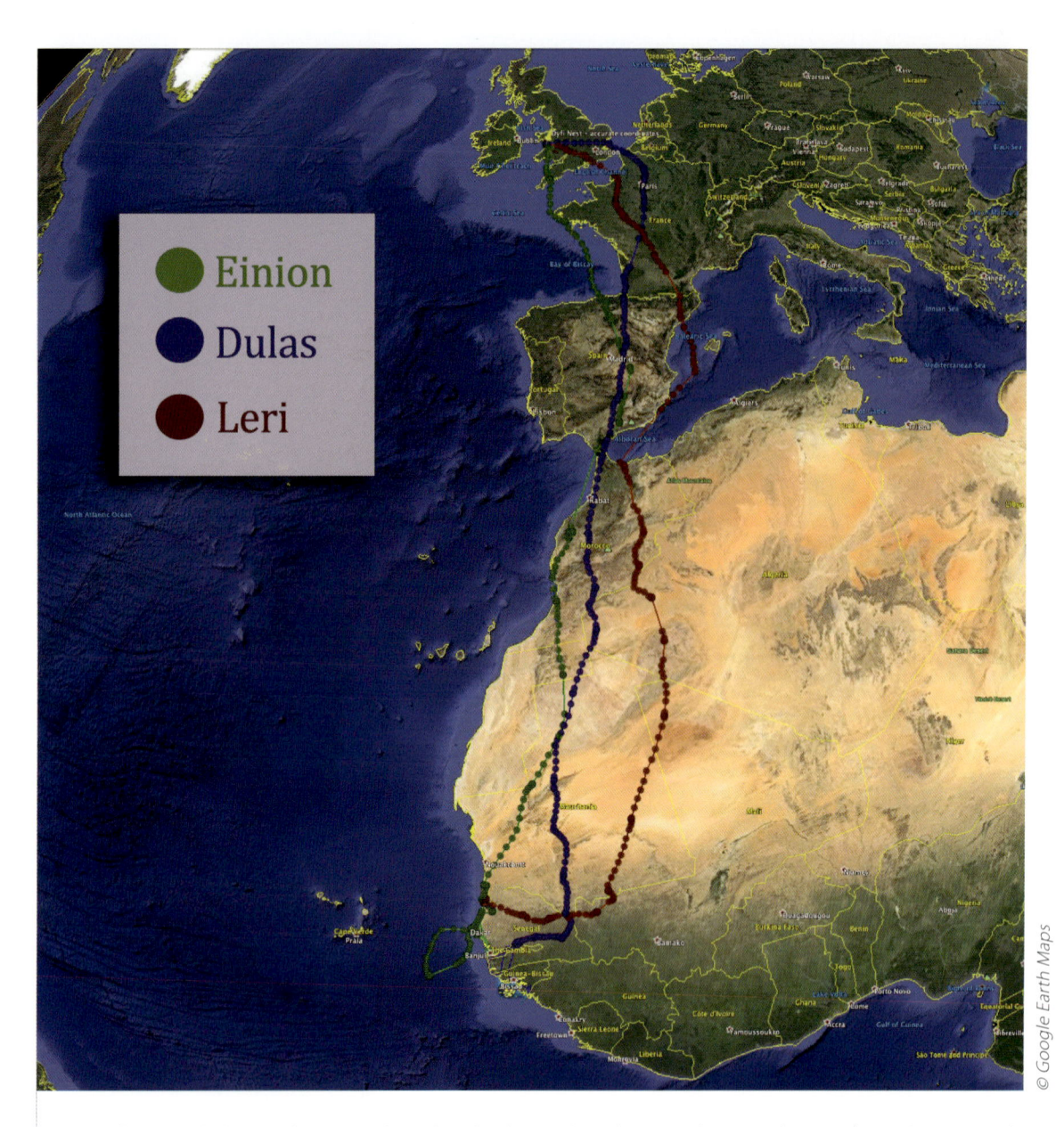

The three Dyfi youngsters are tracked all the way to Africa in 2011, sadly Leri died at the end of October.

Unfortunately her tracker started sending back signals in the same location from 24th October onwards – a mangrove swamp around eight miles inland off the Atlantic coast near St. Louis, Senegal. Leri had been moving around quite normally in this general area for 18 days previously, but of course, we had no idea what condition she was in. She had almost certainly died, having possibly never recovered from her week-long journey over the Sahara without food or water.

We had started 2011 with many questions, but many hopes too. Thankfully, most of those hopes were realised and several of the questions answered. Despite the sad loss of Leri, it had been a good year for ospreys in Wales with two active nests again, producing six offspring for the first time in many centuries. 2011 would be a year for the osprey connoisseur too, with all those remarkable first-time breeding behaviours recorded at the Dyfi, but hopefully 2011 would also be the year that would kick-start osprey colonisation in Wales.

Monty leaves on 11th September 2011 – after years of trying, he had finally become a father.

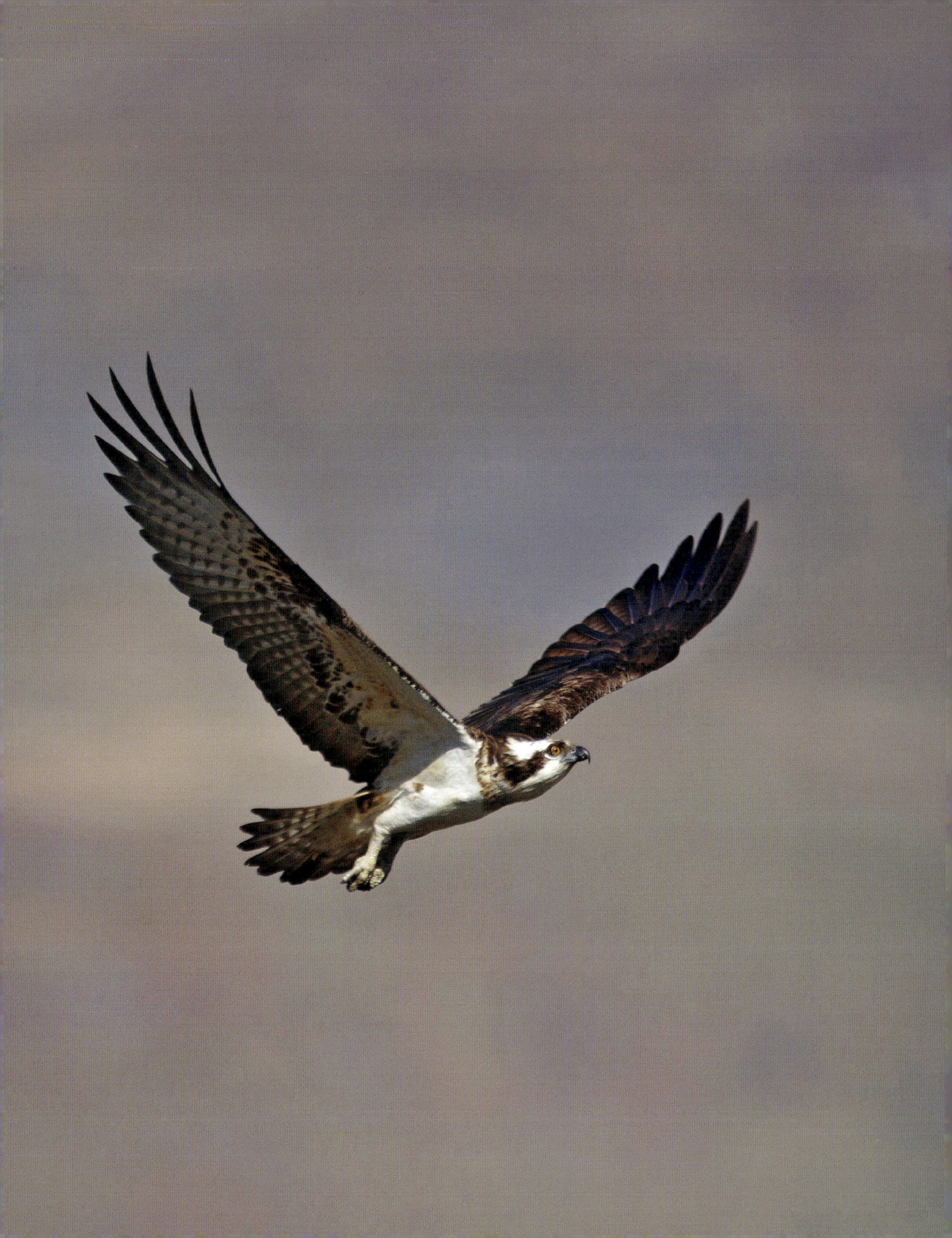

2012

The Big Pull

All those years of going to CCTV trade shows finally paid off in 2012. The funding applications had been successful for new cameras at the Dyfi osprey nest and best of all, they would be in glorious High-Definition. Just as the PTZ camera had heralded a significant step-up in picture quality at the Glaslyn nest in 2007, the new Axis cameras in 2012 would signal a fundamental change in osprey watching in Wales, the UK, and dare I say it, the world at the time. Finally ospreys and High-Definition would meet for the first time and what a meeting it would turn out to be. A marriage made in heaven.

I had also approached Network Rail again over the winter. Trying to transmit enormous amounts of data from four HD cameras via radio transmitters would be hugely costly and logistically nigh on impossible; much better to send the signals via a 'super-armoured fibre optic cable' straight from the

Nora returns on 24th March and takes a look at the new Dyfi camera system. The pictures are out of this world.

nest, under the rail track and directly to the visitor centre at the Dyfi Osprey Project. Network Rail not only facilitated the whole operation, but also kindly donated half a mile of the high-spec cable.

All we had to do at Montgomeryshire Wildlife Trust was to come up with a hundred volunteers to pull the cable across the reserve and hand it to the Network Rail guys who would feed it under the track for us and then onto the nest. On St. David's Day, 106 volunteers turned up from all corners of the UK for 'The Big Pull' event and got thoroughly soaked for their efforts, but it was worth it. Just over three weeks later on 24th March, Nora returned early from migration at 3:34pm and we were all watching on large screens in the visitor centre. The pictures coming back from the nest via the new cable were extraordinary – it was like looking through a window.

The Big Pull – over 100 volunteers pull a fibre optic cable half a mile across Cors Dyfi reserve to connect the new HD nest cameras with the visitor centre.

Nora – the HD cameras are even better than we'd hoped for; it is like being right in the nest with her.

Nora had bred for the first time the previous year so we had no idea when to expect her in 2012 – would she be an early returnee like the Glaslyn ospreys? Moreover, we didn't really know when to expect Monty either, he had consistently returned during the first week of April up to 2011, but he was now a breeding bird himself, would he start to come back earlier?

2012 129

For the next few days the only large bird of prey Nora had for company was a red kite. Interestingly, Nora paid absolutely no attention to the kite despite it being just a few feet away from her on the nest. I remember thinking to myself of the poignancy (and absurdity) of this scene – you would have been hard-pressed to see just one of these birds anywhere in Wales a few decades ago, and here we were in 2012 with both a red kite and an osprey on the same nest!

A red kite watches Nora rebuild her nest in late March, ready for another season.

On 2nd April at 3:35pm, nine days and one minute exactly after Nora returned, so did her mate. Monty had stuck to his usual arrival window and had kept the lady waiting for over a week, but she had stayed faithful to him, and to the nest, rebuilding it after the winter storms, closely watched by the kite.

As soon as Monty returned, both birds got down to business and were mating within minutes. However, there was a subtle change in Monty's behaviour for the first few days after returning to the Dyfi – he was very reluctant to hand over any fish that he caught to his partner. He did look a bit 'lean'; maybe he was just fattening himself up first after his long migration from Africa? *(Although I have harboured a sneaky suspicion for some time that Monty is one of those ospreys that winters in southern Europe and has possibly never been to Africa in his life. I have absolutely zero scientific proof to support this theory however; it's just a hunch.)*

We'd had a very cold March – maybe the fish were deeper than normal in the estuary's waters so were more difficult to catch? Whatever the reason for Monty's reluctance to share his prey, it unquestionably didn't help the early season pair bonding routine. It had taken 16 days between first mating and first egg in 2011, their first season together; so we were thinking this window might be shorter in 2012. It turned out to be exactly the same – 16 days, probably due to the faltering start to the couple's pair bonding.

As the weather finally warmed up during the second week of April, so did Monty's generosity. Mating continued apace once he started sharing his food again and on 18th April, Nora laid her first egg of the season. A second and third followed with the usual three-day gaps.

The HD cameras were giving us amazing views of the eggs; we could make out the finest of details on them. We could even see the tiny scratches that Monty and Nora had made with their talons as they periodically turned all three eggs around while incubating. After pixel-peeping at screens for the last

Monty (right) returns home on 2nd April only to find Nora has beaten him to it – by nine days!

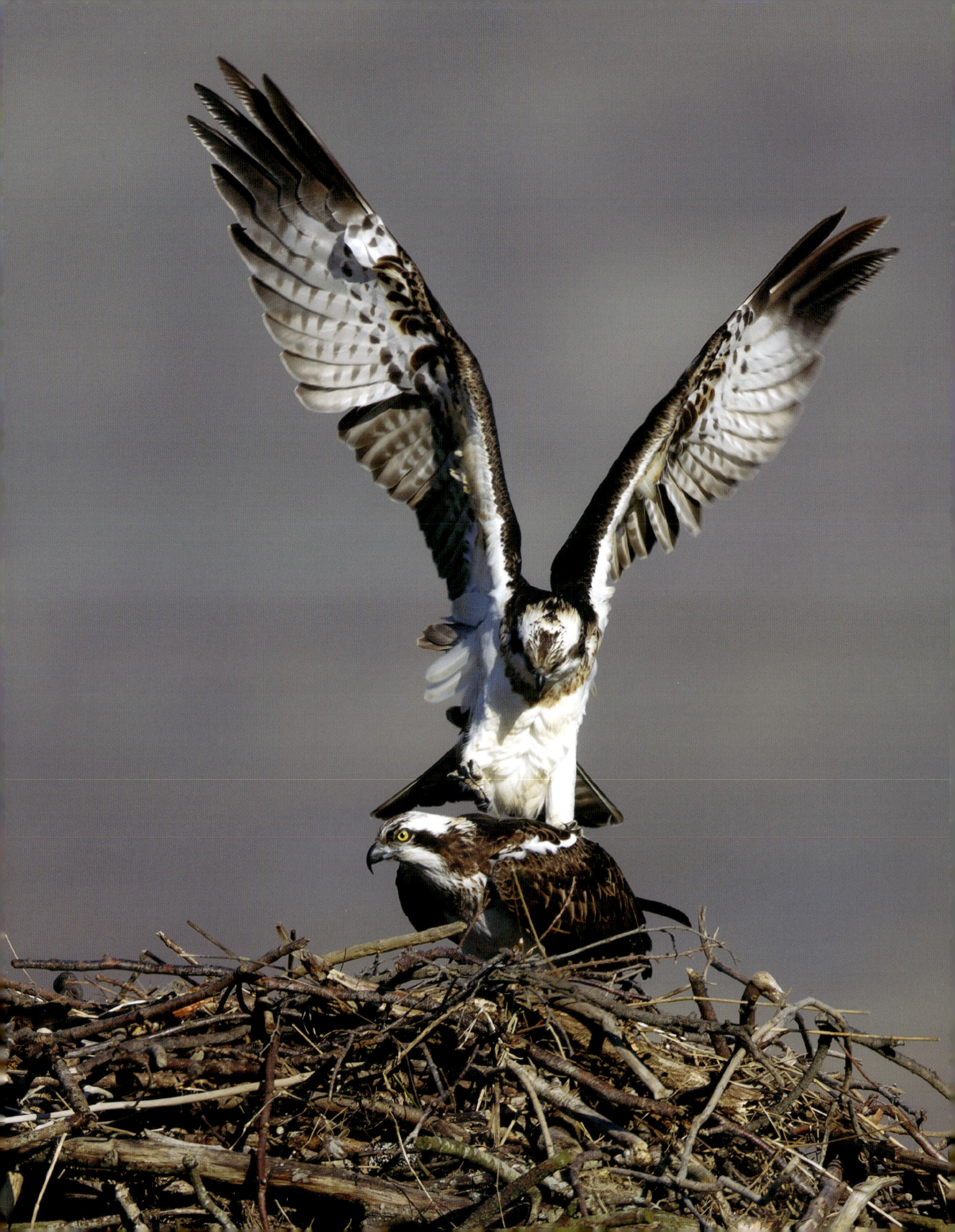

OSPREYS IN WALES *The First Ten Years*

Early morning delivery – Monty brings Nora a sea bass, normal service has resumed.

Nora, talons curled into a ball to avoid damaging the eggs, carefully turns them around to ensure they receive even heat distribution from her body during incubation.

The usual osprey 'fish for sex' arrangement isn't working out in 2012 initially – Monty is reluctant to share his catch for the first few days after returning to the Dyfi.

2012

few years trying to work out which egg was which, that job had suddenly become a heck of a lot easier. The first egg laid was the one with the dark splodge on it (bottom right in the picture – previous page), the middle egg was the Neapolitan-looking one which appeared as if it had been dipped in red paint at one end (top right), and the third egg laid was the one with Australia on it. See it? It's amazing how many countries you can see on osprey eggs if you look long enough.

And Then There Were Three

We'd had a few osprey hat-tricks over the years in Wales, but this next one was by far the most important.

Steve Watson, who had first located the Glaslyn nest way back in 2004, had been erecting artificial platforms in North Wales since that time with the help of 'Friends of the Ospreys' volunteers. A handful of birds had been observed taking an interest in a few of them over the years, but nothing had come of those visits. I saw a male osprey on one particular platform in 2009 and again in 2010, but still no breeding took place. It looked like Monty wasn't the only bachelor in Wales at that time looking for a female.

In 2012 the male osprey (above) finally attracts a female at site ON 4, the fourth breeding nest in Wales since 2004.

The male osprey was joined by a female in 2011 on the same platform, but she kept disappearing so another year went by without any breeding. In 2012 the male, presumably the same bird as in previous years, finally managed to attract a female, who subsequently stayed with him.

This nest is in North Wales, between the Glaslyn and the Dyfi and was the fourth osprey nest of modern times; so without giving its location away, let's call it Osprey Nest Four – or ON 4 for short.

Both the adults at ON 4 were un-ringed, which excluded them from being offspring from the Glaslyn and Rutland nests, where they had been ringed every year. We just didn't know their origins; perhaps they were young Scottish birds?

At last, Wales has a third active breeding nest which produced one male chick. He fledged during the first week in August.

It didn't really matter who they were, but it mattered a lot what Tony Cross saw when he went up a ladder to have a look in the nest on 12th July. There was a single chick in it, a male. Tony quickly weighed and ringed the young bird – Blue 2C; he was around four weeks old and weighed 1,150g. Wales had three simultaneous breeding nests and yet another osprey hat-trick – wonderful news.

Another Glaslyn Osprey – White 91

I received some more good news regarding Welsh ospreys in July 2012. Emma Rawlings, the Scottish Wildlife Trust Ranger at the Loch of the Lowes nest in Perthshire, contacted me with an exciting development.

Ospreys have been breeding at the Loch of the Lowes nest since 1971, but the big news in recent times regarding this eyrie is the provenance of the resident female. She has been breeding at this nest since 1991 and at the time I'm writing this, still is. She has laid 71 eggs in that time and raised 50 chicks

The breeding male osprey (right) at the Loch of the Lowes nest in Perthshire is surprised to find an intruder female land on his nest. She was a three-year-old Glaslyn bird looking for a partner.

– a Superosprey if ever there was one. She is not ringed so her origin is not known, but she must be in her late 20s if not 30 years old by now.

Lady, as she has affectionately become known, was not at her nest early evening on 18th July; her un-ringed male had just returned with a fish and Lady had flown off with it, most probably to consume elsewhere. At 5:41pm another female landed on the nest alongside the male and spent just over four minutes with him, eyeing up the nest and him no doubt. It was White 91, a female offspring from the Glaslyn nest in 2009. She was three years old and looking for a suitable nest and bachelor.

Her White 91 Darvic ring was on the right leg, which was of course the correct leg being Welsh, but she didn't have a small metal BTO ring on her left leg. If absolute proof was ever needed that she was indeed the Glaslyn bird, this was it. Three days after being ringed in June 2009, the BTO ring somehow became loose and fell off. It is extremely unusual for a BTO ring to come off, I have never heard of this happening before, or after.

White 91 was the first female from the Glaslyn nest to have been spotted back in the UK as an adult, White YC and Black 80 (already breeding) being the other two up to that time, both males. Now wouldn't it be great if all three Glaslyn birds would end up breeding in the UK one day...

The Perfect Storm

March 2012 had been exceptionally cold, and April and May had been unseasonably wet, but despite the mercurial Welsh weather, both Monty and Nora had done well to lay three eggs and incubate them for six weeks on the Dyfi. On 28th, 29th and 31st May, for the second year on the spin, all three chicks successfully hatched. The Glaslyn ospreys had also hatched three chicks but during the second week in May – exceptionally early (as usual) and over a fortnight earlier than the Dyfi, which was to prove highly significant in 2012.

the weather had not finished with our Welsh ospreys just yet

The weather had not finished with our Welsh ospreys just yet. At the end of May it started to rain again, and rain hard. On 31st of May it rained for eight hours non-stop and Nora barely got off her two chicks and one remaining egg. By the time she did, the third chick had hatched, but the first chick didn't look good at all. The next time Nora stood up around an hour later it had died – we probably had three chicks alive in the Dyfi nest for just a few minutes. But why was it the oldest chick that succumbed?

Monty (left) and Nora feed their surviving two chicks after the eldest died in the nest at three days old, having succumbed to the weather.

OSPREYS IN WALES *The First Ten Years*

Like all animals, a young osprey is weakest and at its most vulnerable at the very start of life. I always hope and pray for decent weather for a good week or so as soon as ospreys start to hatch; get past that initial seven to 10 days and the chances of surviving increase exponentially. There is a quirk in this paradigm however. For the first 24 to 48 hours after hatching, a young osprey chick will have all the sustenance it needs to survive by virtue of the final absorption of the yolk, pre-hatching: nature's packed lunch to get it through those first few hours and tackle whatever perils lay outside of the egg. The second and third chick still had this sustenance, the oldest chick that died was three days old; his packed lunch had been consumed.

For the next few days everything seemed to be going well, the weather was still miserable, but certainly not anything life-threatening for the young ospreys; the sun even came out for the odd hour or two. On 8th June, all that was to change.

The whole of Wales was hit by one of the worst summer storms in living memory; I had never seen anything like it and hopefully never will again. In Mid Wales we were in an emergency situation with houses and roads flooded, mobile homes and caravans were ripped from their footings and were being washed away; there were police and emergency vehicles everywhere and sirens could be heard

Monty (left) and Nora enjoy a rare break in the weather in 2012.

138 2012

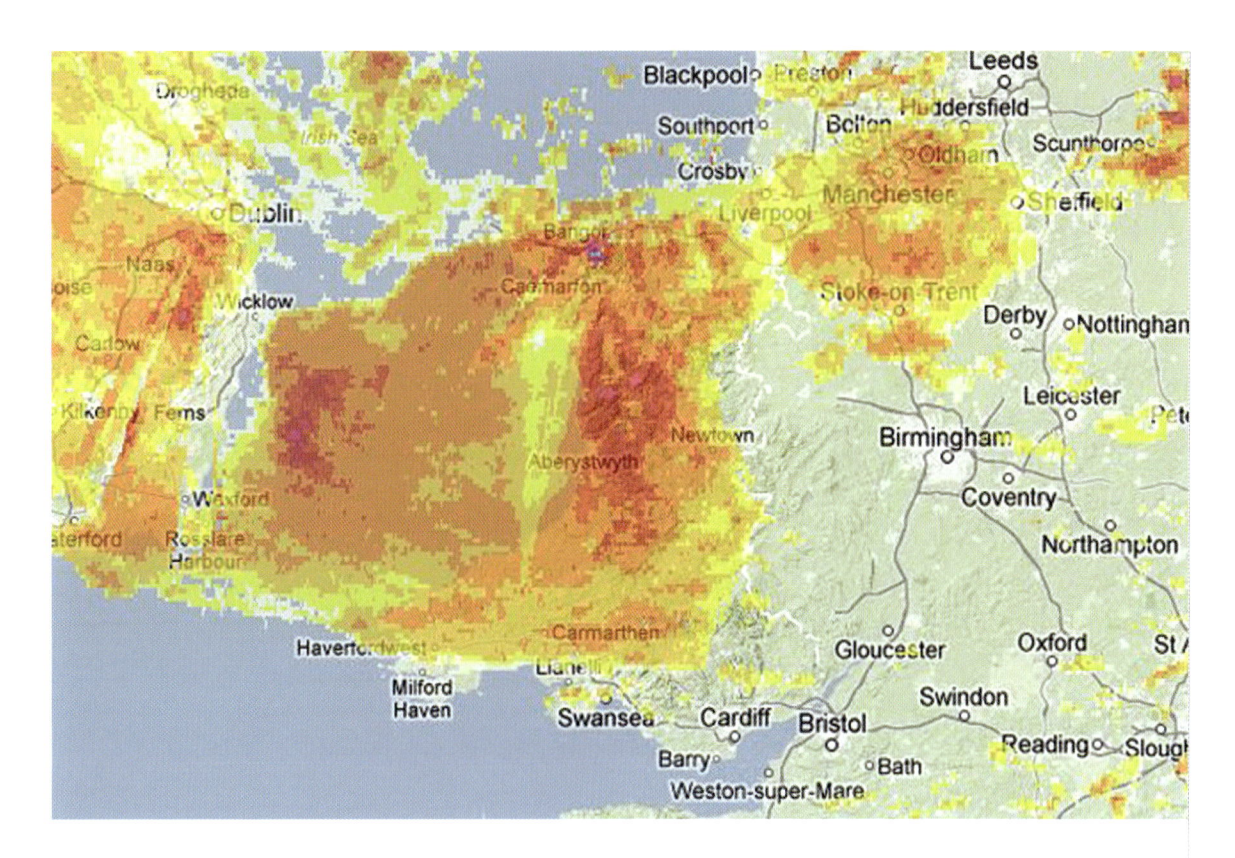

8th/9th June – the worst summer storm to hit Mid Wales in living memory, it rained continually for 36 hours.

The RNLI visit the Dyfi Osprey Project – they had broken down in the floods.

from almost any direction. Even the RAF Sea-King Rescue helicopters were shuttling people from their flooded lowland homes to higher ground. During the afternoon, two guys from the RNLI came to the Dyfi Osprey Project wanting to use the phone, they had broken down trying to rescue someone – the mother of all ironies!

At just after 2pm the inevitable happened, we lost all electrical power to the nest and at the project, the whole area was out. I made the decision to close the project to the public; it was getting far too dangerous and getting worse by the hour. With no live pictures Alwyn, Janine and I gathered in the hide and peered through the telescopes for the remainder of the daylight hours. We could just about see the nest through the pelting rain, but nothing else.

As darkness fell the rain had still not let up; it was raining as hard, if not harder. By this time I had completely lost any hope that either of the two chicks could have survived the storm, I wasn't even thinking about them; I was more worried about Monty and Nora. This wasn't your normal June shower, this was one of January's fiercest storms five months out of synch. The three of us kept saying to each other not to worry, there's nothing we can do

2012

OSPREYS IN WALES *The First Ten Years*

Working as a team – just before the power went off. Monty (left) and Nora stoically try to protect their two remaining chicks.

about it, but it didn't make any of us feel any better. I remember thinking back to the Glaslyn in 2004 – I was just hoping that both adult birds would be alright. I'd have taken that right then.

The roads were just about driveable late on that Friday evening and I managed to navigate the three miles home, but the following morning the situation had deteriorated. I looked out of my bedroom window at first light and I could hardly see anything through the rain, the storm hadn't shifted and by now it had been raining for 24 hours non-stop – on 10th June! The electrical power had gone in my house by now too and my mobile phone was out of charge; at 7am I decided to try and make it down to the project by car – about the only thing that was still left working.

Going to work, the last mile was the wettest!

I got to within a mile away and there was dear old Cathy, who lives in a cottage by the project, at the roadside turning cars around. "Don't go any further Emyr," she said to me, "the road is flooded." I had already squeezed past a yellow 'Road Closed' sign and the police were turning people around further up in Machynlleth where I live. I parked the car by the side of the road and politely explained to Cathy that I was just going to walk around the corner to see how bad it was and to take a picture. I had no intention of returning to the car.

I finally managed to wade through to the dry part of the road just outside the project where volunteer Al Davies, an electrician who lives next door to Cors Dyfi, was waiting for me – with his camera as usual! Hugh Gillings and his young son Justin were also there; they are volunteers who had come up from South Wales in their camper van to help out for the weekend. The four of us looked desperately through the telescopes in the hide, but it was just as impossible to see anything as it had been the day before – how could it rain so much in June?

At 10am the power to the local area was finally restored, but we still didn't have any electricity at the nest. Thankfully, one of the Network Rail engineers had been working to restore the supply for us, "you'll have it back at some point in the day," he said. At 12:15 it came back on and we could see the nest for the first time in over 24 hours. Unbelievably, Nora was still in it trying to shield whatever was

After almost 36 hours, Nora is still valiantly trying to protect her two young chicks from the June storm.

Alive, but only just.

underneath her from the rain. No wonder we couldn't see her from the hide, she was lying down flat as a pancake, the water streaming off her back. The four of us were squished into the tiny office looking at the live screen and I can tell you, there were a few bottom lips starting to go. Talk about trying to man-up and hide your emotions.

By early afternoon, the rain had finally started to recede. As it did, Nora got up to her feet for the first time probably since the storm started some 36 hours before to reveal two wet bundles of feathers underneath her. We all thought they were dead initially, but Justin grabbed the camera joy-stick and zoomed in. They were breathing, but only just.

With one chick close to death and his sibling already dead, Monty tries to grab the fish off Nora to feed it. She is having none of it.

142   2012

Both young ospreys had tried to lift their heads as soon as their mother stood up. They couldn't – they were too weak. The chick on the right, the older of the two, seemed a little stronger than his sibling, but neither could muster enough strength to free themselves from that pathetic looking posture, heads bowed down, completely helpless.

By 2pm the chick on the left stopped breathing, it was a miracle really that he had survived this long. At around the same time, Monty brought a trout back to the nest; Nora swiftly took it off him and proceeded to eat it with her two chicks still in the nest-cup, faces down, just one alive. I've watched a few rugby and football matches in my time and witnessed many a grown man shouting at a TV set, but the four of us were making more noise than Cardiff Arms Park on international day. Why wasn't she trying to feed her only surviving chick? There was a trout and a half eaten flounder in the nest. For heaven's sake, feed your chick – he's dying…

Al Davies and I trying to get to the nest from the Cors Dyfi side, there was too much water.

The Intervention

Hugh, Justin and Al were looking at me asking the same question over and over, "Why isn't she feeding the chick?" Even Monty had realised the desperation of the situation and, having eaten earlier himself, was trying to prise the trout away from Nora to feed the chick himself. Nora kept head-butting him away, even after she had finished eating herself. She had risked her own life to protect her young family from a violent 36-hour storm, but was now choosing not to feed her only surviving chick who was close to death. What a hideous situation; what on earth was going on?

It suddenly dawned on me. I remembered something I'd learnt as a young behavioral ecology student some twenty-odd years before: FAPs – Fixed Action Patterns. In simple terms, an animal will behave in a certain way only when triggered to do so by a 'releaser' or 'sign stimulator'. That 'releaser' for feeding behavior would have been a chick sitting up, eyes open, squeaking, beak open begging for food, etc. Nora could not see or hear any of these things and her Fixed Action Pattern to feed her chick wasn't triggered because the chick wasn't strong enough to food solicit. A desperate vicious circle with only one obvious and inevitable outcome.

The day before, another volunteer, Carol Swales, had bought three fresh trout from Morrisons in Aberystwyth and left them in the fridge at the

OSPREYS IN WALES *The First Ten Years*

project, 'just in case' we decided to leave fish out for the ospreys if Monty couldn't fish for himself in the storm. It was a concept that I had firmly turned down in the past – we should never intervene, these were wild animals and were not to be interfered with, it's nature and nature should take its course. By 3pm that Saturday afternoon however, I was having second thoughts.

"C'mon let's try and get there before we lose the last one," said Al Davies, "we can ladder up to the nest and feed the chick with Carol's trout." I spoke about it with Hugh and Justin and quickly came up with a plan. They would stay in the office looking at the live nest on the screen and Al and I would go to the nest with a walkie-talkie; if the remaining chick died whilst we were en route, Justin would tell us on the radio and we would come back.

We initially tried to get to the nest the quickest way possible – through Cors Dyfi reserve itself, but it soon became obvious that this was a no-hoper. We were wading through two feet of water on the boardwalk itself, by the time we would have had to step off, the water level would have been four feet with just soft peat underfoot. We would have started an emergency situation of our own if we had continued. "Let's go the long way around," said Al. This would take around 45 minutes in dry conditions, but it was the only option we had left.

It took just over an hour to get there and Al quickly laddered up to the nest. I had been radioing Justin back at the project every other minute it felt like; "Is he still alive?" The response was always the same "I think so." Justin was right; the little chick was hanging on to life, but barely. I shouted up to Alan "Bring him down Al," as I hurriedly started to cut up the trout into small pieces below the nest. Al was

In safe hands – getting warmer by the minute.

144 2012

quickly down the ladder with the tiny chick in his hand and we placed him on a small wooden tray where I had cut up the fish. So started the longest 15 minutes of my life, and I dare say, Al's too.

The chick was too weak to stand up and he was shivering. I had never seen a bird shiver before. I tried to feed him but he was limp and wasn't interested in the fish; the best thing to do, I thought, was to try and warm him up a little first. I clasped him with both hands and squeezed him as hard as I thought I could, to try and pass the warmth from my body to his. It was a desperate situation – an electrician and an ecologist in the middle of a reserve trying to feed a young osprey chick on a Saturday afternoon; you couldn't make it up.

After around five minutes I tried to push a piece of fish into the chick's beak, not the easiest of things to do I soon discovered. Nothing was going down, I was too timid, afraid of making the whole situation worse. "You'll have to force it down his neck," came the electrician's response. He was right. The next piece of fish went down its gullet along with half of my index finger. I repeated the same feeding technique again, and again, and again. After just a couple of minutes the chick seemed to acquire a new lease of life – I put him down on a towel on the tray and started to feed him from there. He was now standing up – it was amazing; the food had an almost immediate effect and he had stopped shivering. I would never have believed that such a small intake of food would have such a spontaneous reaction; it was like something out of a film.

After another few minutes the little chick was grabbing fish out of my fingers like there was no tomorrow. Thankfully for him, there would be a tomorrow. "Time to put him back," I said to Al; the chick's little crop was full and our work was done for the afternoon. Al gently placed him back in the nest and put the other chick's dead body in his coat pocket. We later buried him under the osprey hide at the Dyfi Osprey Project.

neither of them smelled good for the rest of that weekend

By the time we got back to the office, Hugh and Justin were beaming with smiles, ear to ear, despite getting their blue bath towel back stinking of fish (neither of them smelled good for the rest of that weekend). I looked at the TV screen and Nora was back at the nest, busy feeding her chick as if nothing had happened. Job done.

Beaten by the weather – we buried the dead chick under the osprey hide.

2012　　145

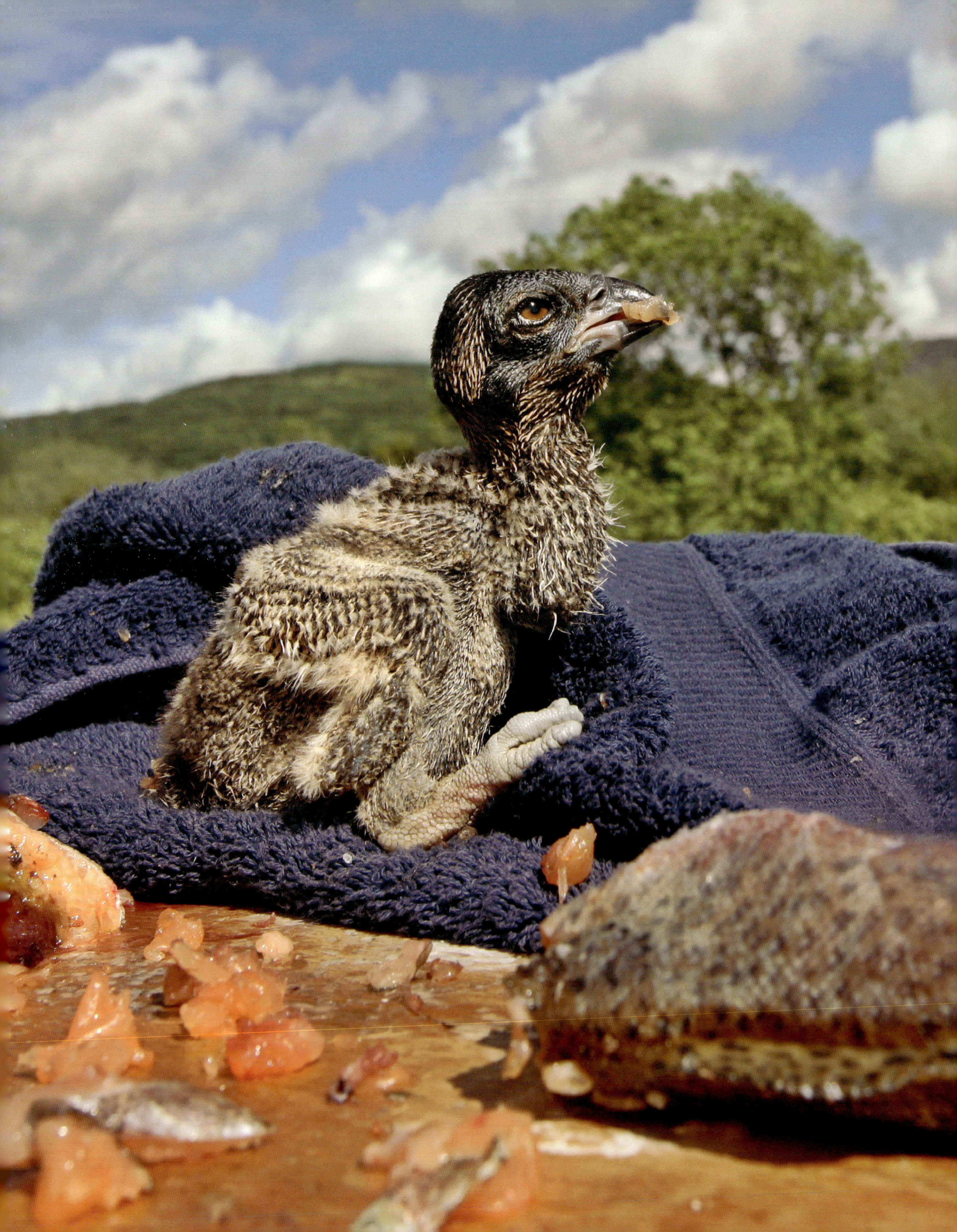

Ceulan

We decided to call our little fighter 'Ceulan' – another tributary of the Dyfi River. I had thought of breaking protocol and simply calling him Survivor, however the Welsh for survivor, 'goroeswr', failed the Posh Pete test, miserably.

By the time Wales's perfect storm had hit, the Glaslyn chicks would have been four weeks old and well out of the dangerous first few days of life window. The chick at the new ON 4 nest however would have been around the same age as Ceulan, or possibly a little younger. We will never know whether Blue 2C was the only chick in that nest that year – he was certainly the only chick that survived the storm if he did have any siblings.

The three Glaslyn chicks are four weeks old by the time the perfect storm hits Wales – it probably saves their lives.

The Jet Stream in 2012 hung around for months on an unusually southerly latitude, bringing with it the unseasonable weather. Being the only chick in the nest would help Ceulan in 2012; this Jet Stream really did bring with it a silver lining. Ceulan reached the grand old age of five weeks and two days before he experienced his first day without any rain at all, that's how aberrant the summer weather of 2012 had been.

Ceulan fledged the nest at 53 days old on 21st July. Just over a week before, Roy had again come down from Scotland and young Ceulan was ringed and satellite tagged. By late August he had grown to be

'Ceulan' standing on his own two feet, crop full and ready to go back to the nest.

Ceulan at five weeks old – he still hadn't experienced one full day without rain.

a healthy young osprey and a strong flier. On 3rd September he set off from the Dyfi at 9:26am and by 15th September he had reached the Senegal-Mauritania border where he would make his home for the next few months.

He had travelled 3,000 miles from Mid Wales to Senegal in just 12 days, a phenomenally quick migration and one of the quickest ever recorded for a British osprey. He was probably trying to get away from the Welsh weather as quickly as he could; I don't blame him.

Sadly on 1st December Ceulan got his legs trapped in local fishermen's nets on the Diawel River, a tributary of the main Senegal River and was unable to free himself; a fisherman spotted him the following day whilst checking his nets. He died just 35 miles away from where his sister, Leri, had expired just over a year before. What a tragic end to an amazing life. There is no fault here; the fishermen were local tribesmen trying to catch fish to eat for the day to survive, just as Ceulan was. His luck had finally run out.

Ceulan touched the hearts of thousands if not millions of people. By the summer of 2012 we had set up a Dyfi Osprey Project website and started streaming live pictures from the Dyfi nest to the world for the first time. Ceulan made it onto Springwatch and countless news programmes; he was even featured in a national Sunday newspaper as a double-page spread. Quite remarkable.

Ceulan in the Sunday People newspaper.

We received more bad news from Africa in 2012 too. The trackers on the Dyfi's two male offspring from 2011 had stopped sending their satellite signals back at almost the same time during the summer. The last transmission from Dulas was received on 13th July from Guinea Bissau, where he had travelled to six months earlier from the Gambia River. Everything had seemed normal up to this time, but there was a large cell of stormy weather passing through Dulas' exact position on this day. Maybe he succumbed in the tropical storm?

The voltage on Einion's tracker started to decrease sharply from 15th July onwards. He was moving around quite normally but by the end of the month, the voltage got so low it didn't have enough power to send back signals; clearly the tracker was packing up, not Einion.

Both Dulas and Einion made it past their first birthday. Just like Ceulan, I rather suspect Dulas' luck ran out when the bad weather caught up with him, but I remain hopeful that Einion is still going. At the time I'm writing this in the autumn of 2014, he would be only three years old, still young with plenty of time to make an appearance in years to come. Einion was a headline story-maker back in June 2011, being the first osprey to hatch on the Dyfi for 400 years; I reckon he still has one big story left in him.

Einion is photographed in Senegal in January 2012 – he looks in good condition.

2012

OSPREYS IN WALES *The First Ten Years*

The Scottish Trip – Part II

On Monday, 3rd September, as Ceulan was starting his long journey south, I embarked on my own journey in the opposite direction. Karl Munday had rung me during the summer to explain all about Black 80's adventures in 2012. His partner of the previous four years had not returned, but he had paired up with another female extremely late in the season. They had produced two offspring, but because they were so late starting, both the youngsters hadn't fledged their nest until the end of August.

It was too good an opportunity to miss. We had come to the end of the season at the Dyfi and Black 80 was still around in Scotland with a new female, who was ringed, but no one could get a photograph to identify her. It was time to go and meet an old friend I hadn't seen since 2006.

Janine had come with me; she would check on Ceulan's progress and I would try and get some shots of Black 80 and his new ringed female – that was the plan anyway. As we settled in to the viewing

Sunset over Black 80's home near Threave Castle in Dumfries and Galloway, Scotland.

hide for the day, we were struck by how beautiful the area was. Black 80's nest was situated close to Threave Castle on the banks of the River Dee, which connected Loch Ken with the Irish Sea. The nest was around 350m away from the hide but for the first few hours, try as we might, we couldn't locate Black 80.

Then suddenly, to the extreme left of us, we heard a commotion. A couple of carrion crows had picked a fight with a Canada goose, which in turn had flushed out several other birds. The only thing that had remained relatively unperturbed by the disturbance was a tiny white speck perching in a tree in the distance. It was an osprey, it was Black 80.

I just stared at him through the telescope for around 10 minutes, thinking about the time I was last with him underneath the Glaslyn nest in 2006 (page 43) and the life he had led in the intervening six years. I wondered where he goes to in the winter and whether he had actually come back to the Glaslyn as a two-year-old in 2008. It sounds ridiculous now, but I felt like I wanted to ask him whether he was that intruder osprey I saw in 2008 when his father was displaying like crazy, upside down with a fish in his talons.

Janine watches Monty on the Dyfi Live Streaming while I try to get a shot of Black 80 and his new blue-ringed female.

I didn't need to see him close-up, that long distance view was fine. I wasn't even bothered that I couldn't take a decent photograph of him either, which was all a bit strange for me. Seeing him there was enough. Maybe I just needed confirmation with my own eyes that it was him, even though I knew it was. Seeing him just made the whole thing real for me. There was a big difference between reading about him over the years on emails and Facebook and actually being there with him, looking at him. It felt like seeing a long-lost friend again for the first time after many years.

We returned to the hide the following day just in time to catch Back 80 delivering a fish to his two youngsters, who had been calling petulantly from the nest. It was a real goose bumps moment. These were Black 80's eighth and ninth offspring and he was only six years old, an age when many male ospreys haven't started to breed yet. What was even more remarkable was that fact that he had bred at all in 2012. Karl told me that the first chick fledged on 25th August, which is the latest date I have ever heard of for an osprey fledging in the UK. Backdating the breeding events meant that the first chick must have hatched at around 5th July, and his egg laid at the end of May or early June. The second chick would have been later still! An incredibly late breeding season.

Try as I might with the longest lens I had, I just could not get enough resolution to clearly see the ring number on the new female. It was time for some Heath Robinson photography.

Two crows pick a fight with a goose as Black 80 looks on in the distance.

Black 80 brings dinner back to his two fledglings at his nest in Scotland.

I attached a 50mm macro lens to the camera and attached this, by hand, to the eyepiece of the telescope, which was set on full zoom. I started clicking away while continuously focusing the lens manually, in the hope that out of several hundred shots, one would come out with enough detail. Janine held the telescope, I held the camera and there was a beanbag in there somewhere too.

The best image from a batch of over 300 would never win a photographic competition, but it did answer one fundamental question. The female had a blue ring on her left leg with the inscription KC. She was a 2008 bird hatched in Stirlingshire from a brood of four, which is exceptional for ospreys. Blue KC had found a mate late in the day in 2012 and had bred, almost certainly for the first time, at the age of three years old.

On our third and last day in Scotland, the sun was shining again and the Glaslyn grandchildren were having some aerobatic fun. They chased each other around for most of the morning, carefully avoiding

Blue KC – a three-year-old female from a nest in Stirlingshire.

a female marsh harrier that was hunting in the area. We left at lunchtime; I had seen all that I wanted to see. Maybe previously there was a bit of me that felt aggrieved that Black 80 hadn't returned to Wales to breed, but at the end of the three days with him, those feelings had turned to happiness. This was his home now, and what a beautiful home he had chosen. Long may he flourish and prosper here.

Two Glaslyn grandchildren take it in turns to chase each other around the Scottish skies.

Ceulan only lived to be six months old, but what a remarkable life he had.

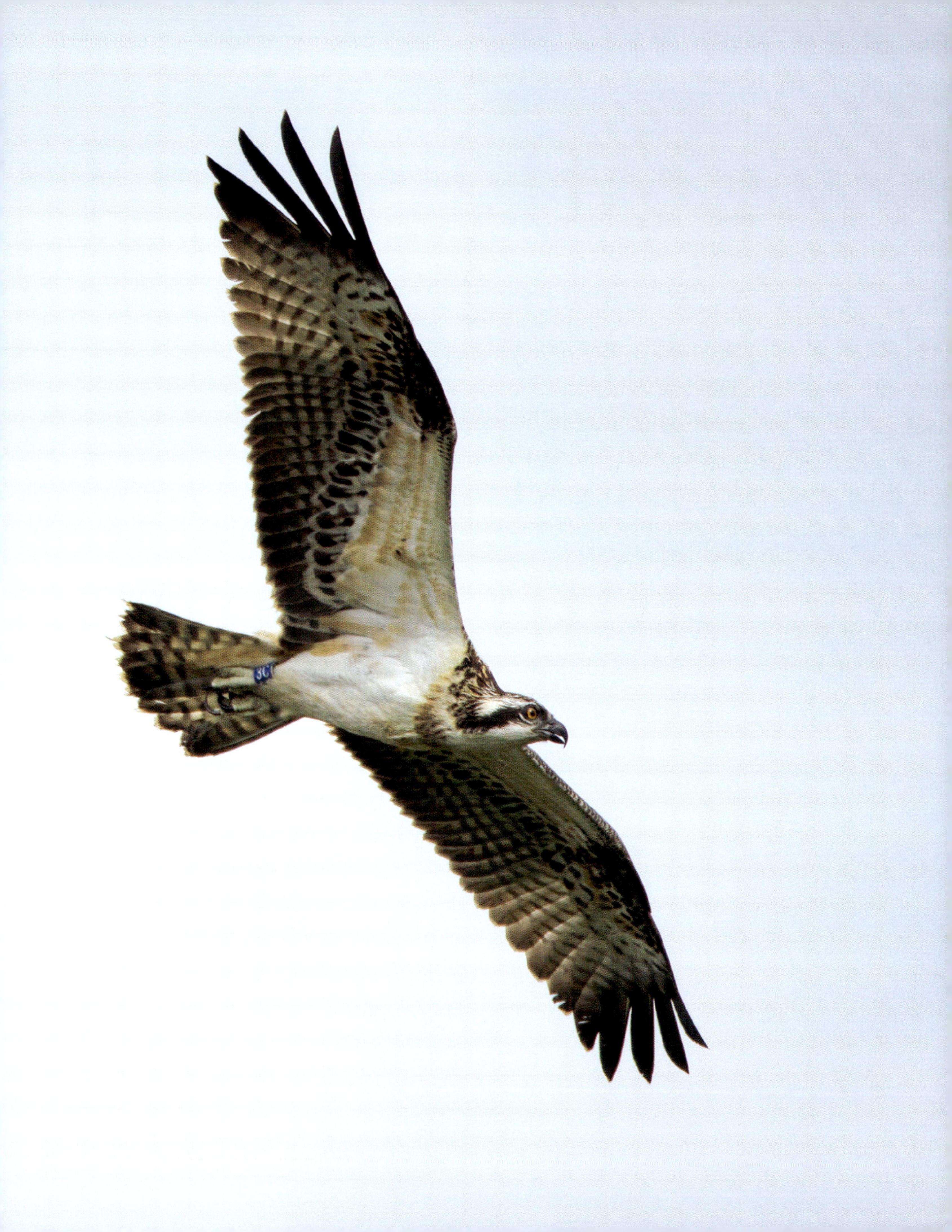

2013

Where's Nora?

We opened the Dyfi Osprey Project early in 2013. Nora had returned on 24th March in 2012, her second breeding year, so we also expected her back early in 2013.

March was even colder than it had been in 2012; there was a biting easterly wind for most of the month and temperatures hardly rose above 0°C for days on end. I wasn't worried too much about the temperature; I was more concerned about the unusual direction our weather was coming from. Strong easterly winds and migrating British ospreys don't mix well.

Nora sees off an intruding osprey in late July 2012 – it is actually her two-year-old niece.

As we entered April, Nora still wasn't back. Maybe her early arrival in 2012 was a one-off? By the middle of the month I was telling people not to give up hope. I had been rummaging through some of the historical Loch Garten return dates going back over 50 years and there were plenty of examples of ospreys returning to their nests in the third and sometimes fourth week in April. Deep down though, I had feared the worst for some time.

One of the last photographs I took of Nora was on 29th July in 2012; she was chasing off an intruder, just a week before she started her migration back south. We'd had several intruding ospreys that year including this Rutland bird – Blue 12. She was a two-year-old, hatched at Rutland's Site N in 2010 and back in the UK for the first time prospecting for nest sites and mates. Blue 12 was actually related to Nora – her mother was a full sister to Nora, making them auntie and niece.

Nora never made it back in 2013. She had only just turned four years old when she left the Dyfi in August 2012, still a young osprey and pretty inexperienced. Whether her immaturity had any bearing on things, or the horrendous weather conditions she experienced in 2012, we'll never know. Maybe she was blown out to sea on her way back home in March by those powerful easterlies? Whatever happened to her, Nora was gone. She had died sometime between leaving on 7th August 2012 and April 2013.

Females Everywhere

Monty returned during his usual slot, the first week in April – on the 7th. During the previous two days a female osprey had spent several hours on the nest; we called her Elin just in case she returned; she had no leg rings. Monty had only just missed Elin by a few hours and spent the next 12 days alone; not a single osprey passed through. On 19th April, Elin was back and showed great interest in Monty's nest, but he wasn't around, he'd gone fishing.

He was back within the hour and immediately started displaying to the new arrival. Following an impressive sky-dancing display lasting some 20 minutes, Monty landed on the nest next to Elin; she wouldn't let him mate with her though. After a couple of hours she was gone.

Next up was a beautiful female on 23rd April with very distinctive black dots on her right iris. This osprey wasn't ringed either, but by looking closely at an osprey's eyes you can sometimes tell one bird from another by their individual iris markings. Seren, as we called her, not only looked interested in the nest, but unlike Elin in Monty as well. The pair spent the next three days mating and pair bonding, Monty bringing lots of fish back to his new partner. The problem was, Seren kept disappearing for several hours at a time – we had a 2011 scenario all over again that was behaviourally identical to Nora's first few days with Monty on the Dyfi.

deep down though, I had feared the worst for some time

OSPREYS IN WALES *The First Ten Years*

Elin: *5th/6th/19th April. She took a great liking to Monty's nest, but wouldn't allow him to mate with her.*

Seren: *23rd April – 1st May. Let Monty mate with her and fought off Blue FS, but kept disappearing.*

Blue FS: *27th – 29th April: "The Stare". Food monster – wouldn't let Monty mate with her.*

White UR: *29th April. Scottish three-year-old; arrived in the middle of a raging battle, she was not interested in joining in.*

Blue 12: *30th April onwards. Nora's niece was back and she was after her auntie's mate and nest.*

Late afternoon on 27th April, yet another female osprey landed on the Dyfi nest. This one had a leg ring – Blue FS; she was a Scottish three-year-old (2010) from a nest near Loch Ness. True to form, she was a monster too, a food monster; she spent the next two days doing nothing but eating and screaming for more food. Monty duly obliged, catching her an incredible 10 fish during one 24-hour period.

This is completely normal behavior for a young female osprey; I call it the "chocolates and flowers" part of a pair bonding relationship. It's essentially a fishing competition for Monty – the more food he can impress her with, the better his demonstration to her that he will be a good provider to her and

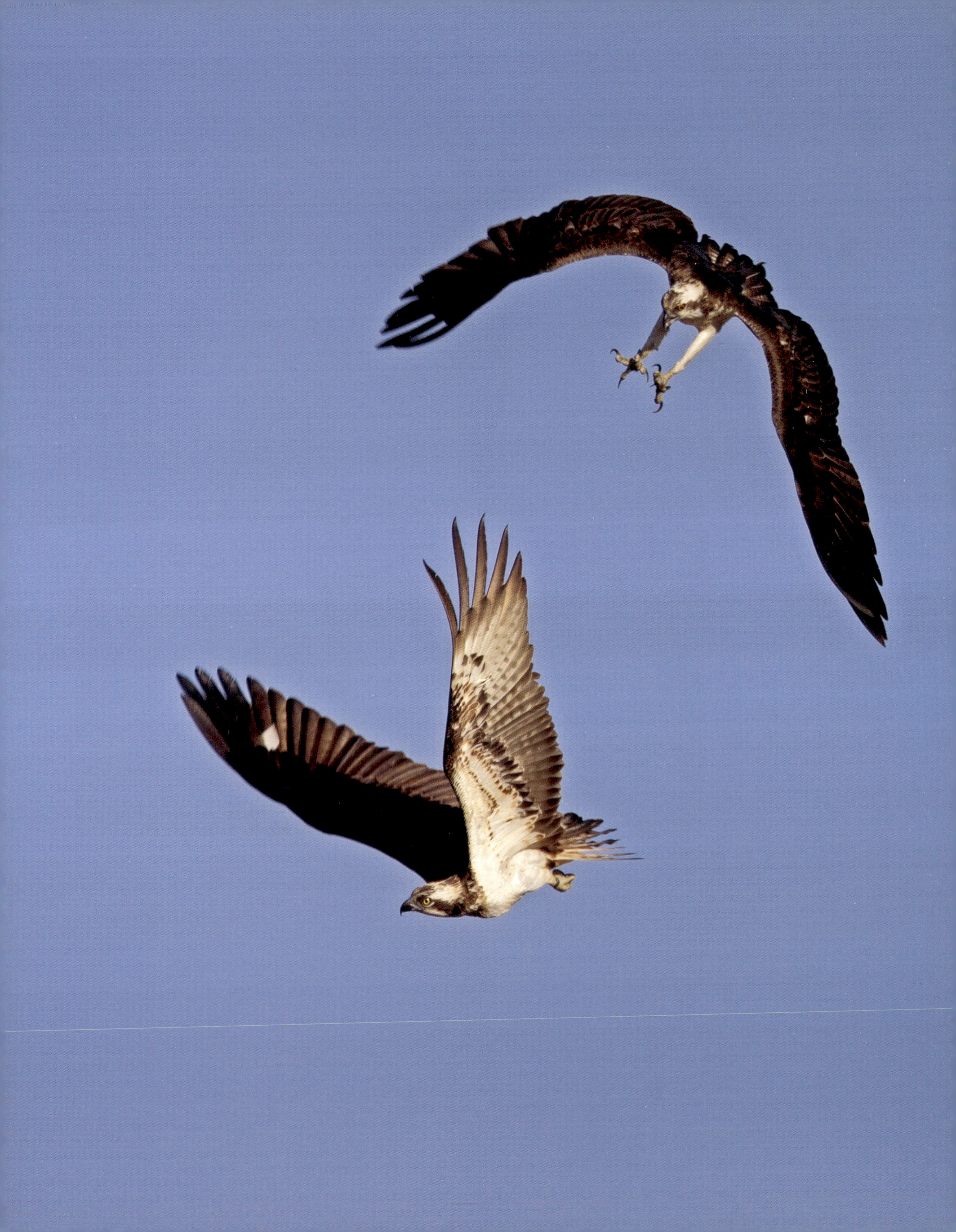

potential chicks in the future. No female osprey wants to invest the next few months of her life and share her DNA with a part-time sardine catcher.

By 29th April, Seren had not been seen for a couple of days and the pair bonding between Blue FS and Monty was going well. At 10am yet another female landed on the nest, an osprey with a leg ring again – White UR; she was also a Scottish three-year-old, from Aberdeenshire. Interestingly, Tim and John from Rutland had photographed White UR as a one-year-old at Tanji Marsh, Gambia in 2011. Before you could say 'holy-mackerel', who decided to return but Seren!

Pandemonium broke out. Just as Nora had done with White DA two years before, Seren saw the newcomer, Blue FS, as a competitor and a threat to her bond with Monty and his nest. Seren started to dive-bomb Blue FS who was standing on the nest, getting closer with each fly-past. Eight large, razor-sharp talons coming at you at high speed from different angles are nothing to be ignored. During her fifth attack, Seren actually caught Blue FS and physically rammed her off the nest and she fell to the ground, 10m below. She managed to get up and flew quickly and directly eastwards – we never saw her again; she had lost her mate to the un-ringed Seren. White UR watched all this happen and soon she was off too, no need to get involved here.

Just as Seren and Monty were getting it together, having been mating and bonding on and off for a week, a fifth and final female osprey made her appearance on the Dyfi on 30th April – Blue 12. Nora's niece was back, but as a three-year-old this time. She looked tenacious, determined and very purposeful. Blue 12 was to be Monty's fourth mate in as many weeks, and the final one. After a three-day battle with Seren, the nest that she had coveted the year before as a nomadic two-year-old had become hers. Monty had little say in the proceedings; male ospreys usually don't.

Blue 12 was new and fresh and blue (ringed); we called her Glesni, which means all of those things.

no female osprey wants to invest the next few months of her life and share her DNA with a part-time sardine catcher

Another Glaslyn Osprey Returns

At the same time as we were looking out for Nora to return during the last week in March, something quite extraordinary was happening at Blagdon Lake, around 10 miles south of Bristol.

A white-ringed male osprey had been spotted fishing in the lake from 25th March onwards for several days – he was obviously on migration back to the UK somewhere, but where exactly? The white ring

Monty (above) fights off Glesni for three days until her determination finally wins him over.

was on his right leg, so that got all of us connected with ospreys in Wales excited, hoping it might be one of the Glaslyn offspring, possibly White YC again. It was even better news than that – it was another bird, White YA, from the clutch of two in 2007 (page 62).

This was the first time that White YA had been positively identified since leaving the Glaslyn as a fledgling in August 2007; he was now the fourth Glaslyn offspring known to have returned along with his brothers Black 80 and White YC, and sister White 91.

Glaslyn's White YA – being ringed in the Glaslyn in 2007 and fishing over Blagdon Lake six years later in March 2013.

White YA hung around at Blagdon Lake for at least 10 days, maybe more; but he kept getting caught up in nets, which are placed over the trout rearing pools to prevent gulls and cormorants predating the fish stocks. He was finding his way in through a few holes in the nets, but was getting trapped trying to get out again. Thankfully he was rescued on three separate occasions before finally calling it a day and recommencing his migration northwards.

White YA was last seen at Blagdon Lake on 3rd April, so started the wait for any news of a re-sighting elsewhere in the UK. It didn't take long for that sighting to hit the osprey newswires. Just four days later on 7th April, he was identified on a nest at Kielder Water in Northumberland, not just passing through though; he was the breeding male at this nest!

With the introduction of a better camera at the nest over the winter, it became possible for the first time in 2013 to read the ring number of the resident male (the female was un-ringed); it was White YA.

White YA is rescued for the third time in a week by volunteers at Blagdon Lake, after becoming trapped under nets overhanging trout rearing pools.

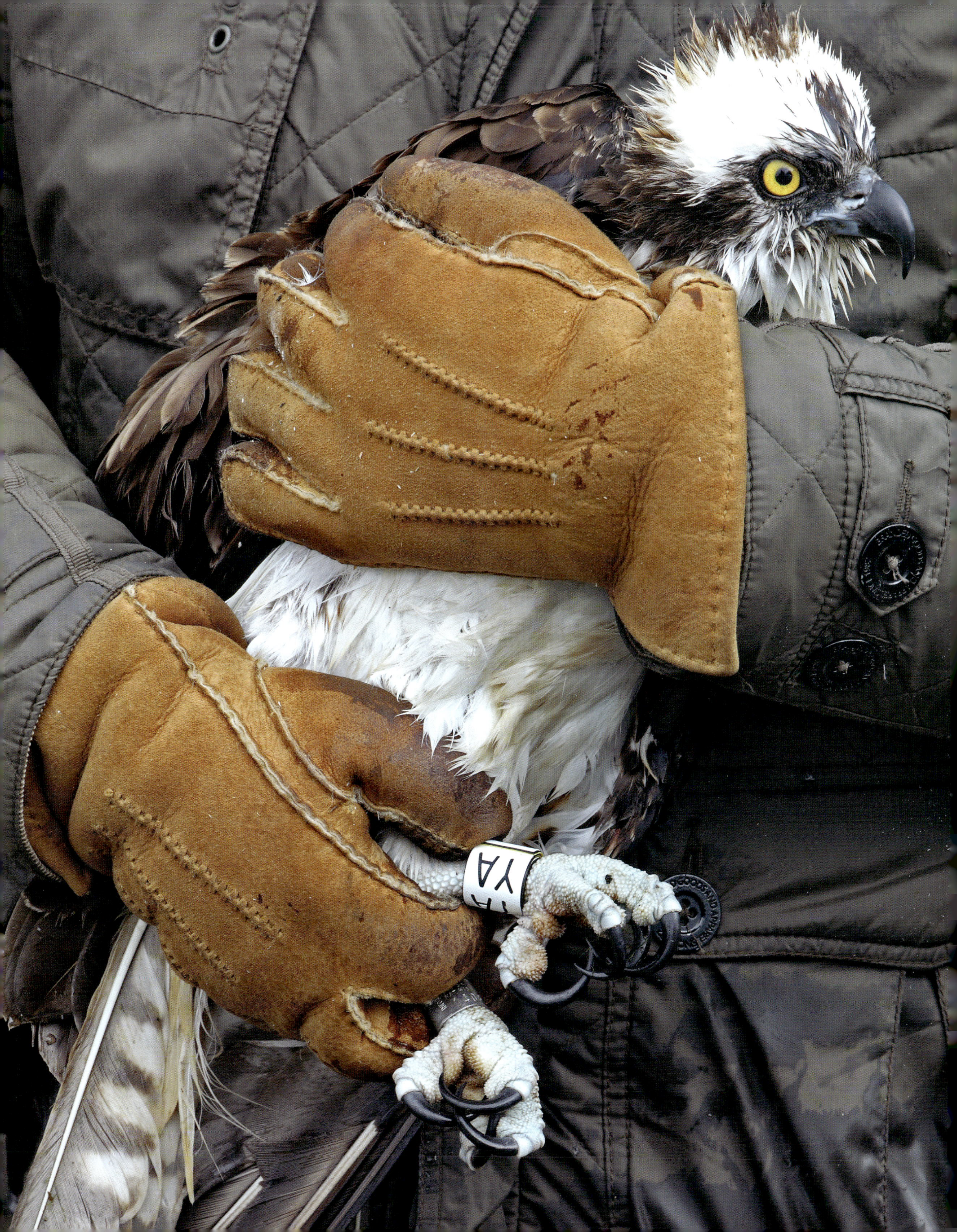
YA

He had actually bred at this nest the year before, siring one chick in 2012. He went on to father another chick in 2013 too, but with a different female to the previous year. The Glaslyn osprey empire was growing.

White YA's 10-day 'staycation' in Somerset begs an interesting question. Upon migrating back in the spring, considering White YA was so close to his breeding nest (around 260 miles away, or more than 90% of the way home if he winters in Africa), why stop off for such a long time if he was only a day's flying time, two at the most, from returning to his Kielder nest?

His extended stay at Blagdon Lake may be explained by the condition he was in when he was rescued on 29th March – the first of the three occasions he got trapped under the nets. Dave Nevitt, the BTO ringer who checked him over, commented, "White YA's breast bone was quite prominent and he was not in the best condition, though he seemed fine otherwise."

This may be an interesting discovery with regard to the migration ecology of our British ospreys. How many more birds do the same thing as White YA? Every year there are numerous ospreys spotted at various reservoirs, lakes and estuaries in the south of England, sometimes staying for several weeks, both on their return journeys in the spring and back down to Africa in late summer and autumn. These birds are clearly taking advantage of good fishing before either the final leg home (usually to Scotland), or the start of their long journeys back to warmer climes. These water bodies serve as re-fuelling pit stops for ospreys on the move. Surely it is only a matter of time before a pair of ospreys finally nest in southern England for the first time in almost 200 years? I hope by the time you read this they will be!

these water bodies serve as re-fuelling pit stops for ospreys on the move

And Then There Were Five

There's only one thing better than receiving news that a Welsh-born osprey has just been sighted back in the UK as a breeding adult many years later: finding out that two have!

This is where things start to sound as if they have been pulled straight out of a science-fiction novel. During the same week that we discovered White YA was back in the UK breeding, we also found out that one of his brothers, Yellow 37 was back – he too was breeding. To make it even more incredible, Yellow 37 had been breeding since 2011 at another nest at Kielder Water of all places – just down the road from his brother White YA!

Yellow 37 is a male offspring from the very first year that the Glaslyn ospreys successfully bred in 2005, so this begs yet another question… He would have been eight years old when he was first identified in 2013; where had he been for all that time? We have advances in technology to thank once again to answer this question, at least partially.

Yellow 37 – a Glaslyn 2005 male osprey breeding at a nest in Northumberland in 2013. Where has he been for eight years?

A nest camera in 2012 had clearly shown the resident male on this other Kielder nest as having a light coloured ring on his right leg with the number 37. It was assumed at the time that it was White 37, but no such ringed osprey existed. It was in fact Yellow 37, the plastic ring had faded over the years to almost white.

Now that Yellow 37's identity had finally been established, it transpired that the Glaslyn ospreys had yet more grandchildren. Yellow 37 had fathered two youngsters in both 2011 and 2012, and in 2013 he went on to produce three more! So add another seven grandchildren to the ever-growing list.

How extraordinary that two Glaslyn male offspring, one from 2005 and another from 2007, were both back in the UK breeding on their own nests, within touching distance of each other in the northeast of England. Was Yellow 37 the 'yellow gold' (page 92) that we saw on the Dyfi and elsewhere in Mid Wales in 2009 prospecting for a nest site and mate? It makes perfect sense in terms of timing, and there aren't that many yellow ringed ospreys around, especially with the rings on the right leg.

Happy Tenth Anniversary

Back in Wales the original Glaslyn ospreys had more to celebrate than just their latest batch of grandchildren; they had returned in 2013 for their tenth successive year of breeding together.

Like clockwork, both birds arrived on the same day, 24th March, within minutes of each other. The first of three eggs was laid 13 days later and everything was going to plan, until mid-May. For the first time since 2005, one of the eggs, the third laid, failed to hatch. For the previous five years these birds had raised three youngsters to fledging age every year – 15 in just five years, a phenomenal productivity

OSPREYS IN WALES *The First Ten Years*

success. It was disappointing that one of the eggs hadn't hatched, but only in the context of the previous few years. The two chicks that did hatch went on to fledge successfully on 6th and 7th July, the 22nd and 23rd Glaslyn chicks to fledge this nest.

The two Glaslyn offspring in 2013 – the 22nd and 23rd chicks to fledge from this nest in 10 years.

Both the un-ringed ospreys at the ON 4 nest also returned in 2013, for their second year together. They were to go one better than they did in 2012; they raised two youngsters to fledging age, both females. Coincidentally, just as in the Glaslyn nest, the ON 4 nest also contained an un-hatched egg, a particularly pale example – maybe it had faded in the searing Welsh sunshine!

Welsh nests have two un-hatched osprey eggs in 2013 – this one is from the ON 4 nest.

166   2013

Glesni's Reign

Despite arriving on 30th April, it took Glesni three days to completely win Monty over. After displacing Seren as the resident female, it wasn't until 3rd May that Monty stopped fighting Glesni off and accepted her as his new partner.

Monty returned to his nest mid morning with a half-eaten fish, hovered over Glesni who was waiting for him, and dropped his mullet straight onto her back! Not the most subtle of osprey chat-up moves, but it was effective; within an hour they were mating. Monty had finally accepted Glesni as the victor of her battles with Seren and she was now his breeding partner-elect. How ironic that Monty had spent some of his early years with another male osprey, females being as easy to come by as hen's teeth. Now he was fending them away, one after another – they all wanted him. Monty had turned from a Jack Lemmon to a Cary Grant in just a few years.

We knew that Glesni was back in the UK before we saw her at the Dyfi; she had been spotted at her ancestral home in Rutland a couple of days before appearing at the Dyfi. She had left it late though. Was 3rd May too late to start breeding? The vast majority of UK breeding ospreys would have been sitting on eggs by this time; the Glaslyn ospreys had already been incubating for a month – they were almost ready to hatch!

The new couple were bonding well, free from the distractions of other intruding ospreys. Glesni was busy bringing sticks and seaweed back to the nest while Monty was in charge of fishing duties. After a week however, Glesni started fishing for herself – was this a sign that the new coalition wasn't as strong as it had first seemed to be? She was catching flounders too – Nora hated these!

The Glaslyn female almost never catches her own food while she is breeding in North Wales, neither did Nora on the Dyfi in 2011 and 2012. Some females do however; this is just a variation we see between individual female ospreys. It must feel alien for a first-time breeding osprey like Glesni to have caught every single fish for herself throughout her life and then suddenly have another bird catch all her meals. The temptation to dive into water if she saw a fish at a catchable depth was possibly too strong an urge resist.

After 10 days of being together, both Glesni and Monty took it in turns to start scraping out an egg-cup in the nest – a large grapefruit sized hemisphere, to lay their eggs in. Things were looking promising and by the start of the fourth week in May, Glesni was acting fidgety and restless, and so were we. On 22nd May she laid her first ever egg in the scrape she had taken so much care to prepare for the big day.

Monty had turned from a Jack Lemmon to a Cary Grant in just a few years

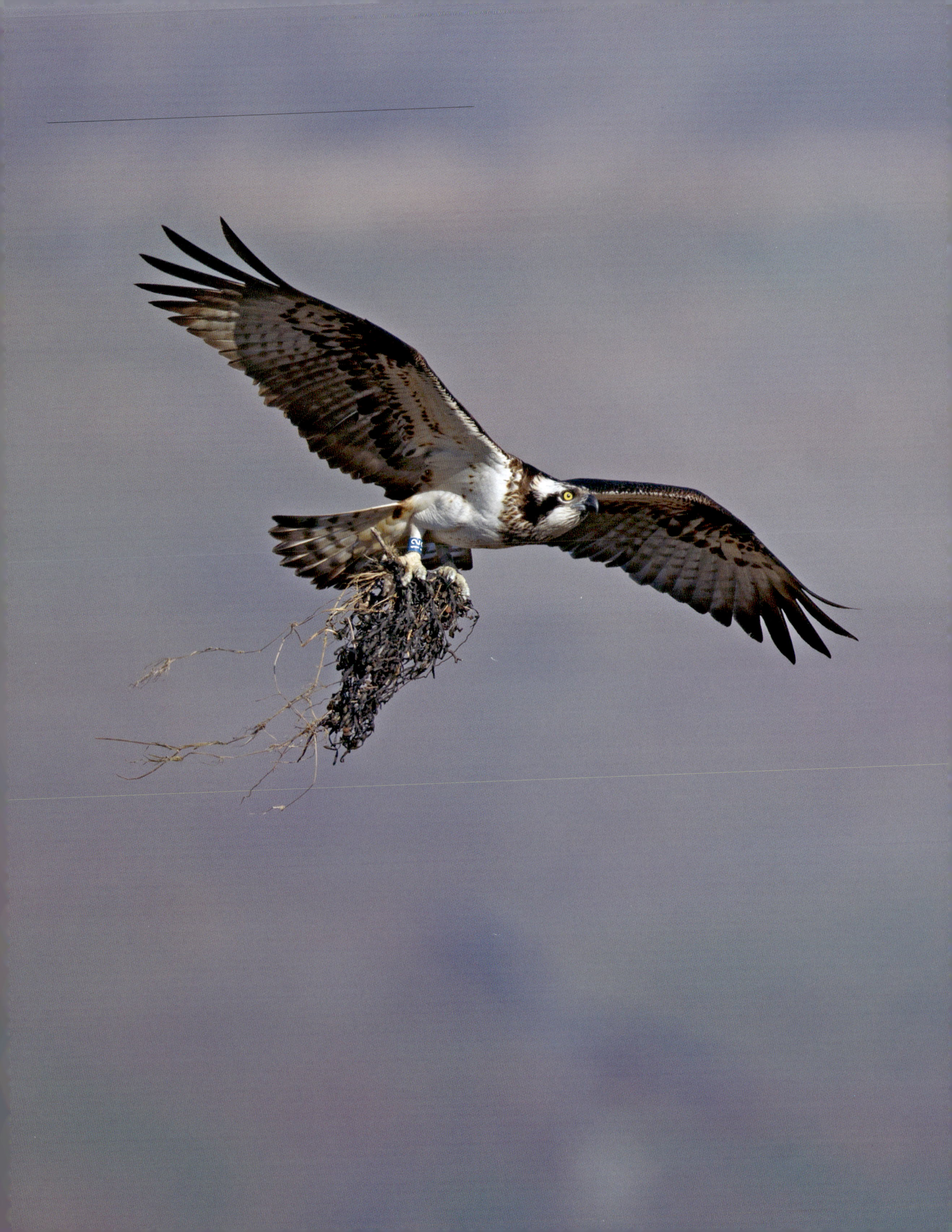

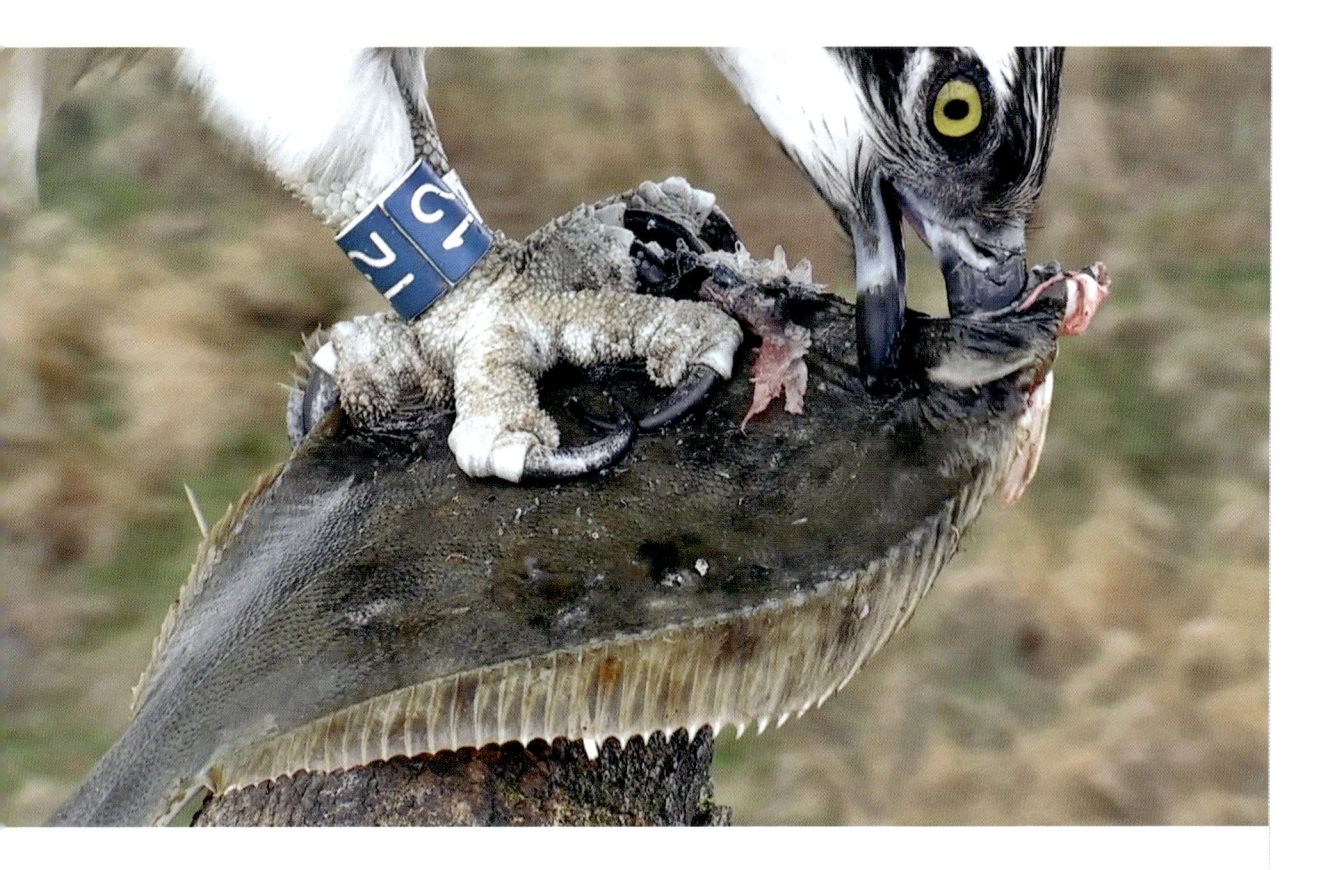

Glesni is fishing for herself a week after pairing up with Monty – is he not catching enough fish for her?

Three days later Glesni laid a second egg, but no third. To lay two eggs is good in any year for any female, but considering she was breeding for her very first time and that it was almost June, she had done pretty well!

Full breeding mode – nest building and mating.

Glesni returns to her eyrie with seaweed as soft nesting material, but is it too late to lay eggs in May?

22nd May: Glesni stands up and looks underneath her – she has laid her first ever egg.

Clarach and Cerist

Following a rather uneventful six-week incubation period, which is always welcome news, Glesni's first chick hatched on 28th June. Two days later on a still and calm day on the Dyfi, we noticed a hole in the second egg.

Montgomeryshire Wildlife Trust had installed a professional microphone system in the nest before the start of the 2013 season, and for the first time we could not only see the ospreys in High-Definition, we could hear them in Hi-Fidelity as well. The tiny chick was making a high-pitched whining sound as she was trying to chip out of the egg – you could hear a pin drop in the visitor centre; it was amazing!

Both chicks turned out to be females and by a huge dose of coincidence, not only did Wales have three osprey nests in 2013, all with two chicks in them, the whole lot were females. Assuming a 50:50 osprey sex ratio, which is true, the probability of all six offspring being females (or all males for that matter) is 64:1!

We named both the young ospreys after local rivers again. Clarach for the first chick to hatch and Cerist for the younger of the two. They were ringed at six weeks old, Cerist was Blue 1R and Clarach, Blue 2R.

OSPREYS IN WALES *The First Ten Years*

We can see the second chick hatching – and hear it.

Cerist (background) has a darker head plumage pattern than her older sister Clarach.

2013

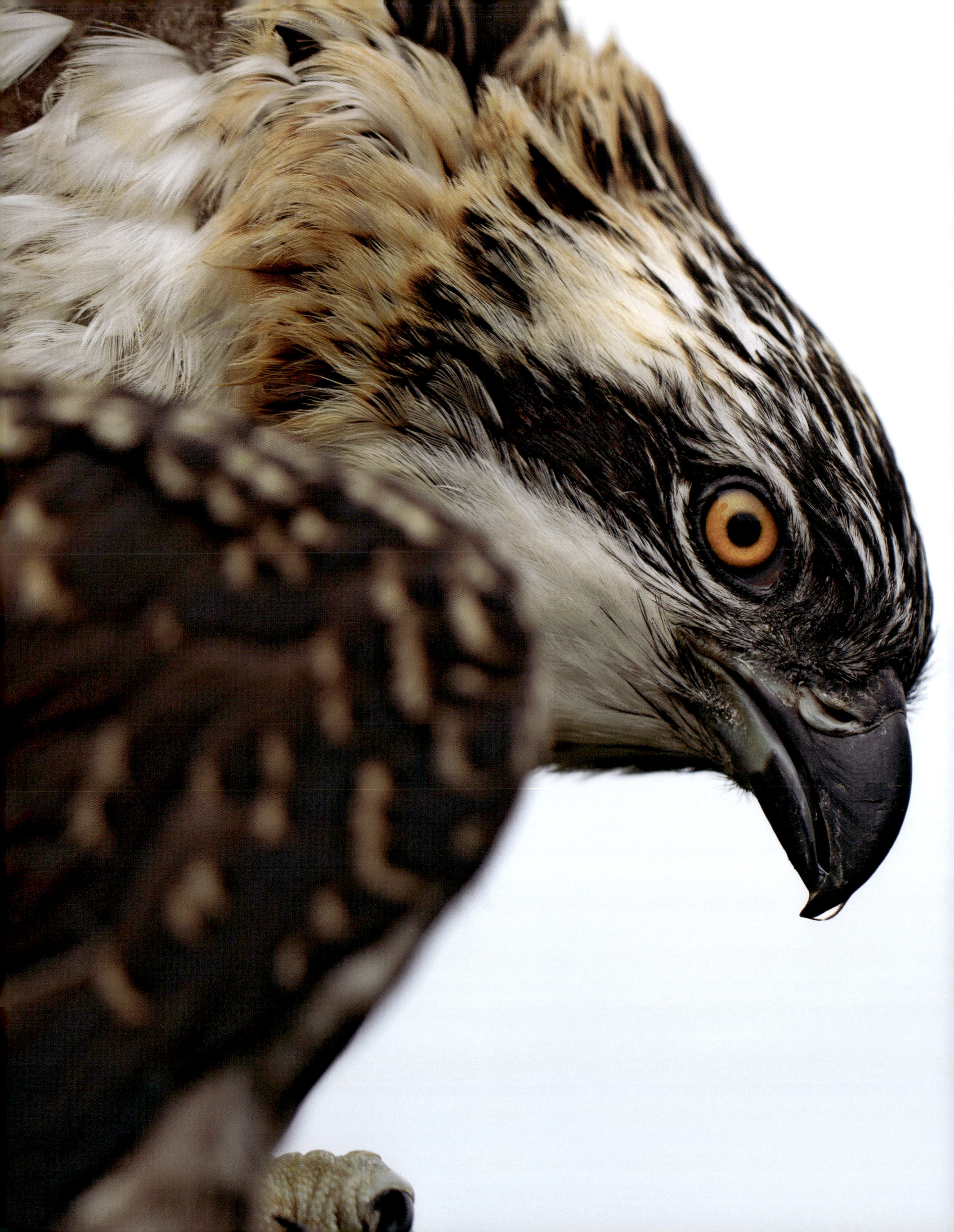

The Search Party

I was so happy that 2013 was going so well following the awful events of the previous season. Considering that Nora hadn't returned in 2013 and Monty and Glesni didn't get it together until May, we were doing pretty well on the Dyfi to get two chicks out. The weather had been helpful too, we'd had Goldilocks weather: not too cold, not too hot, not too wet and not too dry. Just right.

Clarach fledged at the relatively early age of 51 days old – the youngest of any of the Welsh female osprey chicks up to that time. She took off at 8:13am on 18th August, very late in the summer due to the tardy start to the season of course.

She circled over the Dyfi River a couple of times and landed back at the nest two minutes and 13 seconds later – on her sister's back!

If only Cerist's maiden flight had gone so well. Two days later at 9:06am on 20th August, Cerist took to the air for the first time; she too fledged at a precipitous 51 days. The problem was, she didn't come back! We looked up at the skies for her for the rest of the day, as well as trying to search the ground with the osprey nest cameras. Nothing.

16 clean and smiling volunteers congregate outside the Dyfi Osprey Project with a map and some sustenance before the Cerist search. They weren't smiling, nor were they clean for long!

Cerist is one of six ospreys to fledge her nest in Wales in 2013 – and they are all females!

It was the same the following day; where could she be? It is not that unusual for young ospreys to go 'missing' once they fledge; we know of numerous examples of youngsters returning having been away for several days sometimes, following their inaugural flight; severe starvation usually being the trigger for their return. Despite knowing this however, there was no guarantee that Cerist would return, nor in fact that she was still alive. Osprey parents don't tend to feed their young if they are grounded somewhere, and with some of the highest tides of the year approaching on the Dyfi, this was not a good time to have vacated the nest, spending her time on a marsh that would flood over in a couple of days.

The following morning Cerist was still not back so I quickly arranged a search party. Volunteers and staff that were on duty that day would participate in the search itself, a few regular visitors that we knew well would suddenly be upgraded to people engagement volunteers for a few hours.

I wanted to start the search at the very northern end of the reserve, which was the direction Cerist initially flew. I was keen to avoid getting too close to the nest if I could; trying to solve one problem could easily have led to a whole bunch of new ones. The reserve is at its most lush in August; the going was tough to say the least. Nevertheless, by lunchtime we had progressed almost a mile towards the nest, following the Dyfi River.

At precisely 1pm Alwyn's voice came through on the walkie-talkies we had taken with us to communicate with each other. "OSPREY JUST TAKEN OFF FROM THE GROUND," he shouted in his North Walian accent. I looked up towards his position and he had flushed around 25 lapwings into the air, a few curlew and half a dozen snipe. There was also a large white bird of prey amongst them, it was Cerist!

Cerist quickly flew around 600m southwards and landed on the tall telecommunications mast at Dyfi Junction train platform. I was happy that she was there; we had seen Einion, Dulas, Leri and Ceulan

Searching for one osprey in several hectares of marshy wetland is akin to trying to find a needle in a haystack.

perch there in the past – it seemed to be a favourite vantage point for young fledgling ospreys. We quickly called the search off; we had found her and flushed her from the ground. We just had to hope that she would make it back to her nest without any further incidents.

We had all returned to the project in one piece by 2pm, but Cerist was still perching high up on the mast. Half an hour later she plucked up the courage and jumped off – she flew directly towards the nest and following a hostile reception from Glesni, landed on a secondary nest (or *'The Shed'* as we

Cerist lands initially on the 'frustration' nest that Monty had built a few feet above the main nest. She has been away for 56 hours in all.

Cerist (right) is reunited with her sister and apart from looking a little lean, not too worse for wear.

Clarach spends much of her last day at the Dyfi on her dad's favourite ash tree perch. She has become a strong flier in a short amount of time.

called it) that Monty had been building on top of the camera pole in his 'spare time'. She had been away for 56 hours in all, but considering she hadn't eaten throughout that period, she didn't look too bad apart from the odd ruffled feather. A few minutes later she was back on the main nest, reunited with her sister once again.

Thankfully, after this little incident, the remainder of the season went smoothly and without further mishaps. Glesni started her first migration south as a mother on 31st August, but Monty hung around until both his daughters had departed. Clarach was first to go at 10:36am on 18th September, followed by Cerist at 8:36am on 20th September. Cerist had gained height, circling several times before heading southwards at altitude. Once you've seen an osprey start their migration, you know exactly what's happening; the signature is unmistakable and is the same every time.

Monty knew his last remaining daughter had gone. At 9:12, just 36 minutes later, he shot off his ash tree perch and flew straight up, adopting that same flight pattern we had seen him follow before. Within 10 minutes he was a mere dot in the sky and he was also gone, having made sure both his daughters had left before him.

Despite a tense start at the Dyfi and the dud eggs at the other two nests, 2013 had turned out to be a successful season in the end, producing six fledglings in all between three nests, the same number as the previous year. 2013 was the a year for girl-power too, all six youngsters being females. It had also been the year of the 'twos'. We'd had two un-hatched eggs, two chicks fledge from each nest, and most peculiar of all, the first egg Glesni ever laid was on 22nd May, they hatched exactly two days apart, fledged exactly two days apart and migrated exactly two days apart.

Monty waits until both his daughters have started their migrations in 2013. Just 36 minutes later he also departed.

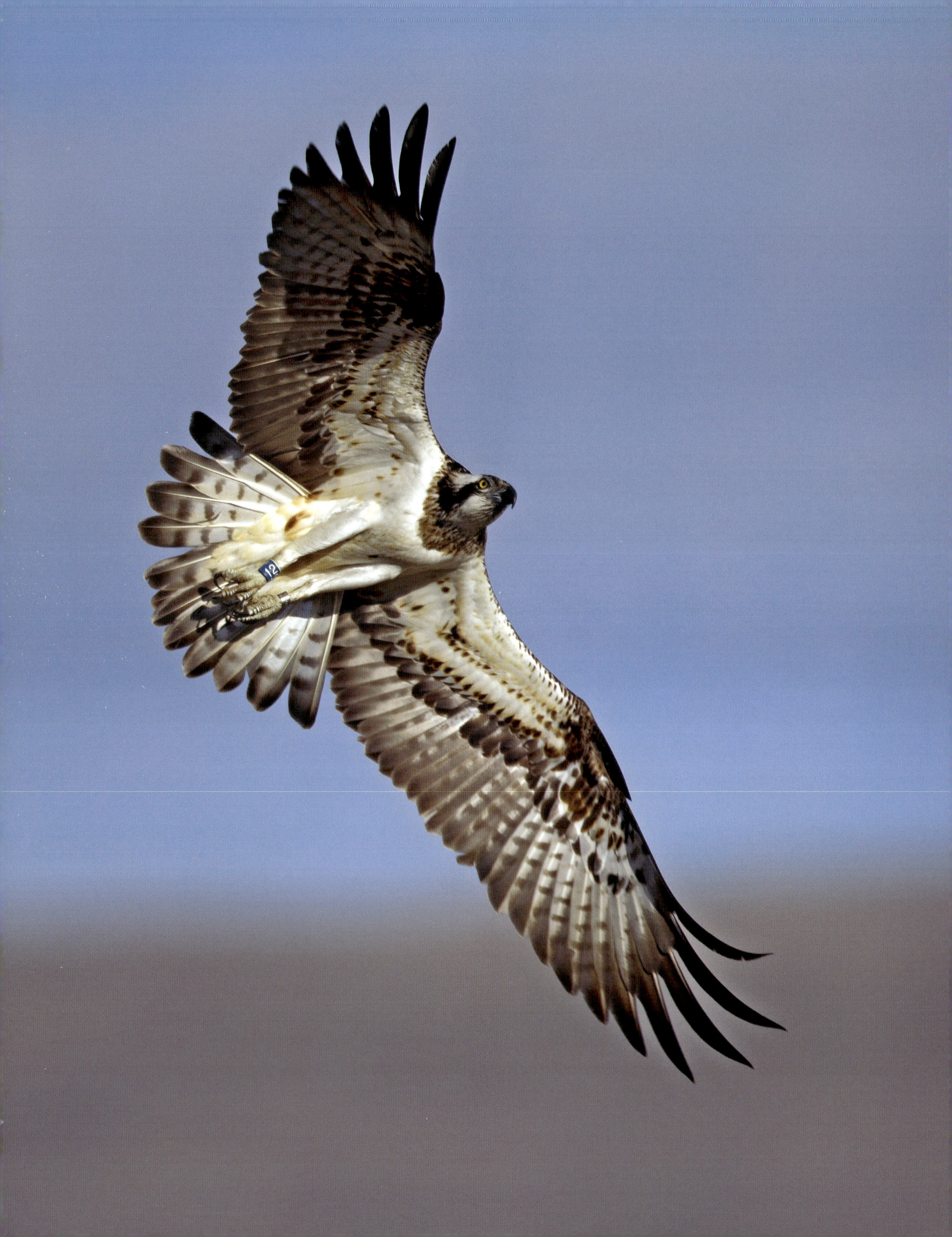

2014

A Room with a View

Back in 2004 when ospreys nested in Wales for the first time in many centuries, watching and learning about them was a simple affair; a couple of volunteers stood in an open field with a telescope and a pocket bird guide. Ten years later in 2014, half a million people had visited the two osprey projects in Wales and many millions more had watched them online.

Montgomeryshire Wildlife Trust's brand new 360 Observatory opens in the spring of 2014.

Glesni migrates from the Dyfi on 31st August in 2013, having become a mother for the first time at three years of age.

Ever since those early ideas, sketches and dreams back in 2010, we had been working hard behind the scenes at Montgomeryshire Wildlife Trust in order to take osprey watching and learning to a whole new level – quite literally. With grants from Heritage Lottery Fund and European Regional Development Fund, the Trust built an iconic 360 Observatory on Cors Dyfi Reserve with a panoramic 360° vista, that would make learning and engaging with ospreys and wildlife a much more thrilling, immersive and fun activity.

The 360 Observatory was built just 195m from Monty and Glesni's nest with breathtaking elevated views over the Dyfi estuary, the Cambrian Mountains and Snowdonia National Park. It was a far cry from those early days fiddling with tripod heads and borrowed telescopes in a soggy field a decade past, but the 360 Observatory would not have been possible without those early years of humble endeavours. No castle exists without its foundations.

Blue 24 and Dai Dot

We were expecting Monty back within his usual window during the first week in April, but Glesni was a first time breeder the previous year, so just like Nora in 2012, we had no idea when to expect her back. What we did get at the start of the 2014 osprey season was the shock of our lives!

31st March 2014 – Blue 24 is back on the Dyfi hoping to snatch Monty and his nest for herself.

We had identified a record number of intruding ospreys on the Dyfi in 2013, one of which was a relation of Glesni's – Blue 24. They were cousins, both born within days of each other in 2010 at different nests at Rutland Water. Blue 24's father, Blue AW (previously ringed Maroon AA, same bird, born 2006 – see page 54) is the brother of Glesni's mum, Green 5N (born 2004). Blue 24 had made a nuisance of herself back in 2013; she was recorded dive-bombing Glesni on the nest on several occasions.

In addition to her ancestry, we knew quite a bit about Blue 24. As a two-year-old she had spent most of the summer of 2012 at Arlington Reservoir, just north of Eastbourne, East Sussex. In 2013 she had been spotted again, at three different locations: back at her ancestral home in Rutland, at the Glaslyn nest and also the Dyfi nest. This is typical early-life behaviour for a female osprey. Blue 24 would return to the UK as a four-year-old in 2014, with a mental map of all the best places to try to attract a mate and set up a breeding home, based on her previous two years research.

On 31st March, Blue 24 landed on the Dyfi nest – the first osprey of the season. She was back again and she was early. Blue 24 seemed in good condition, she stayed around for most of the day, even bringing back the odd bit of nesting material. The following morning she left at 10:30am and didn't return for the rest of the day, but she did reappear first thing the next morning, 2nd April – on the Rutland Manton Bay nest!

By mid-afternoon the following day, 3rd April, Blue 24 was back on the Dyfi nest – she had made a 300 mile round trip to her natal Rutland home and back again in just two days. When she returned to the Dyfi nest this time however, she wasn't alone. A male osprey had arrived, and it wasn't Monty.

Dai Dot is an un-ringed male that has been around on the Dyfi for a number of years. I photographed him in 2011 at the mouth of the estuary and he has been a regular visitor to the Dyfi nest since then. He is always passive, never causes any problems and is tolerated by Monty; the pair have even been observed feeding together on the same perch at Cors Dyfi. I called him Dai Dot back in 2012 because of his two very distinctive and prominent white plumage marks above his beak. Dai sounds like 'dau' in Welsh, which means two. So Dai Dot – two dots!

Dai is quite a dark bird for a male osprey, with a notable and prominent chest plumage that radiates quite a way up his neck; he has heavier than normal under-wing spotting and he also has a very distinctive left eye, with pronounced black iris spots in the four o'clock position. He may have been around the Dyfi before 2011, but assuming he must have been at least two years old then, by 2014 he was a minimum of five years old.

As soon as Blue 24 returned from Rutland, she and Dai Dot hit it off; they got on like a nest on fire. The following day, 4th April, the couple were observed mating and displaying – you just knew there was trouble brewing!

the couple were observed mating and displaying – you just knew there was trouble brewing

Dai Dot with his two signature white plumage spots above his beak.

Just four days into his new, and probably first, relationship, Dai Dot was scraping out a nest cup in readiness for eggs; but he still hadn't worked out the 'fish for sex' osprey arrangement – a sure sign that Dai was a young, inexperienced bird. He never really did reconcile that he needed to share his food for the first time in his life with his new found female; by late afternoon on 8th April, the relationship had come to an abrupt end. Monty was back.

Both males disappeared into the distance whilst circling around each other, gaining height as they did so. Two hours later, just before dusk, Monty was back and he was alone; it hadn't taken him long to dispatch Dai. Both males were familiar with each other of course, no point in Monty fighting an adversary he knew well; they both knew the score.

What would happen now with Monty having returned and a new female on his nest? Monty would have recognised Blue 24 – she was a threat to his nest and chicks the year before, but the dynamics this time around were all different. 9th April turned out to be an interesting day for the animal behaviourists.

Trouble at t'mill: Dai Dot (left) and Blue 24 take ownership of the Dyfi nest – neither Monty nor Glesni is back.

Dai Dot scraping out a nest cup and getting his priorities all wrong.

OSPREYS IN WALES *The First Ten Years*

When Blue 24 first 'met' Dai Dot, she accepted him almost immediately and let him mate with her; by the time Monty showed up five days later, the bond had strengthened and matured. There was one significant flaw in Dai and Blue 24's relationship however; Dai had still not worked out that sharing his dinner was tantamount to sharing his genes a few weeks down the line. We can only speculate as to when the penny would have dropped and Dai would have gifted a fish to Blue 24 for the first time. He was probably quite near to making that connection.

Monty, an experienced breeding osprey by now, knew all about the chocolates and flowers trick. It didn't take him long to present Blue 24 with a mullet, and then another one, and another. Blue 24 soon forgot Dai; this new male was bringing her food and she had probably never experienced that before. At first light the following morning, Monty and Blue 24 were mating.

Monty (left) returns in 2014 and initially pairs up with Glesni's cousin, Blue 24.

The Big Fight

Just to add the last bit of petrol to the fire, at 6:40am the next day, 10th April, Glesni finally arrived back from migration. She didn't like what she saw.

The next few days provided some of the most spectacular, dramatic and interesting osprey watching periods I had ever witnessed. Glesni made a half-hearted attempt at regaining her nest as soon as she arrived back at the Dyfi, but soon gave up. She was clearly not in a fit state to muscle out another female who had already been back 10 days, and had most probably regained all of her strength following her migration. Glesni had not.

For the next five days Glesni made several attempts at displacing her cousin off the nest and as each day passed, she seemed more intent and unswerving in her determination to depose Blue 24. Monty didn't know what to do. He was still mating with Blue 24 but this fight had nothing to do with him; this was a girls only affair. Monty would just have to sit it out and see which female won.

Blue 24: She is determined to hang on to Monty and the Dyfi nest – so is her cousin, Glesni.

OSPREYS IN WALES *The First Ten Years*

Glesni's second attempt on 13th April was delivered with much more gusto and zeal. Her strength was returning and both birds knew it. They disappeared for hours on end with several sightings of them high over the Dyfi estuary, each female circling around the other as if they were sizing each other up. As both females grappled for supremacy it was far from obvious who would eventually succeed. They seemed evenly matched, both in strength and determination – there would be only one way to sort this; they would have to fight it out.

On the morning of 15th April, Glesni launched a vicious attack on Blue 24; their battles over the previous five days had suddenly advanced into all-out war. As one osprey seemed to get the upper hand, the other would come back stronger and more determined. It was fascinating to watch, but also deeply distressing. At just before 2pm Glesni rammed Blue 24 off the nest, she fell to the ground panting hard. Blue 24 eventually managed to fly off, but she was back within the hour.

Glesni was by now holding possession of the nest and as the afternoon wore on, we saw attack after attack. Blue 24 was dive-bombing Glesni, but she held her fort. By early evening, both females looked

The mother of all osprey fights: Blue 24 (left) braces herself for another onslaught from her cousin, Glesni.

After eventually evicting Blue 24 off 'her' nest, Glesni soon gets to work rebuilding it to her own specifications.

186   2014

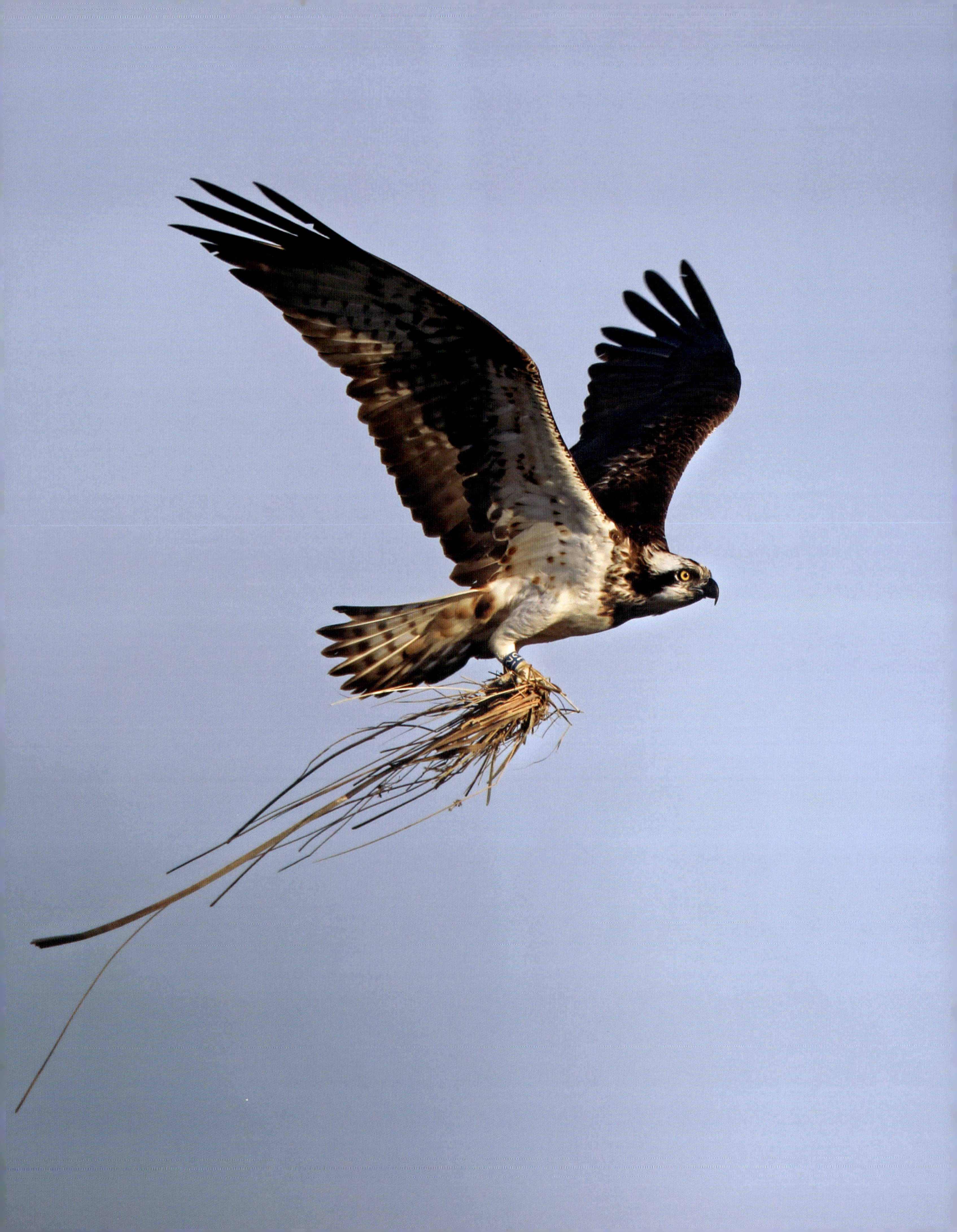

exhausted and jaded; Glesni had regained her nest, but it was a close call. Blue 24 retreated and soon Monty and Glesni were reunited; they were mating by sundown. After five days of stoic persistence and tenacity to win back her mate and nest, Glesni had finally succeeded. This was not the last we saw of Blue 24 however, not by a long way.

Under New Management

Following a hugely successful decade hosting and delivering the Glaslyn Osprey Project, by 2014 the RSPB had decided to pull out of the Glaslyn initiative to concentrate on other conservational objectives in Wales. The goal at the outset was for local people and communities to take over the helm at some point in the future and by 2014, that time had arrived.

Considerately, the RSPB had announced their plans during the summer of 2012, leaving local volunteers almost two years to get everything ready and in order. By the spring of 2014, 'Bywyd Gwyllt Glaslyn Wildlife' had been set up and enough money raised to get the Glaslyn project on the road for its second decade. One of the first items on the action list was a camera upgrade to HD quality and by the end of February, three new cameras had been installed. That £30 camera of 10 years past was a distant memory; the pioneering Glaslyn ospreys would be seen in all their glory for the first time in 2014 – in gorgeous High-Definition.

The Glaslyn female (left) and male in glorious High-Definition for the first time.

OSPREYS IN WALES *The First Ten Years*

Just as HD cameras had opened up another world of osprey watching and learning at the Dyfi back in 2012, the same was now happening at the Glaslyn. As soon as both adults arrived back from their wintering grounds, the lenses were trained and zoomed in on the ospreys; what they revealed was astounding.

We had always known that both the Glaslyn birds were at polar ends of the scale in terms of their plumage, the female being especially dark and conversely the male being extremely light. The new cameras were defining these differences with breathtaking clarity. Both ospreys were as beautiful as we had all perceived them to be, if not more so.

A small portion of the original hide at Pont Croesor was partitioned off as a visitor engagement area, and the video signals from the three nest cameras beamed back by AirFiber, a new wireless transmission technology. The project was entirely run and managed by volunteers and was open every weekend throughout the 2014 summer.

Volunteer Heather shows a visitor one of the Glaslyn ospreys perched on a tree underneath the nest – the new cameras can now see all around the Glaslyn Valley.

2014

Both the adult ospreys arrived at their usual time, the male arriving 20th March and his partner just two days later. By mid-April they had laid their customary three eggs and just to prove that the dud egg of 2013 was a one-off, all three chicks hatched, on 13th, 14th and 16th May.

All three chicks fledged the nest in early July and by the end of August they had all started their migrations south. There were two females in 2014, ringed Blue 7C and Blue 8C; the male was given Blue 9C.

2014 marked the tenth consecutive year that the same two ospreys had successfully produced young to fledging age at the Glaslyn nest, 26 in all. A monumentally successful decade of young osprey production and exactly what Wales needed.

Volunteers Viv and Tony putting in a shift at the protection caravan – the Glaslyn female has laid at least 32 eggs spanning 11 years by 2014.

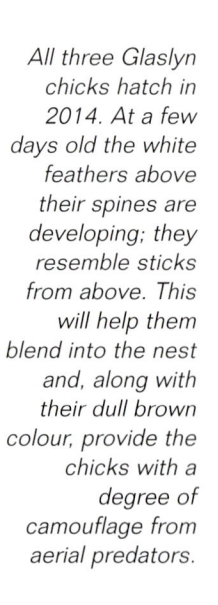

All three Glaslyn chicks hatch in 2014. At a few days old the white feathers above their spines are developing; they resemble sticks from above. This will help them blend into the nest and, along with their dull brown colour, provide the chicks with a degree of camouflage from aerial predators.

OSPREYS IN WALES *The First Ten Years*

Come in White 91

Despite being photographed on the Loch of the Lowes nest in 2012 as a three-year-old (page 136), the Glaslyn 2009 female White 91 wasn't seen again that year. She did return to Scotland the following year however, and paired up with a male on an established nest in a solitary oak tree near Crieff, Perthshire, around 20 miles away from the Loch of the Lowes nest.

The pair failed to breed that year, not helped by having to rebuild their eyrie higher up in the oak tree due to Canada geese taking over their original nest! White 91 returned in 2014 and this time, unhindered by the geese, successfully raised three chicks for the first time. She had bred at five years of age and she is the only Glaslyn female to have been recorded back in the UK as an adult to date.

Blue 8C looks straight into the camera just before she starts her migration at the end of August. The same camera will hopefully pick her up again in two or three years as an intruder at the same nest.

2014   191

Glaslyn's White 91 (top left) perches above her nest in Perthshire, which had to be rebuilt following the ospreys' eviction by a pair of Canada geese the year before!

High Fives – A Fifth Glaslyn Osprey Breeding

Just as this book was about to go to print, I received some brilliant news – just in time! In 2013 a pair of ospreys had attempted to breed at Roudsea Wood and Mosses (National Nature Reserve) in Cumbria for the first time. The pair failed and during the following winter their nest blew down. With the help of local power company Electricity North West, a new platform was erected mid-March 2014, in the hope that the previous year's birds would return.

They did. By 2nd April both ospreys were back and immediately started building a new nest on the platform. They went on to produce two chicks, both males, and when staff from Natural England ringed them in early July, they placed a stealth-cam at the side of the nest to try and establish if either of the adult birds was ringed. It's a good job they did.

Once all four ospreys had left on migration in September 2014, the camera was retrieved and the images analysed. The female was un-ringed, but the male had a white Darvic ring on his right leg – it was White YC!

White YC is one of the male Glaslyn ospreys from 2008 (page 72). We thought we had seen him on the Dyfi in 2010 and he was definitely there in 2011, we photographed him on 18th May (page 116). White YC had also been spotted as a three-year-old at his ancestral Glaslyn nest in 2011. He was the fifth and final Glaslyn offspring to be discovered breeding during the first ten years of Welsh osprey colonisation. Remarkably, by 2014 all five of the Glaslyn offspring that had initially been sighted as returning young adults were breeding, and even more extraordinary, not one of them was nesting in Wales!

Birds pay little regard to artificial, man-made borders of course; at least the Glaslyn children were gradually coming closer, with White YC nesting just 97 miles away from the Glaslyn as the osprey flies. It's interesting that from the first five successful years of breeding at the Glaslyn nest, 2005 – 2009, one bird from each year had returned and was now breeding. That's five returnees from a total of 12 birds – a remarkable 42% return rate, and all of them now breeding. They must have good genes, those Glaslyn birds.

Glaslyn's White YC (2008) breeding for the first time in 2014 at a nature reserve in Cumbria. He sired two sons.

Glaslyn Empire Building

The five Glaslyn offspring had a bumper year in 2014. Black 80 sired another two chicks up in Scotland and his sister White 91 in Perthshire went one better with three at the first time of asking. White YC fathered two chicks for the first time in Cumbria, while the Kielder brothers, Yellow 37 and White YA, both raised three apiece. The Glaslyn empire was expanding, quickly.

In all, 13 'grand-chicks' fledged in 2014 with the total number of Glaslyn grandchildren now standing at an impressive 33. And these are just the ones we know about of course; are there any more out there?

The Glaslyn female takes the ice bucket challenge, completely unaware that five of her children are breeding in England and Scotland. By 2014, she had 33 grandchildren.

Yellow 37 feeds his three chicks at his Kielder nest in 2014; his brother White YA also fathers three chicks at his nest just five miles away.

Notwithstanding other, yet to be identified, offspring that may be around from the 2005 – 2009 years, the Glaslyn parents have produced a further 14 youngsters since then. If 42% of these come back, that's another six ospreys we can look forward to seeing in the future. One may even decide to come back to Wales and breed!

In fact, we have already recorded one of these later birds back in the UK as an adult. On 15th August 2014, Blue 80, a 2012 Glaslyn male offspring landed beside one of the Dyfi fledglings. He just stood there staring at her!

The next batch of Glaslyn ospreys are already starting to show up - Blue 80 (2012) at the Dyfi on 15th August 2014 as a two-year-old.

Blue 80 was just two years old and had only been back in the UK a few weeks no doubt. He was missing (moulting) a primary feather on his right wing at the time, and so was a male intruder that had been spotted around the Dyfi for the previous six weeks – the same bird surely? A blue-ringed (right leg) osprey had also been reported at the Glaslyn during the same period.

Blue 80 had almost certainly been prospecting around North Wales, and possibly further afield, looking for suitable breeding sites for the future – just as his brothers and sister had done in all likelihood during previous years.

Expanding empire moving north, not by the Romans – but Welsh ospreys.

© Google Earth Maps

The Glaslyn Class of '14 – the probability is that at least one of these birds will be back breeding in the UK by the end of this decade.

Dyfi Double

Despite winning her nest and mate back from Blue 24, Glesni was never rid of her cousin completely in 2014. Blue 24 stayed around all summer, constantly interfering and hampering Monty and Glesni's efforts to raise their chicks.

Blue 24 had adopted a few strategic perches close to the Dyfi nest that she would often frequent – she knew exactly how hard to press Glesni's buttons. We never saw an outright attack again, but she remained a nemesis to both Monty and Glesni for the rest of the season.

Two eggs were laid despite all the intrusions – I'm of the opinion Glesni would have laid three if left in peace; the harassment during those few days of egg laying was especially intense. The time gap between the eggs was also very long – almost four and a half days (usually three or less for ospreys). Something had happened. *(After four days and nine hours I had confidently declared to thousands of followers on the Dyfi Osprey Project Facebook page that the time elapsed since the first egg was now so great, Glesni would only lay one egg in 2014. An hour later she laid a second. The 'Ospreys will make you look stupid' rule had struck again).*

Despite all the disruptions from Blue 24, for the second year in a row, Glesni and Monty had produced two eggs and one of them was quite unusual. The first egg laid was almost completely white; it barely had any maculation (pigmentation) at all. We joked that Glesni was in such a hurry to start laying with the incessant interference from her cousin, she forgot to put the final decorations on the egg before it came out. Either that or a Canada goose had dropped in while we weren't looking and laid it!

Monty (left) escorts Blue 24 away from his nest while Glesni protects her two eggs.

Monty eats his dinner on one of his favourite Cors Dyfi perches – Blue 24 is never far away in 2014.

Blue 24 on a nest platform in the Glaslyn Valley on 25th May.

The first 2014 Dyfi chick hatches out of his very white egg.

Blue 24 had opted for a seemingly odd strategy in 2014. She had paired up with Dai Dot for a few days and looked all set to lay eggs a week or so later, before Monty joined the party. Then she started to build a tenuous bond with Monty while she fought Glesni for the nest; now she was defeated, you would have thought the best thing to do was to move on. Obviously not.

The protection volunteers at the Glaslyn had also recorded Blue 24 on a few occasions and rang us at the Dyfi just to make sure she wasn't with us; she wasn't. Blue 24 seemed to have made the Dyfi her home with the odd day trip to the Glaslyn. Why didn't she have another look at Rutland or venture further afield to try and find Dai Dot or another singleton? Her strategy seemed to be to try to unsettle Glesni enough (or the Glaslyn female) so that she could regain a nest she clearly thought of as her own. It will be fascinating to see what her plan of action will be in 2015 and beyond.

Our fears that Blue 24's daily intrusions may have been to the detriment of both chicks hatching were ill founded. On 8th June a tiny little osprey crawled out of his almost pure white egg and three days later the second successfully hatched.

Gwynant and Deri

Thankfully we experienced Goldilocks-type weather again and the two Dyfi youngsters prospered. Monty also caught a rare fish in 2014 – a twait shad. It's a member of the herring family that has no lateral line down its sides. The twait shad is an 'anadromous fish' – meaning it is born in fresh water, spends most of its life in the sea and returns to fresh water to spawn. Monty also caught a twait shad in 2012, although I'm not sure he possesses all the relevant licenses required to catch this species.

By the time the chicks were three weeks old, there existed a discernible difference in the appearance between the two young ospreys. The oldest was developing extremely light coloured feathers whilst the younger of the two was darker, but already the same size by that time, despite being three days younger. It is far from obvious sometimes what gender osprey chicks are in the nest, but in the 2014 Dyfi nest it was pretty clear from early on: one male (oldest and whitest) and one female.

How ironic that the very pale chick had hatched from the very white egg. We decided to call him Gwynant, which means white stream and is also a Welsh river. The female was named Deri, which is a tributary just upstream from the Dyfi.

At six weeks old both chicks were measured and ringed. Deri weighed in at 1,600g whilst her brother, despite being three days older, weighed 80g less, which is what we expected with him being a male.

why didn't she have another look at Rutland or venture further afield to try and find Dai Dot?

OSPREYS IN WALES *The First Ten Years*

Both chicks are fed a rare fish – Monty catches only his second ever twait shad in 2014.

Gwynant reminded me so much of Einion. He appeared confident and fearless with a strong independent streak. He fledged extremely early at exactly seven weeks old, the youngest of any of the Dyfi chicks to fledge. He also started his migration quite early, coincidentally on the morning of 31st August, just as Einion had three years before him.

'The Cwtch'. Just days old the two chicks are miniature eating machines; they will double in weight each week for the next five weeks.

His sister had grown to be another food monster. Deri would stand her ground in the nest, screaming for more fish despite there being enough food for several days in there. Ospreys, especially females, are predisposed to have this gluttonous trait. We hardly ever see young fledglings like this fish for themselves when their parents are still around providing free handouts. They generally start fishing once the filial bond is broken and they get so hungry, there is no other option. Most get the hang of it pretty quickly, although the success rate per dive is significantly lower compared to their more experienced parents.

Tired of 'playing dead' whilst being ringed, Gwynant decides to go for a little walk.

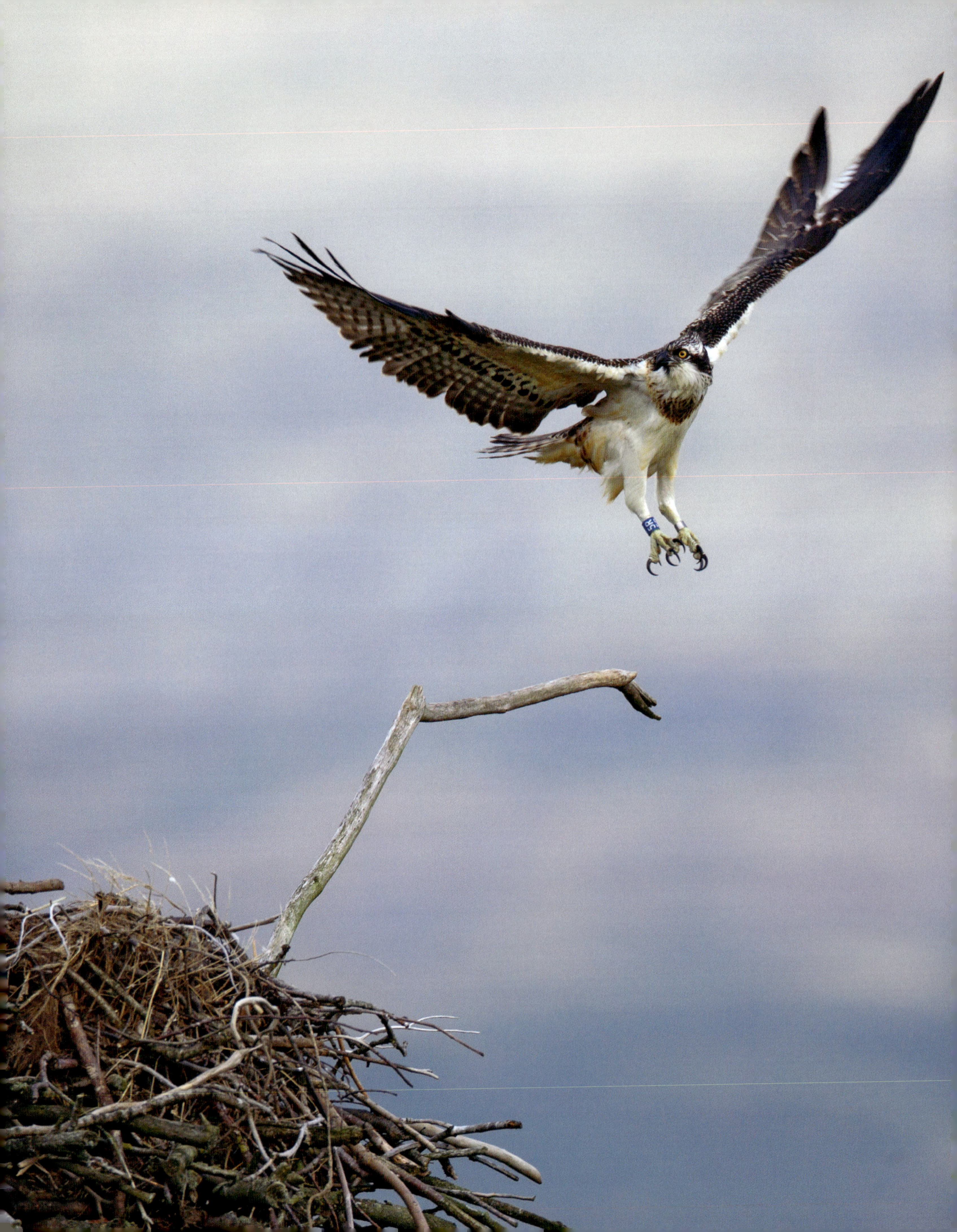

I often wonder how Leri might have fared if she had just eaten an extra mullet or two before she left. A week's journey across the Sahara is a much safer undertaking for a young osprey that is several hundred grams overweight. That pre-migration gluttony is there for a reason.

Glesni started her migration on 19th August, followed by Gwynant and then Deri. Just as in the previous two years, Monty was last to go on 7th September, having seen both his youngsters off. Deri and Gwynant would no doubt have benefitted from not having a third sibling in the nest in 2014; maybe Blue 24 came with a silver lining after all. Blue 24 also stayed around until early September, but made no real attempt at regaining the nest once Glesni had gone. There was no point, it was far too late in the day for that. Someone else did land on the nest in late August however, after Glesni had departed.

Dai Dot was back. We hadn't seen him since 8th April when Monty escorted him off the premises. We used to see him on a regular basis during the summer months of years gone by, generally hanging out with Monty somewhere. There was a very good reason why he hadn't been around. He'd been busy.

Deri, now probably weighing in excess of 2Kg, peers into the Dyfi camera just before she starts the longest journey of her life so far.

Deri takes to the air for the first time at 51 days old.

Dai Dot

Some ospreys are quick learners, some take a little more time to work things out. Just days after being politely escorted away from the Dyfi by Monty, Dai Dot had paired up with another female. He had wasted no time; the experience of pairing up with Blue 24 for a few days had served him well. He must have learnt from his mistakes of not handing over fish and corrected his ways once he had encountered another female calling for food.

By early May, Dai and his un-ringed female had produced three eggs and six weeks later, two of them hatched. On 7th August both chicks were weighed and ringed at approximately five weeks old; one was male and the other female. The un-hatched egg was removed.

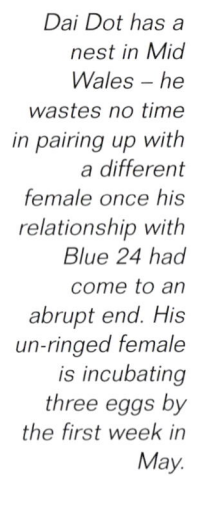

Dai Dot has a nest in Mid Wales – he wastes no time in pairing up with a different female once his relationship with Blue 24 had come to an abrupt end. His un-ringed female is incubating three eggs by the first week in May.

Dai Dot bringing nesting material back to his new eyrie in Mid Wales.

The male weighed a healthy 1,450g and was ringed Blue A2 on his right leg. His sister was 10% heavier and was ringed Blue A1.

By 2014, Wales had its fifth osprey nest, four of them being active with breeding birds. Osprey Nest Five, ON 5, was the newest addition to the growing number of nests in Wales and the combined number of fledged chicks hit double figures in 2014 for the first time in many centuries. Dai Dot had finally managed to secure a nest and produce young after several years of watching Monty do the same on the Dyfi.

Dai Dot's daughter weighs 1,600g at five weeks old; his son is 10% lighter.

Maybe this explains Blue 24's decision not to move on? She would almost certainly have known about her ex-partner's new nest and also the birds breeding at ON 4 further north. All four Welsh nests are within an hour's osprey flying time of each other – maybe after her intense battles with Glesni earlier in the season, which could easily have resulted in serious injury if not worse, her best strategy in 2014 was to sit out the season keeping an eye on the four active nests, just in case an opportunity presented itself at some point.

Deri starts her long migration south from the Dyfi – she is the 43rd Welsh juvenile to do so in 10 years of Welsh osprey recolonisation. She will hopefully be back in 2016.

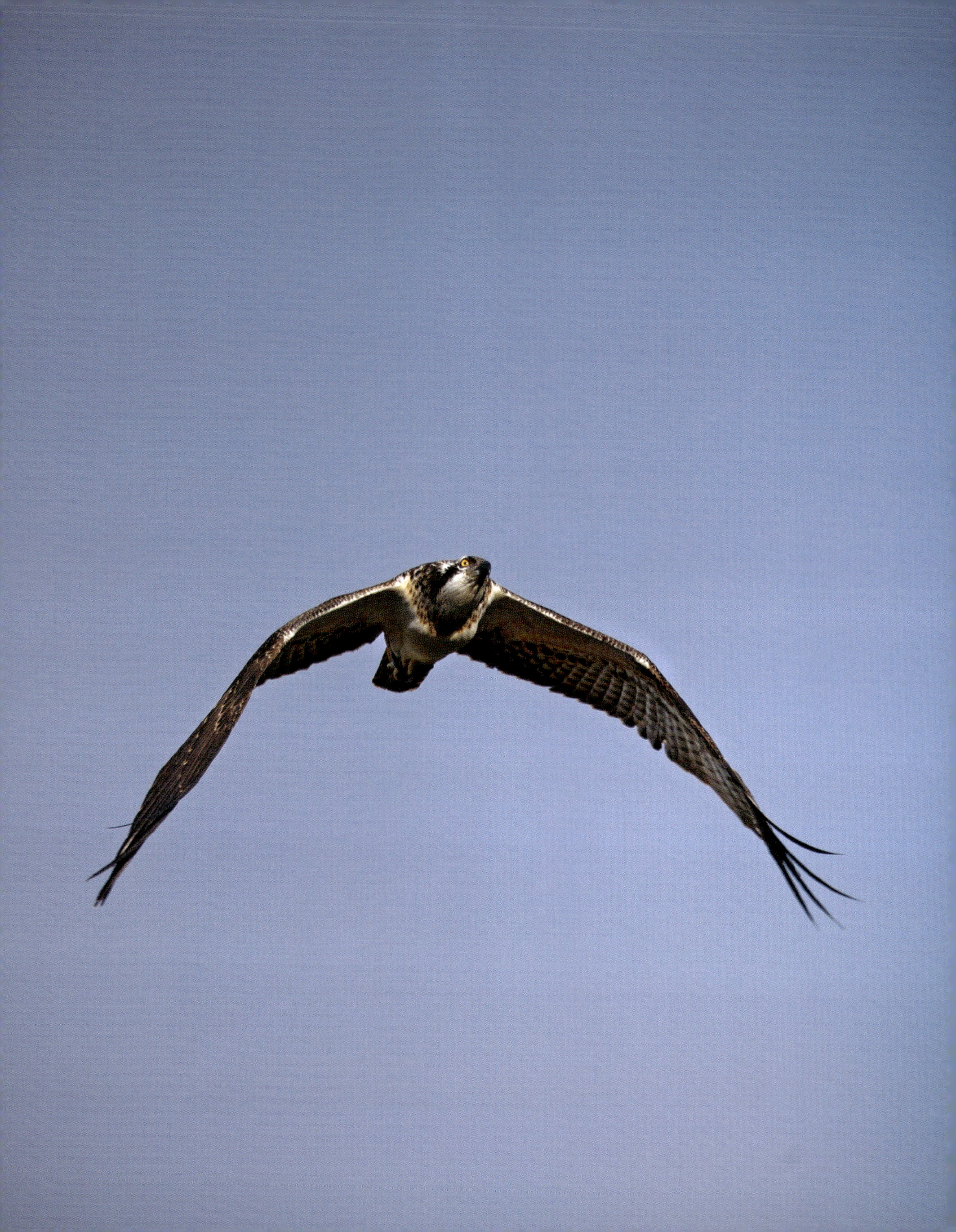

Looking at an osprey's behavior through human eyes, we don't always see the full picture. What looks odd to us at first glance usually ends up not being that bizarre after all. Blue 24 wasn't daft; having missed the egg-laying window in 2014, this was her best strategy looking ahead to 2015. As that expert osprey watcher who visited the Dyfi in 2011 is keen on saying, "ospreys know best." The wily old cat is rarely wrong, neither are ospreys.

So there we have it. From that single Welshpool chick fledging in 2004 to a ten-fold increase a decade later; it has been an exciting beginning to a successful journey for ospreys in Wales. Four active breeding nests by 2014, 43 chicks fledged, five of which are back in the UK breeding having produced 33 Welsh grandchildren.

Yes, we've pinched one or two Scottish and English birds over the years to start us off, but we've rebalanced the books! I can't wait to see what the next 10 years bring.

Glesni's cousin, Blue 24. Where will she end up breeding in future years?

Stats

Marmite

I've always loved numbers and statistics. They help me understand the world and make sense of it. Maths is not everyone's cup of tea I know; I tend to find people either love working with numbers, or hate it!

Statistics have, undeservedly in my view, been given a bad name. Wasn't it British Prime Minister, Benjamin Disraeli, who coined the phrase, "There are three kinds of lies: lies, damned lies, and statistics"? Manipulating or presenting cherry-picked chunks of data to bolster a weak argument by the likes of politicians (and scientists sometimes) has not helped change people's opinion for the better. Statistics have a bad reputation and that's a shame.

I've had to temper my urge to fill the next 100 pages with statistics; I don't think that would be of benefit to anybody! I have tried to find a balance between presenting useful information that is relatively easy to read and digest, and plotting out every graph, table and chart ad infinitum. The next few pages show all the key osprey data contained in the book, and all the major dates and events are included.

I have attempted to make this chapter useful, not just for now, but as a reference point in the future. I've explained some of the most obvious trends and highlights, but there are a lot more goodies in there if you look hard enough. You'll hopefully find the following pages more like jam than Marmite – something that most people like!

Glaslyn and Dyfi Key Dates

These two tables show the all the key dates of the major osprey events each season (apart from Glaslyn 2004 where most dates were not recorded). At the Glaslyn nest, the exact times for all dates are not known, therefore I have not included them. Conversely, all the timings for the Dyfi nest are known, so I have shown them in this table. Here are a few things that stand out:

1. Both Glaslyn adults return on remarkably similar dates, usually within a day or two of each other. By 2009 both birds were arriving by around 21st – 22nd March, a pattern they have followed right through to 2014. These dates are exceptionally early for both birds of a pair to return; the Glaslyn pair has been one of, if not *the* earliest osprey pair to start breeding in the UK every year.

2. Monty typically arrives during the first week in April and despite starting to breed in 2011 for the first time, he has not deviated from this arrival window.

3. Of the 14 combined Glaslyn and Dyfi years represented, a clutch of three eggs was laid in 12 of those years; two eggs were laid during the other two years (Dyfi 2013 and 2014). That is a combined total of 40 eggs at an average clutch size of 2.86 eggs per year. Of these 40 eggs, just two (5%) did not hatch (Glaslyn 2005 and 2013). The true Glaslyn egg count in 2004 is unknown (the nest contained at least two eggs as two chicks were found dead).

4. Including the two 2004 Glaslyn chicks, the combined total chicks hatched at both nests is 40 (30 at Glaslyn and 10 at Dyfi). Of these 40, six (15%) have died in the nest before fledging: two at the Glaslyn in 2004 (nest blew down), one at the Glaslyn in 2006 (reason unknown), one at the Glaslyn in 2007 (reason unknown), and two at the Dyfi in 2012 (weather).

5. Despite being some of the earliest UK ospreys to breed, both Glaslyn birds tend to stay around until September before they migrate. This also makes them some of the longest resident ospreys at their nest site in the UK, at around five and a half months each year. Both the Dyfi breeding females up to 2014 have migrated in August (which is more typical for ospreys). All adult birds in all years have waited until all their chicks have fledged before they migrated.

6. Spanning 11 years and including 2004, the Glaslyn nest has an average productivity (chicks that fledged per year) of 2.36. The Dyfi nest has a productivity of 2.0.

Glaslyn Key Dates for 10 Years							Male 11 (98) & Un-Ringed Female			
	2005	2006	2007	2008	2009	2010	2011	2012	2013	2014
Male arrived	28-Mar	31-Mar	26-Mar	26-Mar	21-Mar	22-Mar	16-Mar	18-Mar	24-Mar	20-Mar
Female arrived	22-Apr	29-Mar	28-Mar	27-Mar	22-Mar	23-Mar	20-Mar	20-Mar	24-Mar	22-Mar
Egg 1 laid	02-May	11-Apr	09-Apr	08-Apr	06-Apr	08-Apr	02-Apr	03-Apr	06-Apr	05-Apr
Egg 2 laid	05-May	14-Apr	12-Apr	11-Apr	09-Apr	11-Apr	05-Apr	06-Apr	09-Apr	08-Apr
Egg 3 laid	08-May	17-Apr	15-Apr	14-Apr	12-Apr	14-Apr	08-Apr	09-Apr	12-Apr	11-Apr
Chick 1 hatched	09-Jun	18-May	16-May	16-May	13-May	15-May	09-May	11-May	13-May	13-May
Chick 2 hatched	12-Jun	20-May	18-May	17-May	14-May	17-May	11-May	12-May	15-May	14-May
Chick 3 hatched	D.N.H.	22-May	20-May	19-May	17-May	19-May	14-May	14-May	D.N.H.	16-May
Chick 1 fledged	30-Jul	Died 30-Jun	08-Jul	04-Jul	06-Jul	08-Jul	28-Jun	05-Jul	06-Jul	03-Jul
Chick 2 fledged	03-Aug	11-Jul	Died 03-Jun	05-Jul	08-Jul	09-Jul	04-Jul	04-Jul	07-Jul	07-Jul
Chick 3 fledged	-	17-Jul	10-Jul	11-Jul	11-Jul	11-Jul	06-Jul	07-Jul	-	08-Jul
Last sighting of a juvenile	13-Sep	06-Sep	24-Aug	01-Sep	02-Sep	26-Aug	26-Aug	02-Sep	24-Aug	31-Aug
Female last seen	01-Sep	04-Sep	18-Aug	04-Sep	03-Sep	24-Aug	02-Sep	01-Sep	26-Aug	02-Sep
Male last seen	13-Sep	06-Sep	29-Aug	05-Sep	03-Sep	29-Aug	02-Sep	02-Sep	27-Aug	04-Sep

D.N.H. = Did not hatch. Two chicks hatched in 2004, but both died on 30th June (storm) at 12 - 14 days old; no other dates are known for 2004.

Dyfi Key Dates	2011		2012		2013		2014	
	Monty & Nora				Monty & Glesni			
	Date	Time	Date	Time	Date	Time	Date	Time
Male arrived	06-Apr	09:20	02-Apr	15:35	07-Apr	09:01	08-Apr	15:13
Female arrived	09-Apr	07:00	24-Mar	15:34	03-May	08:24	10-Apr	06:40
1st egg laid	25-Apr	14:03	18-Apr	19:06	22-May	17:18	02-May	10:19
2nd egg laid	28-Apr	12:29	21-Apr	15:23	25-May	19:06	06-May	20:18
3rd egg laid	01-May	11:45	24-Apr	09:06	-	-	-	-
1st chick hatched	05-Jun	15:35	28-May	21:38	28-Jun	19:14	08-Jun	11:06
2nd chick hatched	06-Jun	06:35	29-May	06:23	30-Jun	20:45	11-Jun	18:53
3rd chick hatched	07-Jun	10:19	31-May	09:58	-	-	-	-
1st chick fledged	27-Jul (Einion)	14:22	Died 31-May	-	18-Aug (Clarach)	08:13	27-Jul (Gwynant)	10:33
2nd chick fledged	29-Jul (Dulas)	08:42	21-Jul (Ceulan)	09:29	20-Aug (Cerist)	09:06	01-Aug (Deri)	13:24
3rd chick fledged	03-Aug (Leri)	16:34	Died 09-Jun	-	-	-	-	-
Female last seen	14-Aug	08:05	07-Aug	14:26	31-Aug	08:06	19-Aug	07:54
1st chick migrated	31-Aug	09:04	-	-	18-Sep	10:36	31-Aug	07:00
2nd chick migrated	12-Sep	06:40	03-Sep	09:26	20-Sep	08:36	04-Sep	10:33
3rd chick migrated	13-Sep	08:00	-	-	-	-	-	-
Monty last seen	11-Sep	16:05	05-Sep	07:23	20-Sep	09:12	07-Sep	10:50

Glaslyn and Dyfi Egg Data

The following two tables show the incubation period for each egg laid at the Glaslyn and Dyfi nests, 40 in all. Additionally, the amount of days elapsed between the adult birds first mating and the subsequent laying of the first egg is also shown. Again, data for Glaslyn 2004 is not shown because other than knowing that there must have been at least two eggs present (two chicks), we know nothing of the other key data.

1. The 'first mating to first egg' interval of British ospreys is generally 10 to 20 days, occasionally longer. Established and experienced pairs tend to have shorter courtship periods than younger birds, as generally they have a nest already built from previous years, plus the male typically shares his food with the female immediately upon meeting at the start of the season. At the Glaslyn in 2005, this courtship time was only 10 days, which is exceptionally short. From 2009 onwards this courtship interval increased by a few days, settling at 13 or 14 days during the last four years recorded. There is no way of knowing for sure, but I would strongly suggest that this lengthening is explained by a gradual increase of other ospreys intruding at the nest, something we know that happened.

2. The picture is somewhat different at the Dyfi. Monty and Nora were both first time breeders in 2011, so we expected a mating to laying interval of a minimum of two weeks; it turned out to be 16 days. It was identical the following year too, possibly not shortened due to the severe weather. In 2013 and 2014 this interval was higher still; Glesni was a first time breeder in 2013 and took a few days to bond with Monty, even fishing for herself during this period hence a protracted 19-day courtship period. In 2014 the mating to laying period was a marginally shorter 17 days, but still slightly higher than average; probably due to the relentless disruptions from Blue 24, who had originally started to bond with Monty following Dai Dot's departure before Glesni returned. Evidence from both Dyfi and Glaslyn nests supports the general consensus that established osprey pairs that experience the least disruptions tend to have the shorter courtship mating to laying periods.

3. The incubation times of the Glaslyn eggs show a remarkable consistency and lack of variation. The incubation period for the first egg was always 37 or 38 days; the incubation period for the second egg was always 36 days (except once: 35 days in 2009) and the incubation period for the third egg was always 35 days (except once: 36 days in 2011). The average incubation periods for egg one, two and three were 37.3, 35.9 and 35.1 respectively. The gradual decrease in egg incubation times results in chicks hatching at closer intervals than their eggs were initially laid.

4. The first two years (2011 and 2012) at the Dyfi with Nora had exceptionally long incubation periods for both years – probably due to Nora choosing not to incubate continuously until the third egg was laid. We also had the unusual event of the chicks hatching out of order in 2011 – the second egg laid was the first to hatch (Einion), resulting in an extremely lengthy 42-day incubation for the first egg laid (Dulas). Incubation times with Glesni were identical in both years and matched exactly the Glaslyn pair.

Glaslyn Egg Data

	Egg order	First mating to first egg laid (days)	Incubation period (days)
2005	Egg 1	10	38
	Egg 2		D.N.H.
	Egg 3		35
2006	Egg 1	11	37
	Egg 2		36
	Egg 3		35
2007	Egg 1	12	37
	Egg 2		36
	Egg 3		35
2008	Egg 1	12	38
	Egg 2		36
	Egg 3		35
2009	Egg 1	15	37
	Egg 2		35
	Egg 3		35
2010	Egg 1	16	37
	Egg 2		36
	Egg 3		35
2011	Egg 1	13	37
	Egg 2		36
	Egg 3		36
2012	Egg 1	14	37
	Egg 2		36
	Egg 3		35
2013	Egg 1	13	37
	Egg 2		36
	Egg 3		D.N.H.
2014	Egg 1	14	38
	Egg 2		36
	Egg 3		35

D.N.H. = Did not hatch

Dyfi Egg Data

	Egg order	Name	First mating to first egg laid (days)	Incubation period (days)
2011	Egg 1	Dulas	16	42
	Egg 2	Einion		38
	Egg 3	Leri		37
2012	Egg 1		16	40
	Egg 2	Ceulan		38
	Egg 3			37
2013	Egg 1	Clarach	19	37
	Egg 2	Cerist		36
2014	Egg 1	Gwynant	17	37
	Egg 2	Deri		36

Glaslyn and Dyfi Chick Data

These two tables show weights and wing lengths of all the Glaslyn and Dyfi chicks, 34 in all. However, because it is practically impossible to weigh and measure each chick at the exact same age, valid comparisons between chicks, years and nests become a little futile. Nevertheless, there still exists some valuable information here.

All chicks are measured at the same time as they are ringed; this usually takes place when the chicks are between four and six weeks old. Females on average are heavier than males by approximately 10% to 15%. As a (very) general rule of thumb, females weigh more than 1,500g at ringing age and males less; but I emphasise that this is a generalisation and there are frequent exceptions to this rule. When we gender an osprey chick we look at other metrics as well, such as the thickness of the tarsi (lower leg – females usually larger), the thickness of the beak (females generally broader) and the 'feel' of the bird to an experienced ringer. Plumage can also be an indicator (females usually darker) as well as behaviour.

Perhaps of more interest in these tables are the fledging ages of all the chicks. Here are the averages:

Chick Fledging Ages (averages in days)	Combined	Males	Females
Glaslyn (26 birds)	52.8	52.1	53.6
Dyfi (8 birds)	52.1	51.8	52.5
Combined	52.7	52	53.4

1. The average age at fledging of all 34 chicks combined is 52.7 days.

2. At both nests, females are on average older than males when they fledge (by 1.5 days at Glaslyn and 0.7 days at Dyfi). Averaged out at both nests for all 34 chicks, females are 1.4 days older when they fledge compared to males.

3. Three males hold the record for youngest chick to fledge – 49 days old (Gwynant in 2014 and the two males at the Glaslyn in 2007: White YD and White YC). Leri (female) was the oldest chick to fledge at 57 days old.

4. The sex ratio at both nests is exactly the same, 50:50 (13 males and females at Glaslyn, four males and females at Dyfi). So a combined total of 17 males and 17 females.

This data supports the consensus that female ospreys fledge slightly later than males (by 1.4 days at these two nests). This is true of many bird of prey species, as females are generally larger than males and therefore require slightly more growing and development time to get airborne.

Glaslyn Chick Data for 10 Years

	Darvic ring	BTO ring	Weight (grams)	Wing length (mm)	Age fledged (days)	Sex
2005	37	1408621	1,430	294	51	M
	39	1408622	1,540	265	52	F
2006	2J	1408623	1,640	327	D.N.F.	F
	80	1408625	1,460	340	52	M
	5Y	1408624	1,350	295	56	M
2007	YB	1408627	1,600	288	53	F
	YA	1408626	1,320	260	51	M
2008	YD	1408629	1,390	315	49	M
	YC	1408628	1,230	310	49	M
	YE	1408630	1,540	272	53	F
2009	90	1431702	1,800	323	54	F
	YF	1431701	1,705	274	55	M
	91	1431703	1,450	268	55	F
2010	93	1431704	1,600	270	54	F
	92	1431705	1,600	273	53	F
	94	1431706	1,370	220	53	M
2011	78	1431708	1,450	293	50	M
	77	1431707	1,670	295	54	F
	79	1431709	1,495	246	53	M
2012	0C	1469801	1,650	337	55	F
	80	1431710	1,420	323	53	M
	1C	1469802	1,290	300	54	M
2013	5C	1469803	1,660	316	54	F
	6C	1469804	1,630	301	53	F
2014	9C	1469807	1,440	315	51	M
	7C	1469805	1,500	316	54	F
	8C	1469806	1,500	295	53	F

D.N.F. = Did not fledge (chick died). One chick died in the 2007 nest at 16 days old.

Dyfi Chick Data

	Name	Darvic ring	BTO ring	Weight (grams)	Wing length (mm)	Age fledged (days)	Age migrated (days)	Sex
2011	Einion	DH	112873	1,470	338	52	87	M
	Dulas	99	112875	1,460	336	53	98	M
	Leri	DJ	112874	1,610	325	57	98	F
2012	Ceulan	3C	1118480	1,415	350	53	97	M
2013	Clarach	2R	1057943	1,710	328	51	82	F
	Cerist	1R	1057942	1,660	300	51	82	F
2014	Gwynant	3R	1112446	1,520	323	49	84	M
	Deri	5R	1112447	1,600	298	51	85	F

2012 - Two chicks died in the nest aged 3 (first chick) and 9 (third chick) days old.

Dyfi Sightings and Glaslyn Offspring

These two tables are pretty self-explanatory. The one below shows all the ringed ospreys that have been photographed on or near the Dyfi nest from 2011 – 2014. These are a tiny fraction of all observed intruder sightings, most are un-ringed and of those ospreys that do have a leg ring, rarely do they land or perch close enough to enable a decent view/photograph.

Of particular interest are their ages; most are just two or three years old. These birds are clearly prospecting for nests and mates; it seems that established breeding birds show little interest in other osprey nests. Also noted here are the two ospreys that eventually became the resident breeding females at the Dyfi nest: Nora (White 03) and Glesni (Blue 12).

The table overleaf shows the Glaslyn offspring with some of their key timescales and events.

Ringed Ospreys Sighted On The Dyfi

Year	Date	Sex	Darvic	Darvic Leg	Origin	Age when seen (Years)	Comments
2011	09-Apr	Female	03	R	England	3	Ringed at Rutland Site B as a chick in 2008. Mother Green 05 (00), Father White 03 (97) - Nora.
	14-Apr	Female	DA	L	Scotland	3	Ringed at Loch Ard near Aberfoyle, Stirlingshire on 7th July 2008 - from a brood of two.
	18-May	Male	YC	R	Wales	3	Ringed at Glaslyn on 20th June 2008, middle chick from brood of three. Mother unringed, Father Ochre 11(98).
2012	21-May	Female	12	R	England	2	Ringed at Rutland Site N as a chick in 2010. Mother Green 5N (04), Father White 08 (97) - Glesni.
	25-May	Female	00	R	England	3	Ringed at Rutland Site B as a chick in 2009. Mother unringed, Father White 03 (97).
	27-May	Female	HZ	L	Scotland	2	Ringed at Loch Ard Forest, near Aberfoyle, Stirlingshire on 14th July 2010 - from a brood of one.
	04-Jun	Female	HF	L	Scotland	2	Ringed at Tweed Valley 2010, second chick from brood of two.
2013	27-Apr	Female	FS	L	Scotland	3	Ringed at Dores, Loch Ness 14th July 2010.
	29-Apr	Female	UR	L	Scotland	3	Ringed Ythan Valley, Aberdeenshire 10th July 2010.
	30-Apr	Female	12	R	England	3	Rutland female seen at Dyfi in 2012 - Glesni.
	22-Jun	Female	91	L	Scotland	2	Ringed 2011 by Roy Dennis in Thurso area of Caithness - sister to satellite tracked juvenile 'Joe'.
	26-Jun	Female	24	R	England	3	Ringed Rutland Site O in 2010, Mother from Argyll, Father Blue AW (06). Seen at Arlington Reservoir, Sussex 2012.
	28-Aug	Female	CF3	L	Scotland	0	Juvenile ringed Flow Country, Sutherland by Roy Dennis 5th July 2013, largest chick from a brood of four.
2014	29-Mar	Female	24	R	England	4	Rutland female seen at Rutland, Glaslyn and Dyfi in 2013.
	15-Aug	Male	80	R	Wales	2	Ringed at Glaslyn on 18th June 2012, middle chick from brood of three. Same parents as White YC.
	20-Aug	Male	CU2	L	Scotland	2	Ringed as a chick near Carsphairn, Dumfries & Galloway on 8th July 2012.

216   STATS

Glaslyn offspring that have been sighted back in the UK as adults up to 2014	Grand-chicks
Black 80 (2006) At Threave Castle, Scotland. **Breeding at 3 years old**	
2008 - July: Black 80 discovered on a nest near Loch Ken, Dumfries taking fish to a female.	
2009 - May: Black 80 and the female returned and raised two chicks. Blue BB and Blue BC.	2
2010 - April 6th: Black 80 and his mate back on Threave nest. Raised three chicks. Blue BK, Blue BL and Blue BM.	3
2010 - September 19th: Blue BK resighted in Pont Grandic Novola, Gulf of Morbihan, France in the Regional Natural Park.	
2011 - April 3rd: Black 80 and his mate back on Threave nest, having won it back from a pair of Red Kites. Raised 2 chicks Blue JE & Blue JF.	2
2012 - March 28th: Black 80 arrived back at Threave nest. Old female did not return. New female arrived 11th May Blue KC. Raised 2 chicks. Blue CU3 and Blue CU4.	2
2013 - March 27th: Black 80 back at nest, bred again with Blue KC. Raised two chicks, Blue CU8 and Blue CU9.	2
2014 - March 30th: Black 80 and Blue KC both back at Threave. Raised two chicks Blue CX0 and blue CX1	2
White YC (2008) At Roundsea Wood and Mosses, Cumbria, England. **Breeding at 6 years old**	
2011 - April 21st: White YC landed on Glaslyn nest at 12:00, remained for around 20 minutes.	
2011 - May 18th: White YC landed on Dyfi nest, May 29th YC landed on Dyfi T perch, possibly sighted on at least two other occasions.	
2012 - May: White YC reported as having been seen fishing in the Porthmadog area.	
2014 - September 30th, White YC reported as having bred in Cumbria during 2014.	
2013 - White YC attempted to build nest in an electricity pylon near Roudsea Wood & Mosses NNR, Cumbria. Fell down over the winter.	
2014 - April 2nd: White YC on new platform in pine at Roudsea NNR with unringed female. Raised two male chicks Blue FS9 and Blue FS0.	2
White 91 (2009) At Loch of the Lowes, Scotland. **Breeding at 5 years old**	
2012 - July 18th: White 91 landed on Loch of the Lowes nest.	
2014 - July 27th: White 91 discovered breeding at a nest in Perthshire. Raised three chicks, unringed as close to fledging. Failed breeding attempt with same male 2013.	3
White YA (2007) At Kielder Water, England. **Breeding at 5 years old**	
2013 - March 25th: White YA photographed at Blagdon Lakes, Somerset, subsequently caught in stewpond nets and released on three occasions.	
2013 - March: White YA confirmed as being the breeding male at Kielder Water nest 1, replacing the previous male in 2012.	
2012 - July: White YA raised one chick Blue H0 (Probably female).	1
2013 - April 7th White YA back at Nest 1. Raised one chick with unringed female, Blue 6H (sex unknown).	1
2014 - April 2nd: White YA returned to nest with same female. Raised three chicks, Blue UV (satellite tagged - male), Blue VV (satellite tagged - female) and Blue VT (female).	3
Yellow 37 (2005) At Kielder Water, England. **Breeding at 6 years old**	
2013 - April 2nd: Yellow 37 confirmed as the breeding male at Kielder Water nest 2. First discovered nest building in 2010.	
2011 - July: Yellow 37 raised two chicks Blue 37 & Blue 38 (male).	2
2012 - July: Yellow 37 raised two chicks Blue 1H - (female) and Blue 2H - (male).	2
2013 - April 4th: Yellow 37 back at nest 2. Raised three chicks, Blue 3H (male), Blue 4H (female) and Blue 5H (female).	3
2013 - July 1st: Blue 38 (2011) - male, youngest of brood, resighted in North Yorkshire.	
2013 - November 14th: Blue 1H (2012) - female, resighted by Frederic Bacuez in the Todde Swamps, Northern Senegal.	
2014 - March 30th: Yellow 37 back at nest. Raised three chicks on new nest with same female, Blue 7H (satellite tagged - female), Blue 8H - (female), Blue 9H - (female).	3
2014 - July 1st: Blue 2H (2012) - male offspring, photographed in Hurworth Burn Reservoir near Hartlepool.	
Blue 80 (2012)	
2014 - August 15th: Blue 80 lands on Dyfi larch perch 09:13.	
Total number of grandchildren	**33**

Welsh Osprey Nests

The top table shows the number of active Welsh osprey nests each year from 2004 to 2014, including the number of young fledged from these nests. The returning breeding offspring are also included.

1. Despite having two nests in 2004, only the Welshpool nest produced young (one). The Glaslyn nest was the only active nest in Wales for the following six seasons (2005 – 2010) producing 12 fledglings during that time.

2. One Glaslyn offspring from each year between 2005 and 2009 has returned and successfully bred, producing 33 offspring combined.

3. The number of active nests started to increase from 2011 onwards, culminating in four breeding pairs in 2014.

4. No offspring from 2010 or later has been recorded breeding as yet, not enough time has elapsed for this to happen.

The bottom table shows the productivity of each of the five osprey nests from 2004 to 2014, including a breakdown of male-female chick ratios.

1. Between 2004 and 2014, Wales had an active osprey nest for a combined total of 20 years. 43 chicks fledged the five nests during these 20 years, giving Wales a combined productivity average of 2.15 per nest.

2. Of the 43 chicks that fledged at the five nests, 21 were male and 22 female.

Welsh breeding osprey nests 2004 - 2014					
Year	No of breeding pairs	No of young fledged	No of young breeding	ID returned	No of grandchildren
2004	2	1			
2005	1	2	1	37	10
2006	1	2	1	80	13
2007	1	2	1	YA	5
2008	1	3	1	YC	2
2009	1	3	1	91	3
2010	1	3			
2011	2	6			
2012	3	5			
2013	3	6			
2014	4	10			
Total		43	5		33

Welsh Osprey Nests (ON) 2004 - 2014	Years active	No of active years	No of fledglings	Productivity	Male	Female
ON 1 (Welshpool)	2004	1	1	1	1	
ON 2 (Glaslyn)	2004 - 2014	11	26	2.4	13	13
ON 3 (Dyfi)	2011 - 2014	4	8	2	4	4
ON 4	2012 - 2014	3	6	2	2	4
ON 5	2014	1	2	2	1	1
Total		20	43	(Av) 2.15	21	22

Dyfi Fish Stats

These four bar charts represent all the fish caught at the Dyfi nest each week for four seasons, 2011 to 2014. The start of each season (week 1) is on the left of each chart and continues to the last week ospreys were around, usually week 23 or 24 in September. Monty caught all the fish with the exception of those shown in the brown bars which were caught by the females. The top two charts are Monty and Nora (2011 and 2012); the bottom two charts are Monty and Glesni (2013 and 2014).

1. These charts clearly show the 'chocolates and flowers' stage of the pair ponding at the start of the season. Once both ospreys are back together, the amount of fish Monty catches is more than is required from a calorific point of view. You could argue that both adults require more calories after returning from a long journey, but increased prey returns to the nest also signal the pair bonding of both birds at the start of the season. This is an important stage for both birds prior to egg laying and demonstrates to the female that the male is in good condition and is capable of providing for her future offspring.

2. For the following six or seven weeks we see more normalised prey returns, closer matching the calorific requirements of each adult – usually between eight and 15 fish per week (depending on the size of the fish caught).

3. From around week 10/11 we see a steady rise in fish caught, which corresponds with chicks hatching and developing. When the chicks are approximately six weeks old we tend to see the prey return plateau off and then decrease a few weeks later when the female departs on her migration followed by the fledglings.

4. During 2012, these differences are less pronounced due to just one chick (Ceulan) surviving, and possibly the freak weather conditions for most of the summer, resulting in slightly restricted prey availability.

5. Nora caught four fish in 2011 and 11 in 2012. Glesni is a more prolific fisher during the breeding season, catching 27 fish in 2013 and 42 in 2014. The females tended to catch most of their fish during the few weeks before they left on migration.

OSPREYS IN WALES *The First Ten Years*

2011
Number of fish caught 2011 — Monty, Nora

Week	Monty	Nora
1	18	
2	19	
3	7	
4	9	
5	10	
6	7	
7	8	
8	13	
9	9	
10	13	
11	19	
12	26	
13	28	
14	23	
15	22	
16	32	
17	30	3
18	28	1
19	27	
20	26	
21	18	
22	16	
23	2	

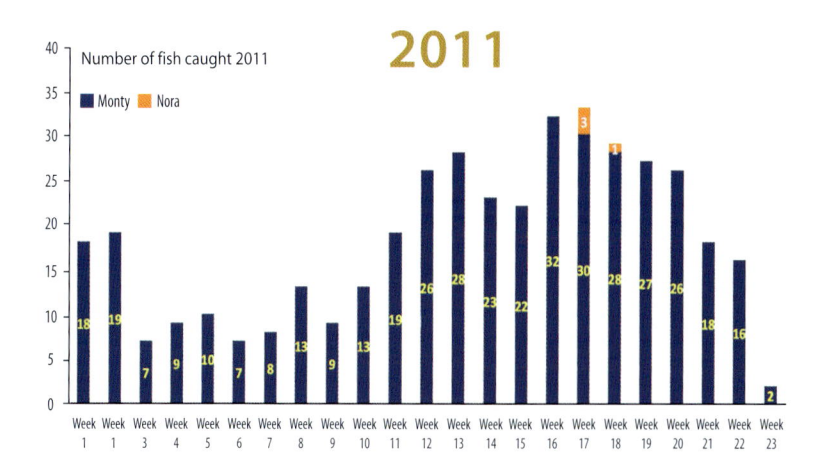

2012
Number of fish caught 2012 — Monty, Nora

Week	Monty	Nora
1	10	
2	11	
3	10	
4	10	
5	12	
6	12	
7	11	
8	8	
9	12	
10	11	
11	17	
12	12	
13	16	
14	18	
15	18	
16	17	
17	11	5
18	18	5
19	13	1
20	15	
21	11	
22	15	
23	2	

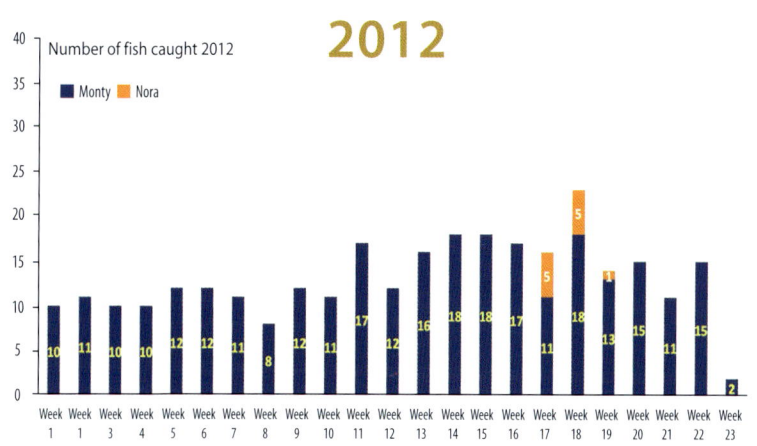

2013
Number of fish caught 2013 — Monty, Glesni

Week	Monty	Glesni
1	11	
2	9	
3	25	
4	25	
5	22	1
6	16	
7	18	
8	15	
9	14	1
10	13	
11	12	
12	9	1
13	27	
14	24	
15	27	
16	23	2
17	27	3
18	28	4
19	25	
20	21	6
21	28	4
22	32	
23	30	
24	13	

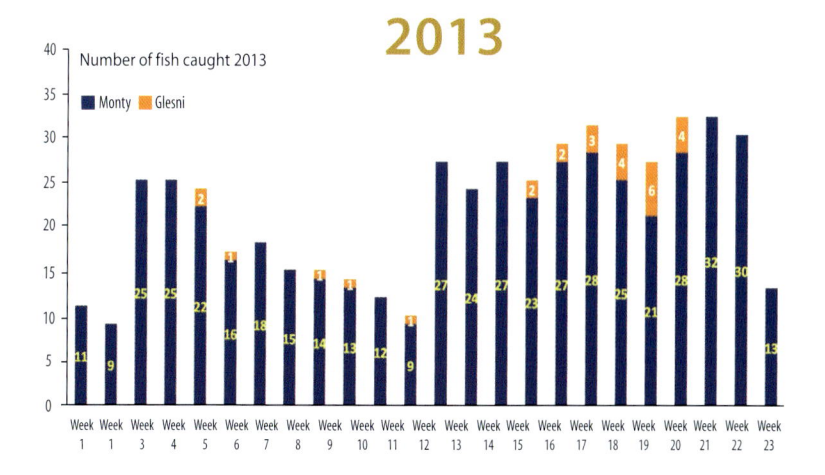

2014
Number of fish caught 2014 — Monty, Glesni

Week	Monty	Glesni
1	11	
2	17	2
3	21	1
4	13	
5	13	
6	15	
7	10	
8	6	
9	13	
10	16	
11	19	
12	20	
13	22	
14	22	1
15	21	6
16	23	3
17	14	10
18	21	11
19	30	8
20	28	
21	30	
22	10	

STATS 221

Fish Pies

No set of osprey stats would be complete without a fish pie! These two charts show the combined fish totals at the Dyfi nest for four seasons, 2011 to 2014. The top chart gives the total amount of each fish species caught over the four seasons, and the pie chart below averages out these species as a percentage of the total catch.

1. Mullet make up almost half (47.4%) of all fish caught. Flounder make up almost a fifth (19.8%) and sea and brown trout make up 29.3% of the diet.

2. Over the four seasons, 11 different fish species have been recorded including twait shad (2), greater weaverfish (1) and garfish (3).

3. Many scientific analyses have been performed on these data sets over the last two years; they all show that there is no major correlation between fish species caught and any other parameter such as weather, time of day, tidal range, rainfall etc. Monty's decision criteria seem to be based mostly on how hungry he or his family are, and prey availability at that time.

Monty brings a mullet back to his two daughters, Cerist and Clarach in 2013.

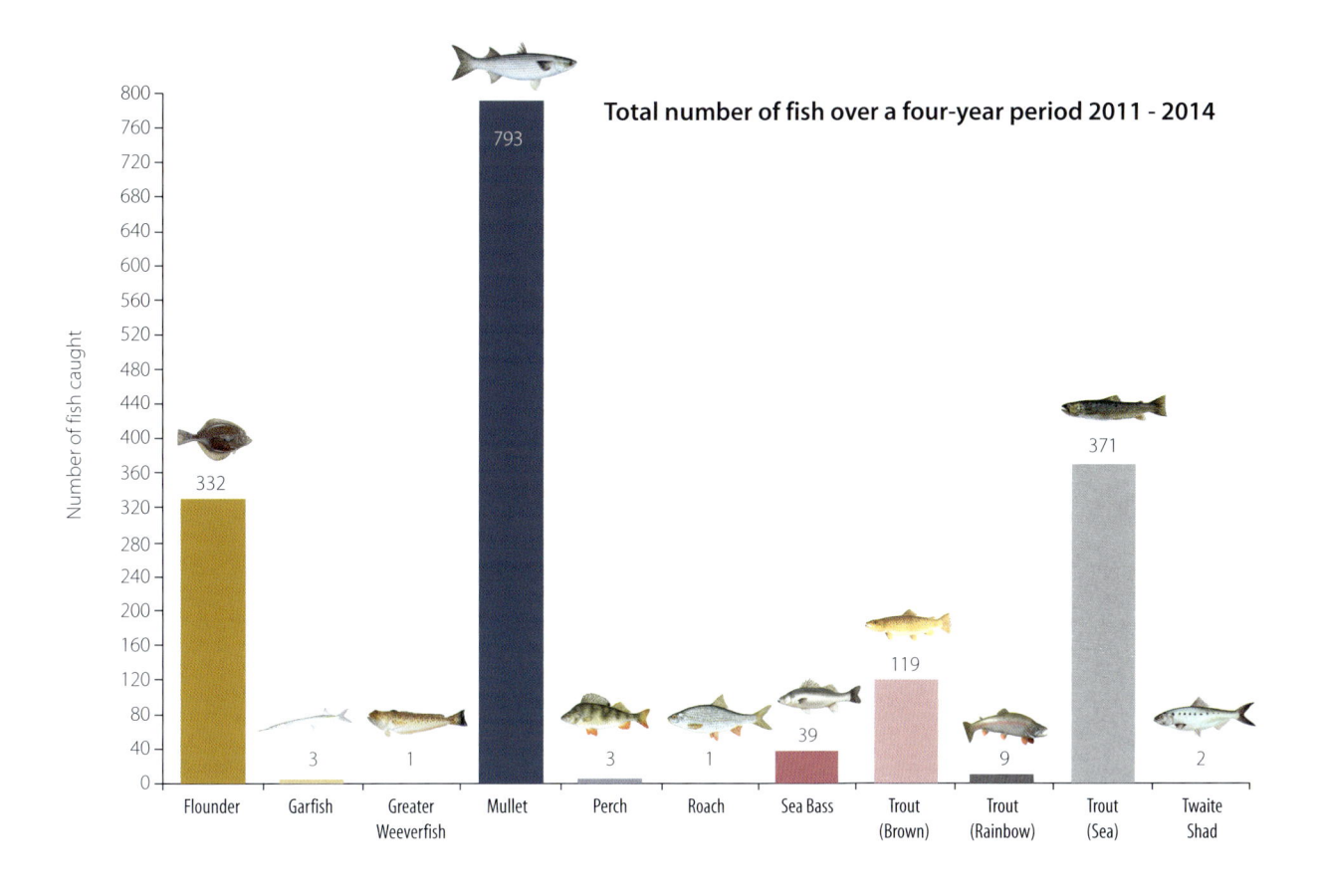

Total number of fish over a four-year period 2011 - 2014

Species	Number of fish caught
Flounder	332
Garfish	3
Greater Weeverfish	1
Mullet	793
Perch	3
Roach	1
Sea Bass	39
Trout (Brown)	119
Trout (Rainbow)	9
Trout (Sea)	371
Twaite Shad	2

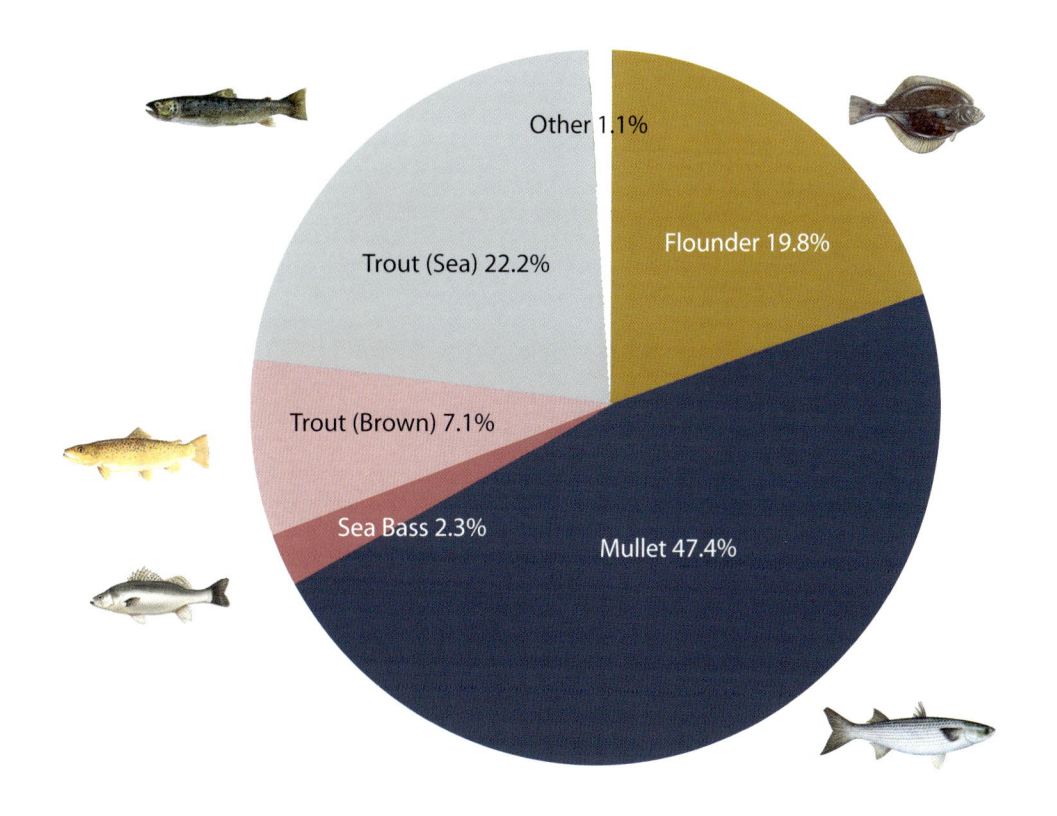

Fish species as a percentage of total diet over a four-year period 2011-2014

- Other 1.1%
- Flounder 19.8%
- Trout (Sea) 22.2%
- Trout (Brown) 7.1%
- Sea Bass 2.3%
- Mullet 47.4%

And Finally...

The Legacies

The importance of the two Glaslyn birds to the success of modern Welsh osprey colonisation is hard to overstate really, the figures speak for themselves. In 11 years of breeding (and it could be more if they were nesting in 2003), they have produced 26 youngsters that reached migration age, six of which have so far returned to the UK. Five of these are breeding in Scotland and England, having produced 33 grand-chicks between them by 2014.

There is also another added advantage to the Glaslyn nest, often overlooked, that is difficult to quantify. The very fact that there has been an active osprey nest in North Wales for over a decade has unquestionably attracted increased interest from other birds, which has resulted in them settling or nesting. Ospreys are practically hypnotised by other nests and are attracted to them like bees to honey. I'm convinced that despite not having a Glaslyn offspring return to Wales to breed yet, there are many more birds around simply by virtue of knowing there is an active nest nearby. Blue 24 at the Dyfi is a classic example of this.

The Dyfi nest – young ospreys are mesmerised by other active nests and are drawn to them like magnets.

As exciting as the news of the first five breeding Glaslyn returnees is, there are surely even greater treasures ahead. Those ospreys were from the first five years of the decade we have been studying, 12 offspring in all; since 2010 another 14 youngsters have fledged. We can conservatively predict that four (30%) of these will return, or possibly even six birds (42%), if the return rate of the first half of the decade is repeated in the second.

When I visited Scotland in 2012 to see Black 80, I was struck by how many ospreys there were in the area. Today there are almost 300 pairs breeding in Scotland and around 40% of their chicks are ringed each year. Four of the five Glaslyn returnees have nested at an eyrie that has a nest camera set up; the fifth, White 91, is nesting at an established site that is visited by an experienced ringer every year. A tiny fraction of UK osprey nests have cameras on them, probably 5% or so – what is the probability of four out of the five (80%) Glaslyn offspring ending up on this tiny 5% batch of camera equipped nests? The chances are, there are more birds out there that we don't know about; the laws of probability tell us that.

Despite a 50:50 ratio of male to female offspring at the Glaslyn nest, is it just coincidence that a relatively high proportion, five of the six (83%) confirmed returnees are males? True, six is not a large enough sample size to draw any valid scientific conclusions, but there may be an explanation for this seemingly high male return rate.

Nesting males are much more likely to be identified than females during the breeding season; it is the males that do most if not all of the fishing, including travelling to and from various water bodies; the females would be far more inconspicuous tucked away incubating or brooding at their nests. So the suggestion here is – are there one or two Glaslyn females out there breeding

The Glaslyn male is 16 years old in 2014, having sired 26 youngsters to migrating age.

And Finally...   225

quietly on a far-away nest somewhere we don't know about, unchecked, unphotographed and unrecorded?

We can't talk about Welsh osprey legacies without mentioning the people behind the scenes here: the individuals and organisations that have put ospreys on the map, in more ways than one.

Volunteers and visitors at the Glaslyn Osprey Project viewing hide at Pont Croesor in 2005.

Many people didn't have mobile phones, computers and emails when ospreys first started to breed in Wales over a decade ago. This was a time before iPhones and iPads, before Facebook, Twitter and social media platforms. It was a time when websites were new and Internet speeds were slow – remember dial-up? It was a time when, if you wanted to take photographs of ospreys, chances were you needed to nip to the chemist first to buy some film. Mention interactive tablets and you would have thought of Moses.

It was against this technological backdrop that the RSPB, with the help of local communities and a range of other environmental organisations, started the osprey project at the Glaslyn in 2004. Five years later, Montgomeryshire Wildlife Trust did the same at their Cors Dyfi Reserve, 30 miles to the south. More recently, we have Bywyd Gwyllt Glaslyn Wildlife running the Glaslyn Osprey Project and between the three organisations, they have kept up with the rapidly changing technological advances, informing and educating people around the planet about the ospreys.

Over 70,000 volunteer hours have been donated to both Glaslyn and Dyfi projects over the first decade that ospreys have been breeding in Wales; literally hundreds of people have given their time for free to help the ospreys. The projects would simply not exist without volunteers. Some of these people are sadly no longer with us, but their legacy most certainly is. The organisations behind the projects, and the ospreys themselves, owe these people a huge debt of gratitude.

And Finally...

Running osprey projects is not an easy thing to do, especially for hard-up charities where every penny is important. Despite this, Welsh ospreys are now known around the world thanks to the tireless work of these organisations. They have taken to the new technologies available and used them to their full potential, continuing the work George Waterston and Roy Dennis started in Scotland over half a century ago.

Finally, if we are talking about legacies in the osprey world, it is important that we highlight the massive contribution that the translocation project at Rutland, started in the mid-1990s, has made to the osprey landscape, not just in Wales or even the UK, but in Europe generally.

Both the Glaslyn and Welshpool males are birds from the Rutland translocation project in the late 1990s. The Glaslyn male has fathered 26 fledglings up to 2014 and he's still going; the Welshpool male sired one (Monty?) in 2004. Of all the ospreys that were translocated from Scotland to Rutland, 13 have been recorded back in the UK including the Glaslyn and Welshpool birds. Of those 13 ospreys, 10 have returned to Rutland, eight of which have bred raising 53 chicks between them up to 2014. Of these 53, 17 have so far been confirmed as having returned to the UK – a 32% return rate. We know two of these 17 birds well of course, Nora and Glesni.

A new osprey project opens in Wales in April 2009.

Volunteers gather for the opening of Montgomeryshire Wildlife Trust's new 360 Observatory in 2014.

The more you think of these numbers and records the more amazing it gets. Combined, those 13 first generation translocated ospreys have raised 89 fledglings between them and countless more grand-chicks, which I'm not even going to try and count! And these birds are just the ones we know about of course.

What started off as a concept and an innovative conservational tool by Roy Dennis and Tim Appleton of the Leicestershire and Rutland Wildlife Trust two decades ago, now looks to have been a stroke of genius; I don't think that even they could have predicted all those years ago the successes that we've seen recently. I said on page 96 that measuring success in conservation is sometimes analogous to turning a cruise liner around 180° going at full pelt – it takes time for things to happen and for hard work to be rewarded. We are now starting to see the dividends of this project, big time.

Undoubtedly, we'll see even more evidence of the success of this pioneering initiative over the next few years, as more and more birds come back to the UK to raise their families. We'll see the same in Europe too. The same basic practices and methodologies of the original Rutland translocation project

228   And Finally...

The Glaslyn male photographed in 2005 before he lost his ochre Darvic ring he received at Rutland in 1998. He has 33 grand-chicks by 2014.

are now being applied in other countries as a direct result of the successes in the UK. Osprey translocation projects have recently been carried out in Portugal, Italy and both northern and southern Spain.

Superospreys

Just now and again an osprey will hatch at a nest somewhere and not only beat the odds and return back to the UK and breed, but much more than that, will do so for a long, long time. I call these birds Superospreys.

These are individuals, maybe just one in every 100 birds, who play a disproportionately large role in propelling the UK osprey population in the upward direction. The female osprey 'Lady' at the Loch of the Lowes nest has raised 50 chicks up to 2014; our own Glaslyn female has 26 fledglings under her belt; many of Roy's birds have gone on to be Superospreys, including another female, Red Z, who had reared 32 youngsters by the time she failed to return in 1998 when she was well in to her 20s. Out of those 13 translocated Rutland birds that returned, (what we now call) the Glaslyn male was not the only one that turned out to be a Superosprey.

White 03 was from the batch of birds translocated from Scotland a year before the Glaslyn male. This 1997 osprey returned to Rutland in 2000 and built a nest on top of an oak tree; in 2001 he successfully bred at this nest for the first time and has done so every year up to 2014. He has reared 32 chicks in all during this time, many of which have returned to the UK to breed, Nora being one of them.

OSPREYS IN WALES *The First Ten Years*

The Glaslyn male – a Superosprey.

Interestingly, White 03's offspring also have a very high return rate, just as the Glaslyn male does (42%). Of his offspring that are old enough to have returned, 40% have been recorded back in the UK. Remarkably, these have raised 43 chicks between them and four of these have produced another generation of 15 birds, making White 03 a great granddad 15 times over!

Two Rutland 'Superospreys' – breeding success up to 2014				
Superosprey	Year born	Chicks	Grand-chicks	Great Grand-chicks
Glaslyn Ochre 11	1998	26	33	-
Rutland White 03	1997	32	43	15

Ochre 11(1998) photographed here at just a few weeks old, perching on his release pen in Rutland in August 1998. Nobody knew it at the time, but this bird would turn out to be a Superosprey breeding in Wales. He has sired 26 fledglings by 2014, five of which (at least) have raised 33 grand-chicks.

And Finally...

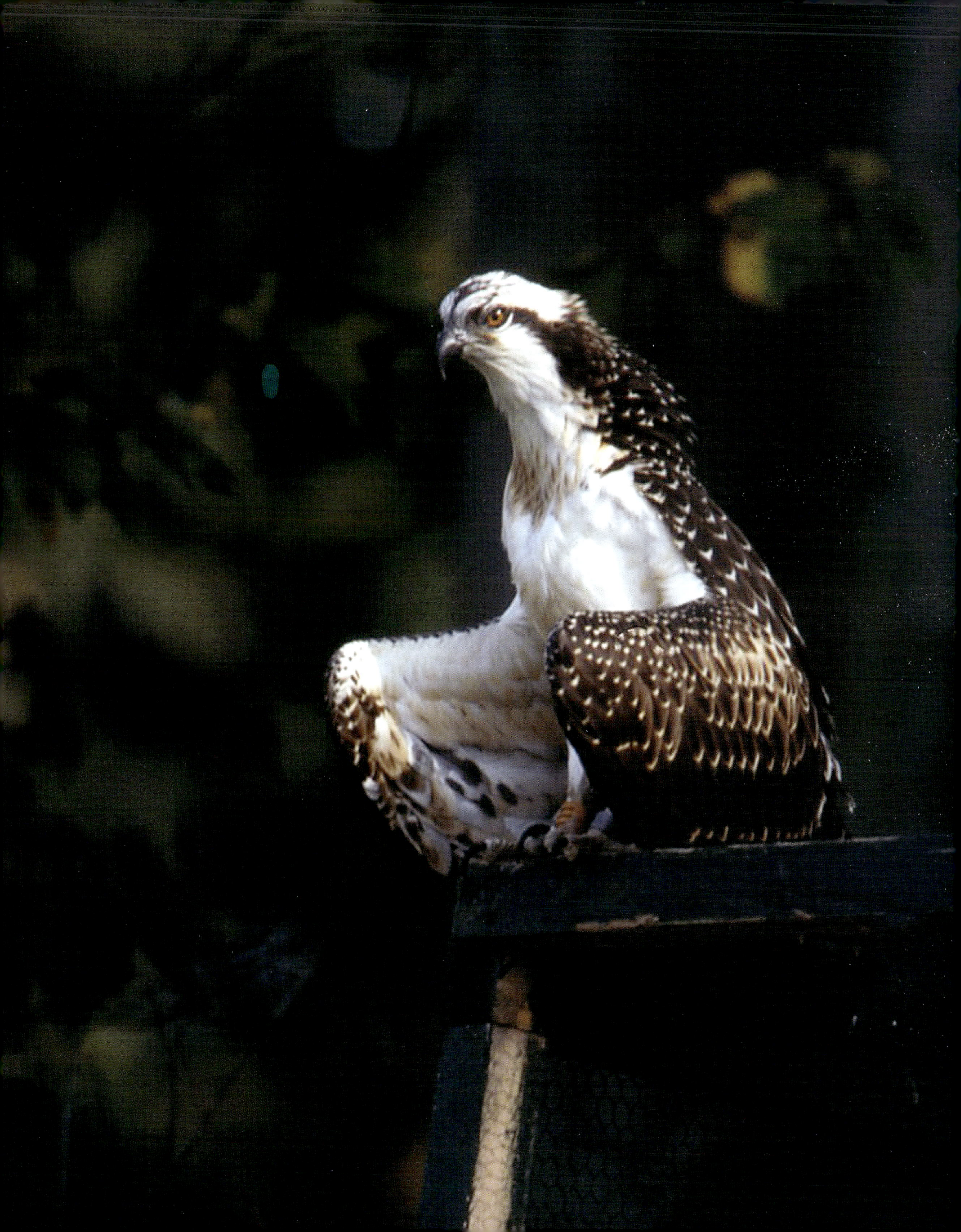

The mortality rate of ospreys is very high; most never make it back to the UK from Africa. In many bird of prey species (and other long-lived birds), particularly where a species is in recovery mode, we see these similar population dynamics play out; a Superbird that defies all the odds and goes on to live for many years, decades sometimes, producing dozens of offspring which eventually make up for those individuals that didn't make it, resulting in a net increase to the population as a whole.

Of course, genetics play a big part here, this is the way Darwinian evolution by natural selection works; but a little bit of luck plays a role too. We've been lucky to have Ochre 11 and White 03, one in Wales and one in England, producing so many youngsters for over a decade – just imagine how the osprey map would look without them. It doesn't bear thinking about.

The Monty Mystery

I have long speculated that Monty might be that sole chick from the 2004 Welshpool nest that couldn't be ringed due to the frustratingly uncooperative cherry-picker. But what if he isn't?

Where are you from Monty?

Let's assume for a moment that Monty isn't the Welshpool chick; we would now have to ask ourselves the question, where *is* he from? He's not a Glaslyn or Rutland offspring – they're all ringed. The nearest possibility then is the Bassenthwaite nest in Cumbria, but these youngsters were also all ringed at the time Monty would have been a chick. He could be a Scottish bird, but it would be fairly unusual for a male osprey from this latitude to start breeding several hundreds of miles further south; three Scottish females have (Blue 24's mum in Rutland is one), but that's about it (we know only of the ringed birds of course). I'm not aware of any ringed Scottish male osprey that has been positively identified as breeding south of the border (notwithstanding the translocated birds obviously, and they were all ringed).

So by a process of elimination, that leaves us with one final option – Monty could be from a nest that we know absolutely nothing about, nada. But if this were the case, wouldn't there be more ospreys around, offspring returning to their natal areas as adults looking for mates and nest sites?

Let's imagine for a moment that there is indeed a mystery osprey nest in Mid Wales, not a million miles away from the Dyfi, which has been active for years; churning out young ospreys, season after season. They wouldn't be ringed of course, because no one would know of the nest's existence. Then we think of all the un-ringed intruder ospreys that have been recorded each year on the Dyfi – where are all these birds from? Sure, some of them are on their way back to Scotland via the west coast of Wales, but all of them? How about those females we've seen on the nest with Monty, the likes of Seren and Elin and many more? How about Dai Dot? How about Scraggly – he called the Dyfi 'home' for at least two years? The final two nests in Wales, ON 4 and ON 5, all have un-ringed adults breeding on them – surely not all of these birds are from Scotland?

The breeding female at the ON 4 nest. Why are so many breeding ospreys in Wales un-ringed?

If only we had a photograph, not of a female, but of a male; we could compare it with those we have of Monty and see if there is a family resemblance – they would be brothers after all, if this mystery nest exists. Enter Dai Dot again.

Monty (left) and Dai Dot – Brothers in Arms?

Dai has been around on the Dyfi since 2011 and possibly longer. He's a male osprey that had been looking for a partner for a few years until he finally nested with an un-ringed female in 2014. If Dai is a Scottish bird, why has he not gone back up there? It would be very unusual for him to stop on the Dyfi for all this time.

We know Dai Dot is quite dark for a male osprey; so is Monty. He has quite a prominent brown chest for a male; so does Monty. He doesn't have any leg rings, neither does Monty. Dai has quite a lot of brown plumage spotting on his under-wings which is unusual for a male; so does Monty. But what about those two distinctive white spots above his beak that give Dai Dot his name, does Monty have these? Well, what do you think?

Perhaps there *is* a hidden nest out there somewhere? A nest so out of sight and inconspicuous, far enough away from people and footpaths, that it has remained a secret for all these years. It would certainly answer the question of where all these young un-ringed ospreys are coming from. Dai Dot and Monty could well be brothers, they look exceptionally similar to me; they may have more brothers and sisters nesting on the ON 4 and ON 5 nests, who knows!

If a mystery nest does exist, let's hope it remains just that, a mystery. After all, aren't the best mysteries the ones that are never solved…?

The Next Ten Years

There's no question that the technological advances of the last decade have helped us humans understand the inner workings of an osprey's life more than at any other time in the past. Iolo made a TV programme a few years ago about the Glaslyn ospreys and described watching them on the three-camera set-up at the visitor centre in Pont Croesor as viewing "the osprey version of Big Brother". How right he was.

Looking at me, looking at you. Ceulan in 2012.

A visitor explained to me in 2012 that she initially got interested in the Dyfi ospreys after sitting next to someone on a tube in London who was watching them live on their smart phone going to work. How mad is that? Phones could barely take pictures a decade before, let alone stream live HD video from a remote osprey nest in Wales!

Learning about ospreys is a much more personal affair these days. By delving a little bit deeper with our new high-tech gadgets, we see what really makes these birds tick, as well as getting to know who's who in the osprey world – that's when things really become interesting. Getting to know ospreys as individuals takes things to a whole different level; it's a much more emotional and intimate experience. It develops into a relationship that is hard to resist; you've been sucked in by the adventure and the stories and now you're hooked.

The Dyfi Osprey Project has taken osprey watching to the next step during the last few years. It's not just on the nest that we see what the ospreys are up to, but also on the whole reserve. To put cameras actually on various perches as well as the nest, increased further our knowledge of the behaviours of the Dyfi ospreys; it filled that hole in our understanding of what their movements and behaviours were away from the breeding site. When Ceulan fledged in 2012 he was away from the nest for 45 minutes, but where had he been? The cameras picked him up on the ground staring at a cow! It was a lot bigger than he had envisaged.

In 2012 Ceulan spends his first 45 minutes of independence after fledging, 350m away from the nest on the ground, staring at a cow. It was much bigger than he thought.

Those visiting female ospreys of 2013 and the colossal fight between Glesni and Blue 24 in 2014 would have been impossible to record with just one static nest camera, let alone try to work out what was happening and which bird was which.

I feel enormously privileged to have worked with ospreys for the last decade in Wales. It's been a rollercoaster ride that's for sure, with plenty of tears along the way; sad ones and happy ones. I still get goose bumps when the Glaslyn birds arrive at their nest very early each season, as I do when Monty thumps down on his Dyfi nest during the first week in April. It's a feeling of exhilaration witnessing a bird you haven't seen for seven months suddenly appear in your life once again.

I think these days I get as much of a thrill watching other people's reactions too – their gasps of delight and joyous elation that 'their' bird has made it back home; jumping, clapping, hugging and all that. That's when the text messages start to come in and the frantic phone calls, the Tweets and everything

236 And Finally...

else. It's like winning the pools and you want to tell everybody, and everybody wants to tell you. It's an unforgettable experience.

The next ten years promise to be just as compelling and enthralling as the first ten, if not more so. The rollercoaster ride hasn't been decommissioned just yet; in fact, it's had a few more high-speed twists and turns installed. Technology and innovation haven't come to a grinding halt either – Ultra High-Definition cameras (4K) are practically already with us, offering four times the resolution of current HD systems. Super-fast broadband speeds via fiber optic cables are coming to Wales too (no, really). Live Streaming with multi-cam views will take osprey learning and watching to new highs again, we'll be able to engage with the birds in ways that were inconceivable just a few years ago. If you missed those two buses back in 2004, there's another one just leaving the depot and it's a great time to hop on and join the journey.

There are so many questions that will be answered during the next decade of osprey watching in Wales. Will Monty end up being a Superosprey himself? He's well on the way. Will both Glaslyn birds still be around? How many more Glaslyn offspring will we see return? When will the first Dyfi youngsters be sighted back in the UK? Cerist and Clarach could well make an appearance in 2015 or 2016. What will Blue 24's strategy be in future years? Is Einion still alive – when will we see him? And arguably the biggest question of them all – when will we see a Welsh born osprey return to Wales to

A personal affair: An intruder (right) lands on the Dyfi nest in 2012 while Nora is away. The single chick in the nest is Ceulan, the intruder is a two-year-old – Blue 12; we now call her Glesni. They are cousins and this would be their only ever encounter.

And Finally... 237

Nora incubating her eggs in 2012 – in High-Definition for the first time.

breed for the first time? It's practically a certainty with so many youngsters out there; the odds are overwhelmingly in favour of it happening, especially as we now have at least four huge magnets pulling them back. We didn't have these when the first five Glaslyn offspring returned in the 2000s.

There is no room for complacency in conservation, that's true; but there really is good reason to be optimistic about the osprey's future for the first time in centuries. You may remember me mentioning this quotation in the Introduction, it's from a letter from one Victorian egg collector, Mr. Dunbar, to another in Scotland in the 19th century, "*I am afraid that Mr. St John, yourself and your humble servant, have finally done for the Ospreys*".

Well, they were wrong. More than a century on from that letter, the osprey population is now very much on the up. They only need a little bit of help; the ospreys themselves will do the rest. Since those days of wanton persecution and needless destruction, we have seen a sea change for the good in people's attitudes to the natural world around them, the plants and animals we share our planet with. Yes, some people still want to do harm, but I honestly believe that the scales are now well and truly tipped more so in the direction of people that want to do good.

Ospreys are not a commodity or a resource; they are just one small piece of a very large jigsaw, and a picture that's not complete without all of its component parts. We have to make sure that all the pieces of the jigsaw survive and are in place for the next generation; we have a duty of care to do so.

First light, just before he starts his migration from the Dyfi in September 2014. Will Monty become a Superosprey in the years to come?

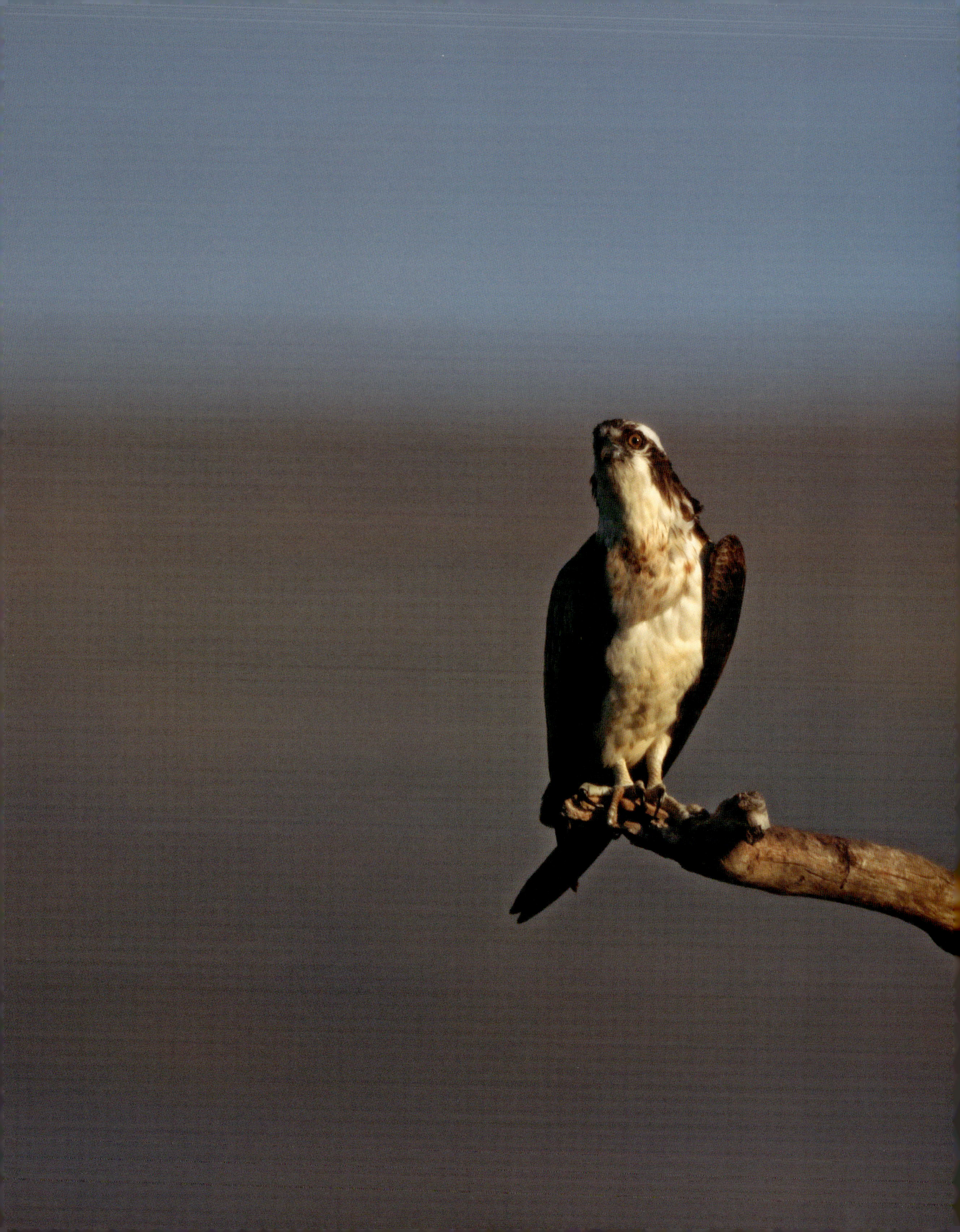

Keeping an eye out – it looks a lot better for Monty and his fellow ospreys than it did a century ago.

These two children are Abby and Oli from a village just down the river from the Dyfi osprey nest. They were the first ever visitors to the 360 Observatory when it opened at 10am on Good Friday 2014; and they wanted to show me a collage. They had been working on an osprey project of their own over the winter, as part of their homework for school. If I were a teacher, I would have given them 11 out of 10.

Abby and Oli weren't born when ospreys first bred in Wales back in 2004, yet they will be adults by the time the second decade of osprey colonisation has passed. They know nothing of Mr. Dunbar or Mr. St John and their ilk, and neither do they need to. Perhaps it is time we stopped focusing on our ignominious past and looked forward. What's past is past and there is nothing we can do to change it; we can change the future however.

These two guys peering out at the Dyfi nest through the huge window in the 360 Observatory somehow made the first decade of Welsh ospreys complete for me. As they looked excitedly at Monty and Glesni for the first time, passionately chattering away, I was looking at them. Abby, Oli and their generation will be the osprey's guardians in the future and for that, I feel very happy.

Abby and Oli – looking to the future

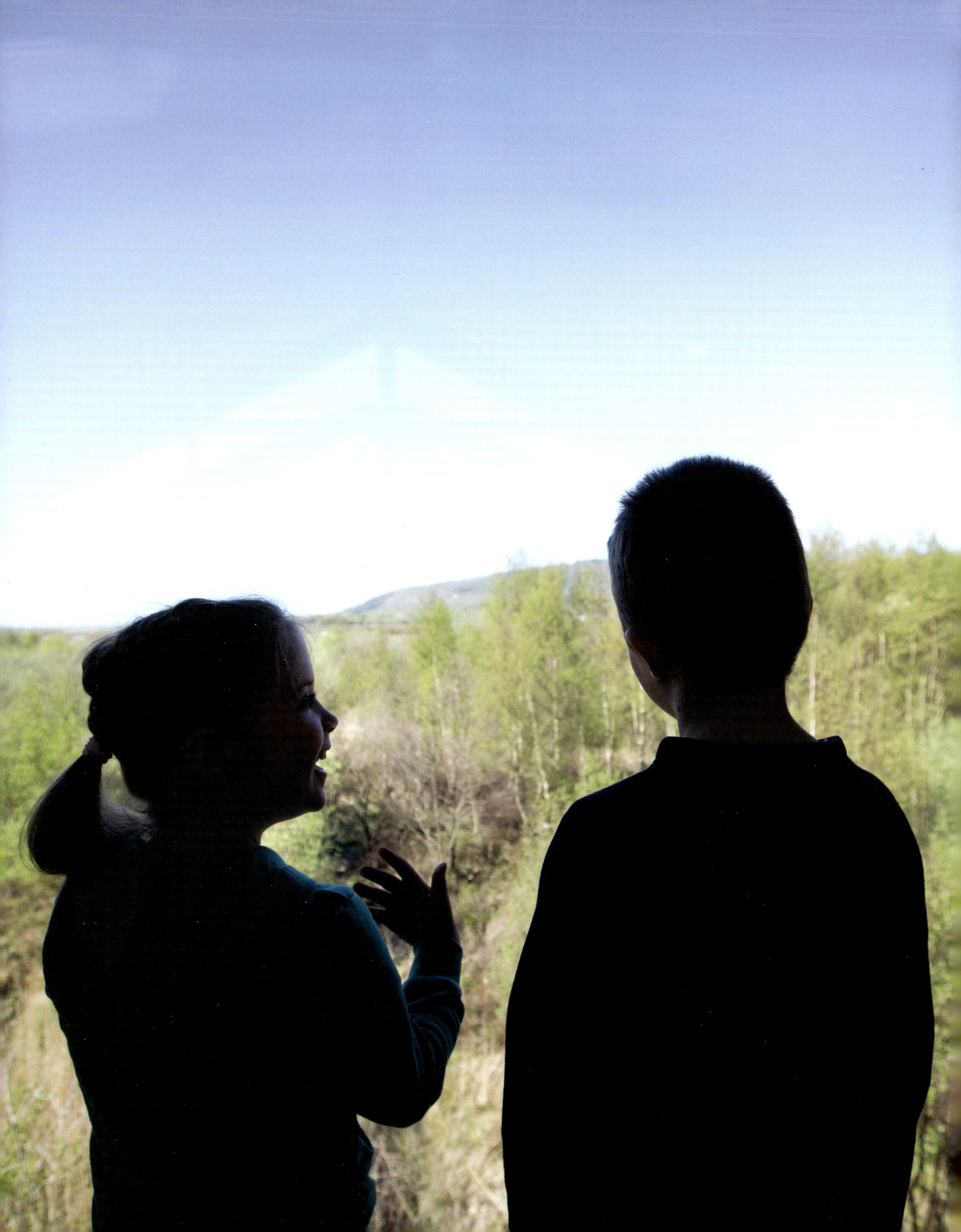

Glossary – Useful Words to Know

These are handy terms to know that you may see or hear when people talk about ospreys. Some are proper scientific terms while others are completely made up, but have managed to wrestle their way in to general osprey talk!

Bobbleheads: Comedic name given to young osprey chicks, especially when they're just a few days old. They bobble their heads a lot!

Crop: A pouch located in an osprey's neck, which acts as a storage chamber for food prior to digestion; it's actually an expanded portion of the oesophagus. Very handy when lots of food arrives in big quantities. Most birds of prey have a crop, but owls don't.

Darvic: A type of plastic that some bird leg rings are made of for ID in the field.

ENS: Empty Nest Syndrome. Suffered by ospreyholics (see below) October – March in the UK.

Fledge: The moment an osprey takes to the air for the first time in a controlled fashion. Usually at the age of seven to eight weeks old for ospreys.

Food Soliciting: A bird calling out for food – usually chicks or a female osprey of a breeding pair.

Gular Fluttering: A thermoregulatory behaviour similar to panting in dogs. An osprey flaps the throat membranes in order to increase evaporation, which cools it down. Same principle as getting cold once you're out of the shower!

Helicoptering: Not proper flight, but young ospreys gliding and hovering whilst sometimes flapping vigorously above the nest. This is pre-fledge practice behaviour and helps the young osprey understand the principles of flight as well as develop flight muscles.

Intruder: In the osprey world, an intruder is any osprey who gets too close to the nest of a breeding family who is not part of that group. Young two and three-year-old ospreys are classic intruders.

Nestoration: Made up name for arranging various materials in a nest – sticks, moss, hay etc. Hybrid of restoration and nest.

Nictitating Membrane: An osprey has a third transparent eyelid that protects the eye and moistens it while the bird still maintains vision. Unlike the two conventional eyelids, the nictitating membrane is drawn across from the side of the eye horizontally, as opposed to up and down. Most birds have a nictitating membrane, as do some reptiles and mammals.

Operculum: A hard bony flap covering and protecting the gills of a fish. This is the only part of a fish ospreys tend not to eat; they generally discard them. See page 56.

Ospreyholic: Self-explanatory!

Ospreyitis: What Ospreyholics suffer from, usually between October and March in the UK.

Philopatry: The tendency of an osprey to come back to the same area to breed as an adult as it was raised. Ospreys are highly 'philopatric', males more so (but not the Glaslyn birds, obviously!).

Productivity: The total number of osprey young that fledge a nest in a particular year.

Siblicide: One chick killing another brother or sister in the nest; extremely uncommon in ospreys.

Spicules: Specialised adaptations on an osprey's feet - the skin is formed into multiple barbs, which helps an osprey catch, carry and hang on to its prey while eating it.

Thanatosis: A form of animal deception whereby an individual pretends to be dead. Between the ages of around two to seven weeks old, this is a young osprey chick's best form of defence from aerial predators. Playing dead increases their camouflage thereby reducing their conspicuousness.

Zygodactyly: Unlike any other bird of prey (excluding owls), ospreys can reverse their outer toe. Normally, they have three toes pointing forward and one back when perching. But when grabbing a slippery fish, they will hold it with two toes pointing forward and two back. This toe arrangement is called Zygodactyly; woodpeckers can do it too.

More Osprey Books

If you are into ospreys and would like some recommendations on other books, here they are!

They are all excellent and despite the first three not being in print any more, they are readily available in second-hand bookshops, on Ebay and other Internet sites. In date order:

THE RETURN OF THE OSPREY
(1962)
by Philip Brown & George Waterston.
Collins

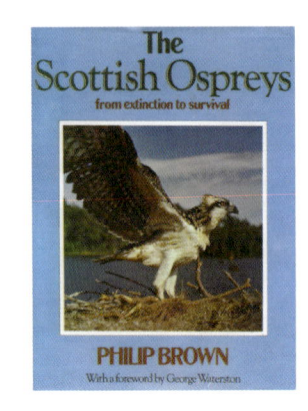

THE SCOTTISH OSPREYS
(1979) by Philip Brown.
Heinemann

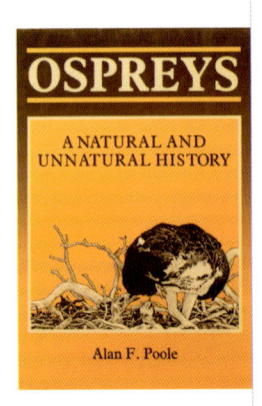

OSPREYS: A NATURAL AND UNNATURAL HISTORY
(1989) by Alan F. Poole.
The Cambridge University Press

A LIFE OF OSPREYS
(2008) by Roy Dennis.
Whittles Publishing

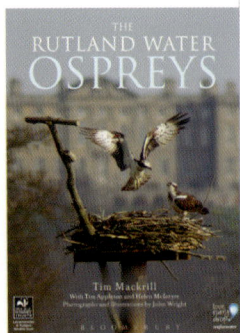

THE RUTLAND WATER OSPREYS
(2013) by Tim Mackrill.
Bloomsbury

Acknowledgements

With special and heartfelt thanks in no particular order to:

Diolch o galon i:

The organisations – Montgomeryshire Wildlife Trust, the Royal Society for the Protection of Birds and Bywyd Gwyllt Glaslyn Wildlife. These organisations have been the guardians and protectors of the ospreys in Wales for the last ten years, as well as their storytellers and educators. Running large-scale osprey projects is a complicated and expensive undertaking and not without significant financial risk. All three should be applauded for their vision and hard work in ensuring the survival and conservation of ospreys in Wales. If you are not a member, please consider joining them.

Volunteers – I have worked with literally hundreds of volunteers over the last decade. The amount of time donated between the Glaslyn and Dyfi osprey projects is now fast approaching 100,000 hours. A truly astounding and humbling figure. In comparative terms, that is equivalent to employing one person, full time, for 70 years. Try multiplying that by the average yearly wage in this country and adding 30%. Many millions. I say it every year, but we couldn't have osprey projects in Wales, or possibly the ospreys themselves, without volunteers.

Network Rail and Scottish Power – for making the impossible, possible.

Heather Corfield – for her unwavering support over the last ten years, for answering all manner of osprey related questions, all the osprey data recording and for proof reading this book.

Janice Corfield – for checking everything before the book went to print.

Janine Pannett – for her unfathomable knowledge of everything osprey related and answering questions at 5am – 7am most days every summer.

Vicky King – for all the number crunching and fish pies, plus the photographic slide scanning work.

Jo Maltman – for her exemplary work proof reading this book and for allowing me to keep some of the Welsh quirkiness.

Andy Rouse – for all the osprey photographs unconditionally donated for this book.

Iolo Williams – for his devotion and passion for Welsh wildlife over the decades and his Foreword in this book. Diolch Iol.

All the ringers and helpers – Kelvin Jones, Adrienne Stratford, Roy Dennis, Tony Cross, Chris Townsend, Dick Squires, Steve Roberts.

Roy Dennis – for all his immeasurable work over many decades in getting ospreys and other species back to viable numbers and populations, and for all his advice for the last ten years.

Tim Mackrill – and all the Rutland guys for all their support and advice over the years (and for 07(97), 11(98), 03(08) and 12(10))!

Alan Davies – for being on-call, permanently.

John Parry – am bob dim JP.

Twm Elias – for his excellent paper on the history of ospreys in Wales. Diolch i chi fel bob amser Twm.

Alwyn Ifans – for his boundless passion for ospreys and teaching me the proper, non-Cofi Welsh words for things. Diolch Al.

Frederic Bacuez – for looking for Leri and Ceulan in West Africa. Merci pour votre passion.

Andy Rouse would like to thank the following people for helping him with his osprey project so far, you have made the difference - Eero and Raisa Kemila, Julian Orsi, Neil McIntyre, Geraint Williams, Carys from CCW, David Trotman, Dana Thomas, Jeremy Gilbert, Rob Cook and Mark Hoskyns.

Photo Credits

I would like to thank all the individuals who have allowed me to use their photographs in this book in order for the osprey's stories to be told. Every single person I asked kindly agreed and sent me the image I was after.

With heartfelt thanks, I would like to acknowledge and credit the following photographers:

Andy Rouse: All photos in the Introduction and pages 94, 95, 105, 115, 230 and 248 (upper).

Montgomeryshire Wildlife Trust: All the Dyfi nest camera images from chapter 2009 onwards.

Bywyd Gwyllt Glaslyn Wildlife: 188, 190, 191, 194 (right), 196.

Steve Watson page 3, **Anne Harrington-Rees** 4, **Reg Thorpe** 8, **Jim Beattie** 10 (both), **Conrad Smith** 11, **Brayton Holt** 13 &14, **Dick Squires** 42 & 62, **Steve Roberts** 70, **Clive Faulkner** 73, **Janet Baxter** 74, **Keith Kirk** (upper) 75, **Janine Pannett** 83, **Ciril Ostroznik** 91, **Martin Trachsel** 98, **Garry Ridsdale** (www.garryridsdale.com) 109, **Tony Cross** 121 & 135 & 166 (upper), unknown 125, **Scottish Wildlife Trust** 136, **Alan Davies** 140 (lower) & 144 & 224, **Gary Brindle** 147, **Arnault Vatinel** 149, **Allan Chard** 162 (right), **Nigel Milbourne** 163, **Forestry Commission England** 165 & 194 (left), **Berni Cavanagh** 166 (lower), **Keith Brockie** 192, **Natural England** 193, **Chloe B** 198 (upper), **Mark Wilson** (www.mwphoto.co.uk) 205 & 234 (right), **Jamie Nicholson** 206, **Leicestershire and Rutland Wildlife Trust** 231, **Paul Leafe** 233.

I took all the rest!

The Glaslyn and Dyfi boys – to the next ten years...